Cornish

A Dictionary of Phrases, Terms and Epithets Beginning with the Word 'Cornish'

Thornton B. Edwards

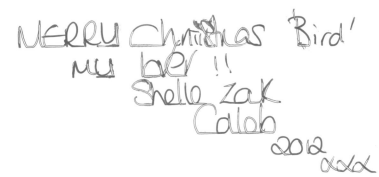

MERRY Christmas 'Bird'
my love !!
Shelle Zak
Caleb
2012
xxxx

First published in 2005 by Truran,
Croft Prince, Mount Hawke, Truro, Cornwall TR4 8EE
www.Truranbooks.co.uk
Truran is an imprint of Truran Books Ltd

ISBN 1 85022 196 0

Printed and bound in Cornwall by R Booth Ltd,
Antron Hill, Mabe, Penryn, Cornwall TR10 9HH

CONTENTS

THE AUTHOR

Thornton B. Edwards was born in Newport, South Wales. He is a folklorist, lexicographer and short story writer. His main expertise is in modern Greek folk customs and rituals about which he has lectured widely and contributed over forty articles to academic journals. He speaks several languages (including Welsh) and has a reading knowledge of Cornish. He has written articles on Cornish folklore as well as a Cornish dialect glossary which have appeared in notable Cornish publications. He is the author of three books; his other two works are similar to this one, but about the words 'Welsh' and 'Irish'. Currently he is completing three new books: a similar dictionary about the words Scotch, Scots and Scottish, a study on Greek Christmas traditions and a collection of Christmas short stories.

INTRODUCTION

It is amazing how many phrases there are with the word 'Cornish'. Almost everyone has heard of the **Cornish Chough**, the **Cornish Elm**, **Cornish wrestling** and the **Cornish Alps**. Yet there are so many similar expressions which are unknown. Perhaps only a few of us know about the **Cornish cut** or the **Cornish Pine**. What is the **Cornish curl**? How tall is a **Cornish Red**? Which school has been called the **Cornish Eton**? Where are the **Cornish pyramids**? And how heavy is a **Cornish ton**? We have all heard of **Cornish diamonds** but what type of stone has been called the **Cornish topaz**? What kind of plant is **Cornish Lime**? What is a **Cornish Sucker**? Why might you find a **Cornish mule** in a pub? Which female animal is sometimes called a **Cornish Queen**? From what animal was **Cornish hair** taken? Why has **Cornish pepper** got milk in it? Apart from a kind of pie, what else does the phrase **Cornish pasty** mean? Who was the **Cornish Carnegie**? Why is a **Cornish fig** very small? What is the difference between **Cornish Time** and G.M.T.? Why wouldn't you like to receive a **Cornish compliment**? Why would you keep a **Cornish organ** in the fireplace? And why would a **Cornish duck** be caught by a fisherman rather than a hunter?

The aforementioned examples are just a few of the phrases which reflect something of the uniqueness of Cornwall and the Cornish. The English language and the Cornish dialect are particularly rich in expressions which contain the word 'Cornish'. When 'Cornish' is prefixed to another word, the resulting phrase invariably connotes that which is distinct in some way from the standard (i.e. English) meaning. For instance, we all understand what a shovel is, but a **Cornish shovel** is a distinct tool. Similarly we know what a hedge is, but a **Cornish hedge** is very different. My purpose in compiling this collection of phrases is to pay a tribute to the rich culture of the Cornish by recording such differences. This is the first time that a dictionary has ever been written with phrases containing the word 'Cornish'. It is my hope that, through this work, many hitherto unknown or unrecorded expressions will be saved. To this end I am inspired by the motto of the Federation of Old Cornwall Societies: *Cuntelleugh an brewyon us gesysna vo kellys travyth* (i.e. Gather the crumbs/fragments so that nothing will be lost).

Since the word 'Cornish' could be prefixed to an infinite variety of subjects, this dictionary contains only those phrases, terms and epithets that have entered oral tradition. I have not included place names of streets, villages or geographical locations like Cornish Terrace (in Truro), Cornishville, Cornishman's Dam yet I have included **Cornish Point** since it refers to a drink as well as a place name. Neither have I been able to include names of newspapers like the 'Cornish Guardian' or certain societies such as the ubiquitous 'Cornish Association' abroad. I have also omitted ships and vessels like the 'Cornish Belle' and local teams like the Cornish Crusaders. However, I have included the

Cornish All Blacks since this is a nickname. Moreover, while this book could not have excluded the **Cornish pasty**, I have had to exclude some new crafts like the Cornish pasty dragon and Cornish pasty money box as well as certain products like Cornish ale mustard. Some forms of the word 'Cornish' have been included like **Cornishry**, yet there is no mention of many compound forms like Cornish-born and Cornish-owned. Nor have I been able to use some of the more abstract academic phrases like 'Cornish anti-metropolitanism' (C.S. 2nd, 1:75) or 'Cornish Celticity'.

One of the most conspicuous uses of the word 'Cornish' is in its application to the wealth of local flora. For instance, there are entries like **Cornish Furze**, **Cornish Mallow** and **Cornish Snow,** not to mention the exotic **Cornish palm** which makes the appellation **Cornish Riviera** sound rather appropriate. There are also varieties of fruit like **Cornish Mother** and **Cornish Giant** as well as vegetables like **Cornish King**. Food is also included. There is, of course, the **Cornish range** and there are traditional dishes like **Cornish underroast**, types of cheese such as **Cornish Yarg**, cakes or confectionary like **Cornish splits** in addition to drinks like **Cornish punch.**

From the animal world there is, of course, the **Cornish Rex** as well as extinct breeds like the **Cornish sheep** and **Cornish Goonhilly. White Cornish** (no relation to **Cornish white**) is a variety of **Cornish game**. Other birds include the so-called **Cornish Pheasant** and the **Cornish Kae** (not to be confused with the **Cornish Kea**). There are also fish like the so-called **Cornish Salmon** and the **Cornish Blackfish.**

Folklore and mythology provide entries like the **Cornish piskey**, the **Cornish Cinderella**, the **Cornish Atlantis** and the **Cornish Bluebeard**. Indeed there are several personal epithets. Many will know who the **Cornish Wonder** was but who was the **Cornish Bunyan?** And perhaps most of us can guess which hero has been dubbed the **Cornish Braveheart**. On the subject of eponymous or toponymous epithets it must be noted that in some cases there is a strange anachronism in that the Cornish example actually precedes the person or thing with whom/which it is compared. For, instance the **Cornish Lourdes**, the **Cornish Titanic** and the **Cornish Carnegie** existed before their famous counterparts.

Since mining was so vital in Cornwall, it is to be expected that we have so many phrases connected with mining and industry. Apart from the **Cornish engine** we have the **Cornish castle** (i.e. **Cornish engine house**) and the **Cornish captain** as well as tools such as the **Cornish wheelbarrow** and machines like the **Cornish boiler**. In the world of transport there is also the **Cornish Mail** and the **Cornish Riviera Express**. In the fishing industry we have phrases like **Cornish taboo names, Cornish Shark** and **Cornish fathom**. Indeed, Cornwall had so many distinct units of measurement like the **Cornish acre** and **Cornish mile.**

Sport and recreation have also provided phrases such as the **Cornish hug** in **Cornish wrestling** and the **Cornish system**. Other forms of entertainment included watching a **Cornish miracle** play at a **Cornish round**. Cornwall's rich musical heritage is also featured with entries like the **Cornish nightingale**, **Cornish piper** and **Cornish bagpipe** but a **Cornish organ** is not a musical instrument. Several entries relate to Cornish dress like the innovated **Cornish kilt** and **Cornish tartan**.

From history we have a wealth of terms like the **Cornish Rebellion** and **Cornish Commotion**. and from politics there are terms such as the **Cornish Nationalist Party**.

Since religion has played such an important role in Cornish history, there are also religious entries like the **Cornish patron saint** (whose flag became the **Cornish flag**), the **Cornish amphitheatre** and **Cornish Quaker saint**.

In a few cases, instead of the word 'Cornish', a phrase pertaining to Cornwall has been called 'English'. For instance, Rawe records (but did not coin) the epithet 'Montpellier of England' to refer to a particular Cornish town (1986:101). In a few such cases I have prefixed the word 'Cornish' in inverted commas i.e. the **'Cornish' Montpellier** but I have also indicated the correct form. In some instances both forms may exist. For instance, the **Cornish Riviera** has also been called the 'English Riviera' but the latter form is not as widely accepted (or acceptable!). Similarly the **Cornish Gretna Green** has also been called 'England's Gretna Green' and 'Cornwall's Gretna Green'. Indeed where a few phrases have the word 'Cornwall' instead of 'Cornish' then again I have tentatively used inverted commas. For instance, I have used the **'Cornish' Titanic** and **'Cornish' London** for what are really 'Cornwall's Titanic' and the 'London of Cornwall'.

Several entries like **Cornish Blue**, **Cornish cream**, **Cornish knocker** and **Cornish pasty** have a few different meanings. I have therefore indicated this by using numbers. In many entries cross references are provided. In the event that a particular category of phrases can have several entries, then cross references are given only in the first entry to appear. For instance, all apple varieties with the word 'Cornish' are listed at the end of the entry **Cornish Aromatic**. For all other apple varieties e.g. **Cornish Honeypin** and **Cornish Longstem** there is only a brief cross reference to **Cornish Aromatic**. A full bibliography is provided of all books cited; however, articles from newspapers, magazines and journals as well as internet sources are acknowledged within the relevant entries.

After the main dictionary three appendices are provided: the first appendix contains phrases in which the word 'Cornish' is the second or final element. For instance, we have entries such as **Buff Cornish**, **Unified Cornish** and **White Cornish** (not the same as **Cornish White**) as well as the slang expression **a bit Cornish**. The second appendix contains phrases with the word 'Cornishman's' as opposed to 'Cornish' like **Cornishman's gift** and **Cornishman's Bible**. The third appendix contains just a few of the many phrases in which the word 'West' (or 'Western') is used. Whereas the word 'North' can often be used for Scotland (e.g. the 'Athens of the North' for Edinburgh) so 'West' is sometimes used to refer to Cornwall. For example, we have the **West Welsh** and the **Falstaff of the West**. Similarly, the nickname 'Cousin Jack' can be synonymous with 'Cornish' in certain phrases such as in the **Cousin Jack chute**, the **Cousin Jack pasty** or **Cousin Jack story** etc. However, in these cases once again I have used the word 'Cornish' with inverted commas. In all these phrases it is clear that the word 'Cornish' is almost as rich as the culture to which it belongs. This collection is therefore a living testimony to the richness of the Cornish people and their unique culture.

ABBREVIATIONS

Bret.   Breton
Corn.   Cornish
C.S.   *Cornish Studies* (the first series)
C.S. 2nd *Cornish Studies* (the second series ed. by Philip Payton)
C.T.   *Cornwall Today* (the magazine)
C.W.   *Cornish World* (the magazine)
C.W.W. *Cornish Worldwide* (the newsletter)
Dev.   Devonshire dialect
Dial.   Dialect (i.e. the Cornish dialect)
Fr.   French
Ger.   German
Gk.   Greek
Ir.   Irish
It.   Italian
J.R.I.C. Journal of the Royal Institution of Cornwall
K.K.   *Kernewek Kemmyn* (Common Cornish)
Lat.   Latin
L.C.   Late Cornish
O.C.   *Old Cornwall* (journal of the Old Cornwall Societies)
O.E.   Old English
O.E.D   Oxford English Dictionary
R.U.C.   Revised Unified Cornish
U.C.   Unified Cornish
U.S.   American English
Sp.   Spanish
Tk.   Turkish
Van.   Vannes dialect of Breton
W.   Welsh
W.B.   *The West Briton* (newspaper)

Cornish!

Cornish Apart from the obvious meaning of that which pertains to Cornwall, the word 'Cornish' is rich in connotations. Sometimes it is applied not only to the *Cornish language* (q.v.) but also to the *Cornish dialect* (q.v.). It is used as a surname and its meanings include: "the ring placed at the mouth of a cannon" (Haliwell 1847:271), a mantelpiece (Wright 1898–1905, Vol. 1, p.734) – i.e. rather like a *cravel* (wooden lintel over a chimney) and as a verb *to Cornish* means to share a glass (see *Cornish a drink*). In American English 'Cornish' refers to the "cornice used by carpenters" (Cassidy 1985:785. Sometimes the word 'Cornish' alone can be used without any accompanying word. For instance, in rhyming slang an attractive girl can be described as *Cornish* (see *a bit Cornish* in appendix 1) and in a few combinations the second element is occasionally dropped. So, for instance, a *Cornish* can, amongst other things, also mean a *Cornish hen* (q.v.) as well as a breed of cattle (Mason 1951:32 – for which see *Cornish cattle*). There are also meanings of the word 'Cornish' which etymologically are not related to the word 'Cornish;' referring to that which is related to Cornwall. For example, 'Cornish' is also an obsolete adjective which meant "of the corn kind" (O.E.D.). Moreover, 'Cornish/Cornishe' an even be used as an alternative spelling of the word 'cornice' (O.E.D.).

Cornish acre The *Cornish acre* is generally regarded as 120 statute acres as opposed to the *Welsh acre* which is only two statute acres (Edwards 1998:7), the *Scots acre* of 1.3 acres (Robinson 1985:588) and the *Irish acre* of 1.29 acres (Edwards 2004:13). The *Cornish acre* was divided into four *farthings*, each *farthing* (Corn. *ferdhyn tyr*) worth thirty acres. However, there was some ambiguity in history since, according to Carew, there were "nine *farthings* a *Cornish acre* and four *Cornish acres* a *knight's fee*" (1602:56). Yet by this calculation a *Cornish acre* would be worth 270 statute acres. Moreover, Sidney Heartland defined the *Cornish acre* as '8 score *lease*' and a *lease* as four *sticks*, and a *stick* as four yards (*Folklore*, 9, 1898, p.189). In Cornish dialect 'he's *in his acres*' means 'in his glory' (Courtney 1880:1). See next entry. For other measurements see *Cornish bushel*, *Cornish fathom*, *Cornish ferling*, *Cornish gallon*, *Cornish hundred*, *Cornish knight's fee*, *Cornish lace*, *Cornish land rod*, *Cornish mease*, *Cornish mile*, *Cornish mining ton*, *Cornish pound*, *Cornish rod* and *Cornish ton*.

Cornish acreage The area measured in *Cornish acres* (the term is used by David Harvey in C.S. 5, 1997, p.339). Yet, according to Harvey, "a *Cornish acre* represented between 40 and 200 English statute acres, and most probably either 64 or 120" (ibid. pp.38–39).

'Cornish' adopted patron saint Rawe refers to St. Piran as *"Cornwall's adopted patron saint"* (C.W. 30, 2002, p.46) for whom see *Cornish patron saint*. He was adopted in the sense that he came from Ireland. See also *Cornish apostle, Cornish miners' saint, Cornish Quaker saint*.

Cornish a drink To drink from the same vessel in turn. A synonym of *to Cornish together* which means "several persons … use only one glass like a *'loving cup'* " (Jago 1882:143). Schoolchildren in St. Ives still all drink from the same silver *Loving Cup* on the third Monday in May when they meet their new mayor (Williams 1987:45). In fact, the verb '*to Cornish*' could also refer to sharing a tobacco pipe as well as a drink (O.C. Vol. X, No. 3, 1986, p.116). According to superstition, by drinking from the same glass one could learn someone else's secret. Jago also mentioned the game *Tom toddy* "in which each person in succession has to drink a glass of beer or spirits, on top of which a piece of lighted candle has been put while the others sing" (ibid. p.295). Yet another shared drink was associated with a phantom druid priest at Linkinhorne who was seen "offering passers-by a drink from a golden cup that could never be emptied" (Underwood 1983:41).

Cornish adventurers 1 Those who invested money in Cornish tin mines. The word *adventurers* is usually sufficient yet some authors prefix the word 'Cornish' (e.g. in O.C. Vol. XII, No.3 1998, p.12 and by Ronald Perry in C.S. 11, 2002, pp.168–169). 2 Adventurers from Cornwall who invested elsewhere. In 1810 Richard Fenton noted that in Aberglaslyn, Wales there was "a copper mine now being worked by some *Cornish adventurers* who are laying out a great deal of money there" (cited by Kirk 1994:136).

Cornish African explorer, the Epithet of Richard Lander (1804–1834) also called 'The Little Christian' (see article by Peter M. Hancock in C.W. 13, 1997, pp.34–35). His statue is in Lemon Street, Truro.

Cornish Afrikanders Cornishmen in South Africa were sometimes called 'Afrikanders' (e.g. in the W.B. Dec. 1899) or as Payton records, 'Cousin Jack Afrikanders' (1999:359). The word *Afrikaner* (and or *Africander*) refers to the white person in South Africa who speaks *Afrikaans* (Dutch dialect). See *Cornish Uitlanders*.

Cornish All Blacks Epithet of Launceston Rugby Football Club. Mickey Stephens writes "this team … has affectionately and universally been dubbed 'The *Cornish All Blacks*' " (C.T. 3, No. 2, 1996, p.45). the All Blacks are the (mainly Maori) New Zealand rugby team who are famous for their opening *haka* war dance. See *Cornish cap, Cornish kiwi* and *Cornish rugby shirt*.

Cornish alphabet The *Cornish language* (q.v.) alphabet varies slightly from form to form: *Unified* Cornish has a 'q' and an 'x' but KK does not. *Late Cornish* has a 'z' but UC and KK do not. The only combination of consonants that is treated as a separate letter is 'ch' in KK (as in Welsh, but with a different sound).The Cornish called the alphabet *criss-cross-row* "as in the old horn books it was always headed with a cross" Thomas 1895:78). *Cornish Alphabet* was also a song by Brenda Wooton.

Cornish Alps Tips in the Cornish clay (q.v.) area. Thurlow explains: "The china clay district was sometimes referred to as the Cornish Alps because of the proliferation of inclined tips, largely composed of white quartz sand which can look very like snow when seen from a distance, particularly in the evening sunshine" (1990:16). They have also been called "The Alps of Cornwall' (Baron 1934:223). By contrast, the Welsh Alps are the peaks of Snowdonia (Edwards 1998:143). Similarly, Hunt referred to "Devonia's dreary Alps" (1881, 1st series, p.22). Perhaps the phrase Cornish Alps, despite being an appropriate description, derives from Chinese etymology. Jenkin says, of Cornish clay (q.v.) "Its proper name is kaolin, which is the name given to the 'white mountain' in China where this type of clay was first made" (1984:35). See *Cornish pyramids.*

Cornish Alps, capital of the The epithet of St. Austell (for this epithet see the internet page http://www.aboutbritain.com/towns/Fowey.asp).

Cornish Alternative to the Structure Plan (CASP) Founded in 1987 to oppose the First Alteration of Cornwall's Structure Plan. This plan was to have new houses built in Cornwall to accommodate the population increase. Although CASP was a non-party group. many memebers were from *Mebyon Kernow* (see Deacon et al 2003:83).

Cornish Amazons 1 Two sisters Jane and Mary Ann Walters described as 'Amazons' assaulted the master of the poor house when he tried to cut their hair (W.B.11 Sept. 1829, cited by Barton 1970, p.190). **2** Henwood (in the "Mining Journal") described the *bal maiden* (see *Cornish isle, sweet thrushes of our*) as 'Amazons' (cited by Scwartz in C.S. 2nd, 7, 1999, p.16). The Amazons were a female tribe of warriors in Greek mythology who to be like men cut off their breasts (the word 'Amazon' is derived from the negative prefix – *a* and *mastos* breast – hence the word 'mastectomy').

'Cornish' American As distinct from the *Cornish English* spoken in Cornwall, there is also another form of *Cornish dialect* which evolved from the Cornish emigrants in America. Alan M. Kent calls this speech '*Cornu-American*' (as opposed to '*Cornu-English*') and it constitutes a different body of "dialect words ... incorporating new concepts and revising old ones" (C.S. 2nd, 12, 2004. p.43 & p.124). Similarly, one could argue that there is also a distinct *Cornish Australian* dialect (a rich glossary of which is to be found in Jauncey 2004:83–107). See

Cornish crake and *Cornish-Yankee accent.*

Cornish American heartland Epithet of Mineral Point, Wisconsin due to the presence of Cornish mining families there from C19th (C.W. 28, 2002, p.46). See *Cornish capital, Cornish ecclesiastical capital* and *'Cornish' London.*

Cornish amphitheatre, John Wesley's As Joan Hellyar Shaw calls Gwennap Pit, the venue of Wesley's preaching (C.W. Vol. 2, No.11, 1996, p.21). See *Cornish Methodism, open air cathedral of.*

Cornish and pasty tea A *Cornish tea* (q.v.) with a *Cornish pasty* (q.v.). Traditionally it was only when eating a pasty that sugar would be taken with tea.

Cornish anthem Term used by some writers (e.g. Caine and Gorton 2001:24) for Rev. Hawker's *The Song of the Western Men* ('And shall Trelwny die? ') – for which see *Cornish national anthem.* There is also a Cornish language anthem *Bro goth agan tasow* (literally the 'wild' [i.e. untamed and therefore free] land of our fathers) which, like the Breton, is a variation of the Welsh national anthem *Hen Wlad fy Nhadau* ('Old Land of my Father' – see Bowen 1991:415). See *Cornish battle hymn.*

Cornish Anti-Nuclear League (CANA) launched in 1980 as a response to the Atomic Energy Authority's decision in 1979 to build a power station at Luxulyan, Gwithian or Nancekuke. Unlike the English branches, the CANA had an alliance with *Mebyon Kernow* (see Deacon et al 2003:79)

Cornish Antipodes Those Cornishmen living in the Southern Hemisphere, particularly in 'Little Cornwall' of Australia (the word 'Antipodes' is used with reference to them C.S. 2nd, Vol. 3, 1995:66). The word 'antipode' means literally 'opposite feet' (Gk *anti-* + *podos* foot).

Cornish apostle Or rather the *Apostle of Cornwall.* William Young who opened a chapel at Bodmin (Rawe 1986:153).See *Cornish patron saint.*

Cornish apparatus Another name for the *Cornish range* (q.v.).

Cornish apple pound See *Cornish pound.*

Cornish apron A *Cornish apron* was not always a souvenir garment. In Cornish dialect a *towser* is a hessian apron and a *wrapper* is also an apron (Phillipps 1993:55 and 60). A smart woman's apron was a *sogget* (Jenkin 1945:103). In Cornish *raglen* is a fisherman's apron while *apern* is a normal apron (Nance 1978). This word in dialect is *apernt* (Thomas 1895) or *apperne* (Ivey 1980; cf. Dev. *apern*). By contrast, an *apron* is the fat layer around a pig's kidney (Phillipps ibid. p.19).

Cornish archaeology, the father of As William Borlase has been called (for his epithet see internet page http://www.st.just.online.freeuk.com/pendeenvau.htm). Borlase was one of the greatest Cornish scientists of C18th. He is celebrated not only for his contribution to Cornish antiquities but in his work on Cornish natural history.

Cornish archers (Corn. *an waregoryon gernewek*) The archers who marched with An Gof in the *Cornish Rebellion* (q.v.). *Cornish archers* had also fought at Crècy (1346). In Cornish the word for archer is either *gwaregor* or *sethor* (from *seth* – arrow). See *Cornish arrows*.

Cornish – Armorican That which pertains to both Cornwall and Brittany. Since the British Celts went to 'Brittany' (hence the name – as opposed to 'Great Britain') there has always been regular contact between Cornwall and Brittany. The Cornish and Bretons share a common heritage of the saints and their languages are very similar. In Cornish the name *Kernow* can mean either Cornwall or Cornouaille in Brittany (to clarify the Cornish can say *Kernow Breten Vyghan* – i.e. the 'Cornwall of little Britain'). By the same token the Bretons' name *Kernev* refers to their own place of Cornouaille and to refer to Cornwall they would qualify it as *Kernev Veur* (i.e. 'Great Cornwall'). See *Pidgin Cornish* and *Tudor Cornish* in appendix 1.

Cornish arms (Corn. *Cota arvow* or *Scos* – literally 'shield') The black crest with fifteen *bezants*. According to G.A. Stevens, these symbolize the gold coins (*bezants* or *besants* minted in C9th Byzantium – hence the name) which the Saracens demanded as ransom for a Duke of Cornwall who had been captured in the Crusades (p.11). The Cornishmen's joint effort in collecting the ransom accounts for the motto written below the *Cornish arms*: 'One and All/ Onen hag Oll'. Pearse and Fry also suggests that the "fifteen gold balls has been linked with Jewish pawnbrokers" (2000:47). See *Cornish ensign* and *Cornish flag*, *Cornish independence flag*.

Cornish army See *Cornish host*.

Cornish Army, Free (FCA) Name of a probably fictitious group of extreme Cornish nationalists. They were cited by the press in the 1970s with bogus photographs showing students in quasi-military training gear. It is commonly believed that such media coverage was designed to bring the main Cornish movement into disrepute (see Deacon et al 2003:62). The name was possibly derived by allusion to the Free Wales Army (who like the MAC) in the 1960s were actively involved in a spate of acts of vandalism and sabotage, destroying government buildings but never endangering human life. For the shadowy group An Gof see *Cornish Braveheart*.

Cornish Aromatic A mid-late variety of Cornish apple for eating not cooking (Spiers 1996:58). For other apple varieties see *Cornish Garden Cooker*, *Cornish*

Giant, Cornish Gilliflower, Cornish Honeypin, Cornish Longstem, Cornish Mother, Cornish Pine and *Cornish Wine Apple.*

Cornish arrows Peter Waterfield cites Londoners at the time of the *Cornish Rebellion* who were impressed by the '*Cornish arrows*' that were "the length of a tailor's yard, so strong and mighty a bow the Cornishmen were said to draw" (C.T. summer 1997, p.10). According to Cunnack, in the *Hal an Tow* song (see *Cornish Furry*), the 'grey goose feather' intended for the Spaniards refers to arrows (1975:15).

Cornish assembly (Corn. *Cuntelles Kernow*). It has also been translated as *Senedh Kernow* (C.S. 2nd, 10, 2002, p.280) a term that would mean 'Cornish Parliament'. The independent assembly that the *Cornish Nationalist Party* (q.v.) and many other Cornish people demand. See *Cornish parliament* and *Cornish Stannators.*

Cornish Atlantis Lyonesse, the fabulous land situated between Cornwall and Scilly where, legend has it, 140 villages and churches were flooded (for this epithet see http://www.uktouristinfo.com/yuk/yuk1.htm). There is also the Cornish legend of *an eglos kellys y'n tewennow* (i.e. the church lost in the sands) at Perranporth. Similarly, the Breton equivalent was the land of *Ker ys* (which in both Breton and Cornish means 'lower fort/city'). The *Welsh Atlantis* was *Cantre'r Gwaelod* or the 'Lowland Hundred' (Edwards 1998:12–3). Even though Cornish uses a different word for hundred (see *Cornish hundred*), the Welsh *cantref* (literally '100 towns') is seen in the Cornish words *cans* + *tre(f)* and the Welsh *gwaelod* is like the Corn. *goles*. Moreover, the *Irish Atlantis* was *Hy Brasail* (Edwards 2004:18–9). Atlantis was the lost civilization mentioned by Plato and it is believed to be somewhere in the Altlantic.

Cornish attic Or rather '*Cornwall's attic*' as Bude and Stratton have been called (C.T. 8, 1995, p.4).

Cornish auction A type of 'candle auction' which "requires the auctioneer to insert a pin one inch below the top of the candle. As long as the pin stays in place, the bidding can continue. When the pin drops, the auction is over" (see Kate Reynolds' internet article *Auction Offshoots*). In Cornwall an auction was called a *survey* (Jago 1882:285 and Thomas 1895:127). In Cornish an auction is *stryfwerth* (*stryf* – contest + *gwerth*– sale).

Cornish Autonomist Party As Bernard Deacon calls *Mebyon Kernow* (*Planet 72*, Dec./Jan. 1988–9, p.6). See *Cornish Political Party.*

'Cornish' Azores S.P.B. Mais drew an analogy between the Atlantic islands of the Scillies (of Cornwall) and the Azores (of Portugal). With reference to the *Cornish Riviera* he wrote in 1928 that "Penzance is proving a formidable rival to Madeira, the Scilles to the Azores and Mullion to Monte Carlo" (cited by Ronald Perry in C.S. 2nd, 7, 1999, p.101). It was off the Azores that in 1591 Sir Richard

Grenville fought the Spanish fleet in the 'Revenge'.

Cornish bagpipes (Corn. *pybow sagh*)The Cornish form of the bagpipes which is similar to the Welsh *pibgorn* and Breton *biniou*. It has a left hand chanter (f# to d) and a right chanter (c to g) as well as a drone which rests on the left shoulder. Unlike the *Cornish kilt* (q.v.) and *Cornish sporran* (q.v.), the *Cornish bagpipes* were not borrowed from Scotland and are even shown in a carving on the bench-end of a pew in St. Nonna's church, Altarnun in Bodmin (c.1510–30). Often the bag is covered with *Cornish tartan*(q.v.).

Cornish bagpiper Phrase used by Jane Bowden-Dan (C.W.W. 1997, 21, p.7) for the *Cornish piper* (q.v.).

Cornish ball game, the As *Cornish hurling* has been called (Payton 1996:18).

Cornish bal-maiden The *bal maiden* was the woman who worked at the surface of the mine (Cornish *bal* – not to be confused with the Cornish dialect *bal* meaning 'noise'; another Cornish word for mine is *wheal*). She wore the distinctive *Cornish gook* (q.v.). The word 'Cornish' often precedes the term (e.g. see Schwartz in C.S. 2nd 8, 2000:78 and Ince 2001:28). The *bal maiden* would work on the *dressing floor* (where ore was dressed) and do *spalling* (breaking large pieces of ore), *cobbing* (breaking waste away from the ore) and *bucking* (final crushing of ore). The *clay maidens* or *scrapers* were women employed at the clay works (Jago 1882:134).

Cornish banana belt, the Area around the latitude of Falmouth where it is possible to grow certain varieties of bananas (the term is used in the Royal Horticultural Society internet page: http://www.rhs.org.uk/publications/pubs/gardens0502/bananas.asp). Merton even suggests a 'banana pasty' (2003:18).

Cornish bank, the The original name of the Gothic building in Truro built 1848 which was the Coinage Hall (C.T. 2, 9, 1996, p.15). With a small letter 'b' the phrase *Cornish bank* is frequently used to mean the Cornish side of the Tamar.

Cornish banner A synonym of the *Cornish flag* (q.v.). The word is similar to the Cornish *An Baner Kernewek* (which, incidentally is also the name of the *Cornish Nationalist Party's* newsletter).

'Cornish' banshee With reference to the Irish *banshee*, St. Clair writes "in Cornwall sometimes she takes the form of a phantom tree" (1971:21). Weatherhill & Devereux compare a woman of the *fogou/vuggo* (cave) near Penwith with the *banshee*. She had a red rose in her mouth and "any who chance to see her will surely die" (1994:iv). The *banshee* (Ir. *bean sidhe* – 'fairy woman') wails outside the house of one about to die.

Cornish bantam A synonym of *Cornish game* (C.W. 22, p.21). In Cornwall the word *mabyers* meaning 'chicks' could also be applied to the equally small bantams (Ivey 1976:42).

Cornish bard A poet in the *Cornish Gorsedd* (q.v.). (the word bard is a cognate of the Corn. for poet *barth*, pl. *byrth*; cf. W. *bardd*, pl. *beirdd* and Bret. *barzh*, pl. - *ed*). A lady poet or poetess would be a *bardhes* (pl. *bardhesow*). In the *Cornish Gorsedd* (q.v.) there is also the rank of ovate (Corn. *ovydh*, c.f. W. *ofydd*).

Cornish bardic name (Corn. *hanow bardhek*) The special name that someone uses in their capacity as member of the *Cornish Gorsedd* (q.v.). For instance, the bardic name of R.Morton Nance was 'Mordon' or 'Sea wave'. Bardic names are also used by bards (W. *beirdd*) of the *Welsh Gorsedd* and called *enw barddol*.

Cornish barm A mixture containing flour, mashed potatoes, water, sugar and raisins – to be kept for a week before use (Pascoe 1995).

Cornish baronet, the little As Sir John Aubyn of the *Cornish Mount* (q.v.) has been dubbed (Payton 1996:165).

'Cornish' barrel roof Type of roof once common on Cornish churches of the Perpendicular period. Michael Fisher mentions a watercolour (c.1858) of Launceston showing "the old 'horse-box' pews, slate floor, *Cornish-style barrel roof* and brass chandeliers" (O.C. IX, 7, 1982, p.318). Daniell calls it the *Cornish wagon or barrel roof* and describes it as having "curved braces to the rafters and a division of the whole into panels infilled with lath and plaster" (1988:27).

Cornish barrow No relation to a *Cornish wheelbarrow* (q.v.). Salmon refers to 'the *Cornish barrows*' (1903:34) of which there are at least 200 according to his calculation. A *barrow* is a prehistoric mound and by confusion (or perhaps by association with the ancient *Cornish Jews* q.v. in old mine works), the word *burrow* (often used interchangeably with *barrow* – e.g. see Jago 1882:125) also refers to old mine workings (Ivey 1976:11). Clemo calls 'clay dumps' *burras* (p.101).

Cornish Bastilles The workhouses in Penzance were called 'Bastilles' because of their terrible conditions (W.B. 21 July, 1837, and see accompanying note in Barton 1971, p.37). The allusion here is to the Bastille or prison fortress which was destroyed in the French Revolution in 1789. Perhaps a similar fate was desired for the workhouses.

Cornish battle hymn, the As Brian Redley calls Trelawny (*The Times Weekend*, Sat. May 1999, p.30). See *Cornish national anthem*.

Cornish beam engine Type of steam engine used for pumping, winding and giving power for ores to be crushed. It was housed in the *Cornish engine house* (q.v.).

Cornish beam pumping engine A *Cornish beam pumping engine* "has no rotary motion, its valve gear consists of a fascinating array of deadweights, trips and handles for starting and is known as gearwork" (Brown and Acton 1994:138).

Cornish beehive huts The *crellas* which were the ancient ruins of rounded huts. In the *Cornish language* (q.v.) the word *crellas* is the correct singular form, not *crella* (c.f. *Cornish double plural*). The same word in *Cornish Dialect* also connotes an excavation in a bank roofed over to serve for an outhouse (see Bottrell 1873:156). They are also called *piskies' crows* (Corn. *crow* – hut).

Cornish Bellflower (*campanula alliariifolia*) An edible flowering plant found in rough ground, especially at the side of railways in South England.

Cornish Bells A carol by Stubbs mentioning Cornish places:

> "Merry ring the bells
> Across the western Land
> From Launceston's town to Michael's Mount
> From Bude to Sennen sand" (cited by Rowse 1942:147).

Cornish bezants (Corn. *besont*, pl. – *ns*) The fifteen gold coins on the *Cornish arms* (q.v. for the origin of the bezants). The word *bezants* is often preceded by the word 'Cornish' (e.g. by Deane and Shaw 1975:17).

Cornish Bible (Corn. *Bybel* or *An Lyver* – i.e. 'the Book' c.f. the Gk. word for 'Bible' *Biblos* which literally means 'book') One of the greatest blows to the Cornish language was the lack of a *Cornish Bible* and a *Cornish Prayer Book* (see *Cornish Prayer Book Rebellion*). However, while no *Cornish Bible* was generally available, some scholars e.g. Malte W. Tschivschky postulate that a *Cornish Bible* may well have existed (C.S. Vol.11, 2003, p.308). This is because a copy of the *Tredegar Homilie* (c.1555) included quotations from the Bible in Cornish. See *Cornishman's Bible* (appendix 2).

Cornish Bible Christians Denomination which emerged from the *Canorums* (as the Cornish called the Methodists). In Cornwall this denomination can be called simply *Bible Christians* but the preferred form is to precede it with the word 'Cornish' (e.g. by Rawe 1986:131 and in C.S. Vol. X, No.11, 1990, p.565). They were also called *Bryanites* as the group was formed in 1815 by William Bryan (later changed to O'Bryan) of Luxulyan. He established several chapels and went to America. Notable members included the preacher Billy Bray (see *Cornish tin mining evangelist*). One Cornish reply to someone enquiring about their health was 'All owver alike like a Bryanite' (Hawke 1973:13).

Cornish bilingualism 1 Term used by Myrna Combellack Harris to refer to the ability to speak both Cornish and English (*Contact Bulletin*, Vol. 5, No.3, winter

1988/89, p.4). **2** The ability to speak *Cornish dialect* (q.v.) as well as standard English. Cyril Noall refers to *Cornish dialect* speakers who are "as it were, bilingual, 'speaking proper' when the occasion requires, and reserving their own homely speech for conversations with friends" (intro. of James 1979:3). To speak in such a refined way is to *cut up* (Phillipps 1993:26) and is similar to what Devon dialect speakers would call *telephone English* (Downes 1986:49).

Cornish bird 1 One of the names of the *Cornish Chough* (used by Dale Jackson in C.W. 27, 2001, p.14). **2** The *'Cornish Bird'* is the boat that takes visitors on fishing trips from Padstow (see Caine and Gorton 2001:13 and 37).

Cornish biscuits See **Cornish wafer**. In dialect biscuit is *biskey* (Jago 1882:116).

Cornish Black See *Cornish Cattle*. No relation to the *Cornish Large Black* (q.v.).

Cornish black cake Rich fruit cake that is called 'black' because its dark colour is derived from the currants, raisins, sultanas, cinnamon and brandy and because the colour of the cake contrasts with the white icing (e.g. see web site *Connie's Cornish Kitchen Recipes*).

Cornish Black Country Areas of Cornwall where there are many *knackt bals* or disused mines which Bird calls 'Cornwall's Black Country' (1989:76). Another dialect name for an abandoned mine was a *balscat* or *scat bal*. The analogy was also seen by du Maurier who argued that the revival of the tin and copper trades would not mean "turning Cornwall into a Black Country, full of belching smoke, concrete factories and grey slums" (1967:202).

Cornish Blackfish Name applied to two species of fish (*schedophilus medusophagus* and *centrolophus brittanicus*). See *Cornish Jack* and *Cornish Sucker*.

Cornish black ship Alexander refers to two such ships: **1** A phantom ship with black sails which haunted a notorious wrecker at Priest's Cove. **2** A similar vessel seen off Porthcurno which was 'regarded as a harbinger of evil' (2002:24). See *Cornish cloud ship*.

Cornish Bladderseed (*phylospermum cornubiense*) A rare kind of plant.

Cornish blight A potato blight which attributed to the famine in Cornwall in the 1590s (C.S. Vol. 4, 1996, p.110).

Cornish block pavers Term for paving stones used in *Cornish paving* (q.v.) (see internet page http://www.pavingexpert.com). See *Cornish cobbles*.

Cornish Blonde A light beer brewed by Skinners, Truro. See *Cornish knocker*, *Cornish Rebellion* and *Cornish Saxon*.

Cornish Blue 1 Type of ceramic crockery ware with blue and white stripes, also called *Cornish Kitchen*. See *Cornish Green* and *Cornish Yellow*. **2** A type of grey blue slate. See *Cornish Hellan*. **3** A variety of cheese. See *Cornish Capra*, *Cornish Feta*, *Cornish Herb and Garlic*, *Cornish Pepper*, *Cornish Soft*, *Cornish Trelwney* and *Cornish Yarg*. **4** A subspecies of the ferret also called the *Cornish Blue Ferret* (see http://homepage.ntlworld.com/ferreter/mixture.htm).

Cornish Bluebeard, The Tregeagle who, according to Cornish folklore, sold his soul to the Devil and murdered heiresses to take their estates. As a punishment he was doomed to empty the Dozemare Pool with just a limpet shell (called a *croggan* – in which there was a hole). His epithet is mentioned by many writers (e.g. Brewer 1870:1134; Courtney 1890:72; Tregarthen:176 and Martin 1951:75). A howling wind is still said to be Tregeagle whistling. Bluebeard was a character in a tale by Charles Perrault in *Histoires et Contes du Temps Passé* (1697) who murdered his wives. His last wife Fatima was given a key and told not to open one locked room (when she did she found the corpses of her predecessors). Because of Tregeagle's pact with the Devil he has also been called the *Cornish Faust* (q.v.).

Cornish bodhrán Neil Davey refers to the *crowdy crawn* as 'equivalent to the Irish *bodhran*' (C.W. 38, 2004, p.29). The *bodhrán* is a kind of tambourine and the word also means a kind of sieve or 'winnowing drum' in Irish. Similarly the Cornish term *croder croghen* meant a "sieve-rim with sheepskin bottom, used as tambourine, measure." (Nance 1978:227), a meaning which is also conveyed in the dialect word *croud* (Bottrell 1873:156). Moreover, the same Irish word *bodhrán* also means 'deaf' (and as such is the cognate of the Corn. *bodhar*).

Cornish bogey, the W. S. Lach-Szyrma's name for Tregeagle (cited by Penn 1906: 22) for which see *Cornish Bluebeard*.

Cornish bogeyman As Bird (1989:23) and Caine and Gorton (p.23) call Tregeagle (p.23) for whom see *Cornish Bluebeard*.

Cornish boiled cake Cake in which the ingredients are first boiled (before the eggs are added) and then baked (Butcher ansd Annand 1994:50–51).

Cornish boiler A type of cylindrical flue boiler which could withstand greater pressure and replaced the old 'haystack' or 'wagon' boilers of copper, lead or wrought iron which suffered leaks that the boilerman had to patch with tallow. The size of the fire was reduced, enabling the oxygen to reach the fire. The *Cornish boiler* could also be mounted on wheels (see Cowley 1976:19).

Cornish bonnet A *gook* (See C.W.19, 1996) for which see *Cornish gook*.

Cornish booys Spelling used by Jenkin (1945:404) for *Cornish boys* (q.v.).

Cornish border The River Tamar marks the border between Cornwall and England/Devon. Grand Bard Ron Lyon wrote recently that "Having held the first two *Gorseddau* in the west of Cornwall, it was decided that the next should be somewhere in the east as 'The Tamar is the boundary of Cornwall, not the Fal' " (cited in C.W. 36, 2003/4).

Cornish boss A proverbial hard task master. In America *Cornish bosses* had a reputation for being strict. Whetter writes "no class of 'bosses' act so meanly towards the men under them than '*Cornish bosses*' " (1977:118).

Cornish Bouillabaisse Or 'Bouillabaise Cornish version' Soup of fish stock, garlic, thyme, orange peel, bayleaf and saffron (Heard 1984:17–18).

Cornish boulter Nance refers to 'the *Cornish boulter* and *spiller*' which are fishing tackles (1963:42). The former is a longer line used for conger, ling and cod whereas the latter is used for smaller fish.

Cornish boys Courtney wrote "There are no men in Cornwall; they are all *Cornish boys*" (1880:6). Just as in Irish English, in *Cornish Dialect*, the word 'boy' is often used for a grown man (cf. the *Warsail boys* in the entry *Cornish wassailers*). The opposite is sometimes not 'girl' but 'child' as Joy Stevenson observes, hence the expression "Issa a boy or a cheeld?" (i.e. Is the new baby a boy or a girl?) (C.T. 2, 7, 1996, p.8). Yet girls are also called *maids*. An inscription on the door of the Tinners Arms, St. Hilary (and obviously for men) read:

> "Come all good *Cornish boys*, walk in,
> Have a brandy, rum and shrub, and gin"

(cited by Deane and Shaw 1975:67).

Cornish Braveheart As Michael Joseph/Myghal Josef An Gof ('the Smith') has very appropriately been dubbed (by Payton 1996:125). An Gof was the leader of the *Cornish Rebellion* (q.v.). The original 'Braveheart' was William Wallace (1270–1305) enemy of Edward I and victor at the battle of Stirling Bridge (1297) who was also tortured like An Gof. Alan M. Kent has extended this term by referring to "the *Cornish bravehearts* Michael Joseph 'An Gof' and Thomas Flamank" (C.S. 11, 2003, p.118). The name 'An Gof' was also used by a group claiming resposibility for the bombing of a magistrate's court in St. Austell in December, 1980 and other acts of arson and vandalism, including planting broken glass on tourist beaches. Many believe that this group did not really exist but was part of a 'dirty tricks' campaign to attack decent Cornish nationalists (who would never condone violence) (see Ellis 1985:144; Deacon et al 2003:77–78). See *Cornish Army, Free*.

Cornish breakfast The phrase 'a full *Cornish breakfast*' (C.T. November 1998, p.68) is mainly synonymous with a cooked English breakfast – unless, of course, a Cornishman wanted to serve something different like pilchards. See *Cornish tea*.

Cornish bridge A bridge made with several large pieces of granite (Leggat 1987:55). In dialect this is called a *clam*. In the Cornish language a bridge is *pons* (cf. W. / Bret. and Fr. *pont*, It. *ponte* and Sp. *puente*). It is most probably a legacy of the Roman invasion and the Corn. *pons* is also a cognate of English words like 'pontificate' (literally 'build bridges').

Cornish Brie A type of cheese. The original Brie is called after Brie in N.E. France. See *Cornish Blue*.

Cornish brigade Cornish South Africans formed "the self-styled *Cornish brigade* as an instrument to keep the peace and defend Cornish interests in Johannesburg" (Payton 1999:356). There was some hostility towards the Cornish as their neutrality in the Boer-War (1899–1902) was viewed by some as being pro-Boer. See *Cornish Uitlanders*.

Cornish broccoli Mentioned by Jack Richards (p.24) perhaps as a separate variety. Yet in dialect they can "use the term 'broccoli' for a white 'single' cauliflower" (see O.C. Vol. XII, No. 9, p.22). One *Cornish dialect* form is *broccolow* (see Courtney 1890:46 under the entry *rare* i.e. early). In fact due to the early harvest of *Cornish broccoli*, the *West Briton* recorded on 9.1.1939 that 41,500 tons of broccoli were 'dispatched by rail' from Cornwall (see Ince 2001:8). There is also a *broccoli pasty* (Wright 1986:16).

Cornish brogue Phrase which has sometimes been used to describe the Cornish accent (cited by Payton 1999:239). The word 'brogue' (Ir. *bróg* means a coarse leather shoe) is applied to a broad Irish accent. Yet its usage is interesting in that it emphasizes the Celtic quality of Cornish speech. By coincidence, the *Cornish dialect* also uses the word *broog* as a wood-soled boot worn by *lappiors* (O.C. IX. 11, 1984, p.570).

Cornish broiler (U.S.) a supermarket *Cornish game* (q.v.) chicken. Not to be confused with *broil* which in mining was the back of a lode (Jago 1882:122).

Cornish browney The word 'Cornish' often appears before the name of this fairy creature from Cornwall who can settle the bees (e.g. see internet glossary http://hedgewytchery.com/denizens.html). See *Cornish guardian of the bees*.

Cornish brownies Plural of *Cornish Browney* (see Barber and Riches 1971:29). The plural 'browneys' is less common. Cf. *Cornish piskies*.

Cornish burnt cream See *Cornish scalded cream*.

Cornish bucca Often the word 'Cornish' is prefixed to this fabulous creature in Cornish folklore (e.g. Rose 1998:58). The *bucca* exists in two main forms: *Bucca Gwidden* or the good 'White Bucca' (from *gwyn*– white) and the *Bucca Dhu* or evil 'Black Bucca' (Corn. *du*– black) as the Devil is sometimes called. Like the original Cornish word *bucca* (pl. *bukkyas*), the same word in Cornish dialect also means scarecrow (J.R.I.C. Vol.1, part 3, 1864–65, p.46).

Cornish buccaboo As W.S. Lach-Szmyrna refers to the *Cornish Bucca* (q.v.) "who is usually rendered in the medieval manner as the devil" (W.S. Lach-Szyrma in *Folklore* 1, 1883, p.364). Moreover, he explains that Newlyn fishermen threw fish to the *Buccaboo* and have therefore had the nickname Newlyn Buccas.

Cornish bugle (*ajuga genevensis*) A unique variety of wild flower.

Cornish bucket The *kibble* (see *Cornish kibble*) has been called the '*Cornish bucket*' (see the internet site *Reed Gold Mine–Glossary of Mining Terms*). Buckets were used in the *Cornish water wheel* (q.v.) and there is also a *draw bucket* (Ivey 1976:22) to draw water from a well (see *Cornish peath*). The Cornish words for bucket were *buket* and *kelorn* (for a milk pail). There were two buckets in a house – one for drinking water and the other for *coddling* water (i.e. washing floors or clothes) (Jenkin 1984:82). For the use of a bucket on *Dripping Day* see *Cornish elm*.

'Cornish' Bunyan Jack Clemo (1916–1994) poet and novelist has been dubbed 'The John Bunyan of the century' (C.T. 3,1994, p.21). In 1970 the *Cornish Gorsedd* (q.v.) crowned him *Prydyth an Pry* ('Poet of the Clay'). Clemo was both deaf and blind. John Bunyan (1628–88) was the author of *Pilgrim's Progress* and the writing of both Bunyan and Clemo has a distinct spiritual emphasis. Moreover, like Clemo, Bunyan's daughter Mary was also blind. See *Cornish Pilgrim's Progress*.

Cornish Bureau of European Relations (CoBER) Pressure group formed by Roger Holmes et al, seeing Cornwall as a European nation in cooperation with other European countries.

'Cornish' Burns, the John Harris (b.1820) Bard of Bolenowe, poet and writer of religious tracts and social issues such as slavery and drink. His more common epithet which is also written on his tombstone is *The Cornish Poet*. Elwyn Rees also dubs him '*The Robbie Burns of Cornwall*' (C.W. 29, 2002).

Cornish burnt cream Not *Cornish scalded cream* (q.v.) but a dessert with alternate layers of custard and *Cornish cream* (see internet page: http://www.recipeview.com/Corn41.htm).

Cornish burr Phrase used by Dave Neville for the Cornish accent (O.C. X. 5, 1987:224).

Cornish burying tune Song sung at a funeral, eg. for a dead miner (Payton 1996:218). Courtney refers to 'singing funerals' or *buryings* (pronounced *berrins*) (1890:168).

Cornish bush At Christmastime in Cornwall there would be "the traditional '*Cornish bush*' or 'kissing' bush' hung in the windows of many houses" (C.T. Vol. 3, No.2, 1996, p.2). As its name suggests its purpose would be the same as the mistletoe. The *talking bush* was a branch of holly (see *Cornish Christmas tree*) tied to the mast of a ship (Nance 1963). In *Cornish dialect* the word *bush* was an object like a balloon on a stick waved by the *huer* (lookout on the cliff) who gave his *scry* (report on seeing the shoal of pilchards) with the shout '*Hevva!*' For other Christmas entries see *Cornish carol service*, *Cornish Christmas tree*, *Cornish guisers*, *Cornish wassail* and *Cornish yule log*.

Cornish bushel The equivalent of three Winchester bushels for measuring barley, wheat and potatoes (W.B., 10 April, 1812 and 4 July, 1817). A bushel of wheat was the price of a swarm of bees (Couch 1871:84).

Cornish butt In Hiberno-English there was 'the old *Cornish butt*, a dung cart' (ÓMuirithe 1997: 58). In *Cornish dialect* the word *butt* refers to the body of a cart (Hawke 1989), a beehive (Thomas 1895:72) or a buttock of beef and in the plural *butts* was a horse disease (Ivey 1976:11). Also in Cornwall an animal does not 'butt' but *bunch* (Phillipps 1993:23). See *Cornish wain*.

Cornish by adoption Term used by Jenkin (1984:67) and by Barry Kinsmen (O.C. XII, 11, 2002, p.1) as opposed to the native Cornish (i.e. Cornish by birth).

Cornish by marriage A category of non-native Cornish lovers or *Cornuphiles* whose children, of course, will be Cornish (Payton 1996:267). See *Cornish by adoption*. There are baseball caps with the words '*Cornish by marriage*'.

Cornish by post (Corn. *Kernewek dre Lyther*) Correspondence course to learn *Kemmyn Kernewek* (or *Unified Cornish* if specified). The course is designed especially for those outside Cornwall (both the *Cornish diaspora* and non-Cornish learners) without the benefit of attending Cornish classes. Ray Edwards provides carefully graded lessons at all levels and the correction of students' work is always analytical and meticulous. A similar Cornish By radio (*Kernewek dre Radyo*) was also proposed by Agan Tavas in 1994.

Cornish cake, the traditional As Butcher and Annand (1994:54) call the *Cornish saffron cake* (q.v.).

'Cornish' camomile There is an endemic Cornish variety of camomile called *Treneague* – "a variety … discovered in Cornwall that produced no flowers and had a less scrambling habit, making it suitable and affordable for ordinary country gardens" (hitherto before early C20th it was only for the rich). It is drunk to calm the nerves (see C.W. 37, 2004, p.25) and 'camomile liquor' was used by fair-haired people as a shampoo (Hawke 1973:30). It was also boiled to relieve rheumatism (Day 2003:238). In Cornish it is *camyl* and in dialect *camels* (Hawke 1989:24). The word 'camomile' literally means 'earth apple' (Gk. *chamaimelon* [even in modern Gk. *mílo* is apple] and thus it has the same meaning as the Fr. word for 'potato' *pomme de terre*).

Cornish Camp The settlement of Cornish miners at New Almaden, Cailfornia (C.W.W. gwaynten, 1995, p.9). *Cornish Camp* was also called Englishtown as opposed to the Spanishtown inhabited by the Mexicans. (Payton 1999:207).

Cornish Cantata Song written by David Gilbert in 1828 which is also called 'Lapyor Tom's Song'. The lyrics are just a list of Cornish place names which gives the impression that the song is sung in Cornish (see Davey 1983:59 and O.C. June 1990:32).

Cornish cap An award for rugby (C.T. Oct. 1998, p.72). See *Cornish All Blacks* and *Cornish rugby shirt*.

Cornish capital Truro which is Cornwall's only city (see Rowse 1986:278–84).At one time it was Launceston (Payton 1996:91). Talking of capital, one of Oswald Pryor's Cornish cartoon captions features a miner who says: "Capital! What is capital? If you was to ask we to come'n'ave a drink, lad, that would be capital" (quoted by Payton in C.S. 2nd, 9, 2001, p.174). See *Cornish ecclesiastical capital* and *Cornish London* and in appendix 3 see *Bath of the West, the*.

Cornish cap'n The words *cap'n* or *cappen* (see Thomas 1895:132) mean captain. Treenoodle used the word *kepen* (1846:95). See *Cornish captain*.

Cornish Capra A soft chesse produced by Paxton &Whitfields from goats' milk (the name '*capra*' is It. for nanny goat ; cf. Sp. *cabra*, W. *gafr* and therefore related to Corn. *gavar* – hence our word 'Capricorn'). See *Cornish Blue*.

Cornish captain 1 A work manager, especially in a mine. There were a few types of captain: *mine captain* and *grass captain* (who was on the 'grass' i.e. surface – hence also called *surface captain*). Inside a mine the overseer was the *underground captain* (Jago 1882:302). There was also the *captain dresser* in the milling department (see Orchard) and a *clay captain* (who supervised a clay pit) as well as a captain for an engine house and, of course, for a boat. The wives of the *clay captains* and *mine captains* were addressed as *Mrs Cap'n* (Phillipps 1976:33). **2** Or *Captain of the Cornish* – as Michael Joseph is known (see Best in section 'Men and Women', question 6). The Cornish word for 'captain' *kembrynkyas lu* literally meant 'leader of an army or host' (see *Cornish host*). See *Cornish Braveheart*, *Cornish March* and *Cornish Rebellion*. **3** The captain of a fishing boat. According to Day, "the Cornish believed that the souls of dead sea captains never rested, but turned into albatrosses or gulls" (2003:264). Thus neither bird (like the robin or wren) were killed by Cornish people.

'Cornish' Captain Courageous John/James Silk Buckingham (1786–1855) of Flushing has been dubbed 'Cornwall's Captain Courageous' (Selleck 1992). Buckingham was a traveller, adventurer, social reformer and author.

'Cornish' Caravaggio John Opie (for whom see the *Cornish Wonder*) whom Sir Joshua Reynolds likened to Caravaggio (byname of the Italian painter Michelangelo Merisi 1573–1610). By coincidence, on his death in 1807 he was buried next to Sir Joshua Reynolds. See *Cornish Velásquez*.

Cornish card, play the To appease the Cornish people. Payton uses the phrase with reference to Henry VII who tried to gain acceptance by the Cornish by using his own fellow-Celtic (i.e. Welsh) roots and naming his son Arthur. (1996:123).

Cornish Carnegie, the John Passmore Edwards (1823–1911) 'The *Cornish Carnegie*' or 'Mr. Great Heart' as he was dubbed by Sir Henry Irving. Born in Blackwater, Edwards began his career as a journalist writing about social reforms. He later became a newspaper editor and then owner. From 1880–85 he was Liberal M.P. for Salisbury and from 1990 began his philanthropic work, financing hospitals and other public buildings but mainly libraries. His epithet is derived from the Scottish-born benefactor Andrew Carnegie (1835–1919) who built libraries throughout U.S.A. and is also known for the Carnegie Hall.

Cornish carol service A service with Cornish carols or *curls* (in Cornwall *curls* also means 'neck glands').Treenoodle called them *carlls* (1846:92). Even in Australia Cornish people are still famous for their *curling* or carol singing (Davey and Seal 2003:81). The Cornish words for carol are *can carol* or *can Nadelek* (i.e. Christmas song) whereas *carol* means 'choir, round dance sung to music' (Nance 1978:220). Cornish carols were completely different from the carols sung elsewhere in Britain, the most popular were by Thomas Merritt (d.1908) and Davies Giddy (see the *Cornish Philosopher*). Carol singers went from door to door and even the *Cornish knockers* (q.v.) sang carols in the mine on Christmas Eve. Also on Christmas Eve the *Curn Dilly* or 'Dilly Carol' was sung at midnight when the *Dilly bird* (saffron currant bun) was eaten (see Gendall & Gendall 1991:5). Nance also records the word *pelgens* for a 'midnight service on Christmas Eve'. The same word had connotations of 'dawn' and 'cock crow' and corresponds with the Welsh *plygain* carol service before dawn on Christmas morning and Bret. *pelgent* (from Lat. *pulli cantus* 'cock's crow' – i.e. reflecting the earliness of the service). It is analogous with the Catalan *misas del gall* (i.e. 'mass of the cock') and the Manx *Oei'l Verney* (with *carvals* or carols). According to Cornish superstition, "it is unlucky to sing carols before Christmas or before the *arish mow* (i.e. stack of corn sheaves) is made" (Courtney 1890:171). Another version dictates that it is permitted to sing carols after 21st December – i.e. St. Thomas' Day/Midwinter Day (Day 2003:376). See *Cornish Bush* for other Christmas entries.

Cornish cart Synonym of *Cornish wain* (O.C. XII, 9, 2001, p.60)

Cornish casserole As Heard calls *Cornish under-roast* (q.v.) (1984:57).

Cornish castle The *Cornish engine house* (q.v.). The term is used by several writers (e.g. Trevail 1990:38; Brown and Acton 1994:7 and Pearse 38).

'Cornish' cathedral Or *'Cornwall's cathedral'* is Truro Cathedral. Also Altarnum is the 'cathedral on the moors' (see Stevens p.33). The Cornish word for cathedral is *peneglos* (literally 'head church') yet 'cathedral' (from Gk. *kathedra* or 'chair' – since it is the seat of a bishop) is related to the Cornish word for 'chair' *cadar* (cf. W. *cadair*, Bret. *kador* and Ir. *cathaoir*). The 'Cathedral' was also the name for the bottom level of South Condurrow/King Edward Mine (Buckley 1989:28). See also *Cornish Methodism, open air cathedral of*.

Cornish Cattle A distinct black breed of cattle that were quite small and extinct in C19th (C.S. 1st, 12, 1984, p.27). They were mentioned by Carew (1602:14).They were also called simply *Cornish* (Mason 1951:32) or *Cornish Black* (q.v.).

Cornish caudle chicken pie Unlike other chicken pies (with pieces of small meat) this has a drum stick of chicken and the pie filling has egg and cream. In Cornish dialect the word *caudle* means 'mess'.

Cornish cavaliers Term used by Peter Lane (O.C. IX. 12, 1985, p.602) for the *Cornish royalists* (q.v.).

Cornish Cave-Man Mathematician, the Epithet of Daniel Gumb, C18th eccentric troglodyte who built a house of *Cornish granite* on Bodmin Moor, near the Cheesewring. He was noted for his "scientific prowess" (the epithet was recorded by W.H. Paynter in O.C. 2, No. 4 1932 and cited by Jason Semmens in *Folklore* 116, April 2005, p.92).

Cornish Celtic Society As the *Cowethas Kelto-Kernuak* has been called (C.S. 2nd, 3, 1995:86) for which see *Cornish Society, Celtic*.

Cornish Celtic tongue The *Cornish language* as opposed to the *Cornish Dialect* (the phrase is used by Donald Rawe in C.W.W. c1995,16, p.27).

Cornish chair A large rock. According to Rundle the term *Cornish chairs* refers not only to actual chairs but to 'nature's chairs' and 'giants' chairs', church, historic chairs and saints' chairs (J.R.I.C. Vol.15, 1902–03, p.384). These are unique to Cornwall: e.g. St. Mawnan's Chair and the Lizard chair.

Cornish charmer Term used by Deane and Shaw (1975) for a *white witch* who used spells for healing and helping someone *ill-wished* or *overlooked* (i.e. under the spell of the evil eye) as well as *piskey-led* (bewildered and lost). Formerly called a *peller* (pl. *pelloryon*), he would give *soons* (from Corn. *son*, cf. W. *swyn* spell or charm) (written or spoken charms – see Ivey 1980). The word *peller* conveys the idea of one who removes/takes away charms (form *pell* far away). The other Cornish word is *huder* (pl. *hudoryon*) who was literally an enchanter or magician (from *hus* –magic, cf. W. *hud*). The charmer was distinct from the *pomster* or quack doctor. As in Greece, in Cornwall the charmer had to learn his/her charms from a person of the opposite sex and he/she should not be thanked for his/her services. Moreover, no payment should be received (Hawke 1973:29).

Cornish Charter 1 Produced by the Cornish branch of the Celtic League. This charter (distributed to all candidates in the 1987 district council election and subsequently in the General elections) made devolution and Cornish identity an election issue (see Deacon et al 2003:85). **2** The fragment of land charter dated 1340 on the back of which was written what Ray Edwards believes was either a Cornish play or a long poem (*The Celtic Pen* 3, 1, 1995/6, p.17).

Cornish Chartist As William Lovell is described (C.T. 5, pp.32–33). The Chartists (fl. 1830s) sought electoral reform (secret ballot, male suffrage and no property qualifications for M.P.s.).

Cornish Chatters Service provided by Richard Woollard to distribute tapes for disabled people to hear (C.T. 11, June 1995).

Cornish chaw A synonym of the *Cornish chough* (q.v.). *Chaw* also means 'cattle house'(i.e. *bowjy* – which also refers to a sheep pen) or 'chew' (Hawke 1975:10).

Cornish chawk A name for the *Cornish Chough* (q.v.). The name is probably derived from the Cornish words *choca, chok* and *chogha* (i.e. jackdaw or chough). These dialect forms are derived from O.E. *ceo*, which meant chough, jay or jackdaw (Hall 1894:67).

Cornish cherry choclets Tiny chocolate cakes with glazed cherries. See *Cornish burnt cream*.

Cornish chert. A variety of black stone. Usually flint (associated with limestone), chert is associated with chalk. *Cornish chert* is black (Ferris p.16). It is interesting to postulate whether there may be a relation between 'chert' and the Slavic word for 'black' (e.g. in Bulgarian *cherno*).

Cornish chess set Unique chess set designed by Dennis Lammerton of An Lyverji

Kernewek. The pieces are made of pewter (an alloy which is mostly *Cornish tin*). *Cornish engine houses* (appropriately called *Cornish castles*) are used in place of castles, swords with the *Cornish coat of arms* take the place of knights, *Cornish crosses* are bishops, lighthouses are pawns and the king and queen are a *Cornish tin miner* and a *Cornish bal maiden* respectively. In Cornish the words for chess are *chekker* (which is also a bird – the stonechat or wheatear) or *gwythpoll*. This was the ancient form of the game and similar to the W. *gwyddbwyll* and Bret. *gwezboell*.

'Cornish' chief patron saint Or rather '*Cornwall's chief patron saint*' as Caine and Gorton dub St Petroc (2001:45). See *Cornish saints, father of.*

Cornish Chime Kenneth Pelmear's musical composition for Ecclesiastes 3. See *Cornish Grace.*

Cornish china 1 The type of chinaware (Davey 1983:77n.1) also called *Cornish kitchen* (q.v.) **2** See *Cornish clay.*

Cornish china clay See *Cornish clay.*

Cornish china clay cap'n Term used for a captain of a Cornish china clay works (O.C. Vol. XII, No. 12 spring 2003, p.5). See *Cornish captain.*

Cornish Chough (*pyrrhocorax pyrrhocorax*) **1** a black bird with a distinctive red beak and red legs. Even though (with the exception of recently introduced protected specimens) the bird has disappeared from Cornwall, it is the *Cornish national bird*. Whereas Welsh legend believes that King Arthur (like Owain Glyndŵr) is asleep in a cave waiting to rise, according to Cornish legend the soul of King Arthur resides in the *Cornish Chough*. Hunt suggests that its red legs and beak are indicative of Arthur's bloody death (1881, 2nd, p.309). Under the emblem of the *Cornish Chough*, there is often the motto *Nyns yu marrow Myghtern Arthur* (King Arthur is not dead). For this reason in Welsh one name for the chough is *brân Arthur* (Arthur's crow) and Cornwall is called 'King Arthur's Land' (Payton 1999:374). The motif of a hero's soul taking the form of a bird is also seen in Welsh legend when the slain Llew Llaw Gyffes becomes an eagle. Similarly in Guatemala the *rahual* (double) of Tecún Umain was the *quetzal* bird. Moreover, Carew described the *Cornish Chough* as prone to "filching and hiding money and ... somewhat dangerous in carrying sticks of fire" (1602:56). In Cornish superstition it was bad luck to kill one (Courtney 1890:58) as it was unlucky to kill a *rabin/ruddock* (robin) or a *wranny* (wren).The *Cornish Chough* has several names, some of which contain the word 'Cornish': *Cornish chaw, Cornish daw, Cornish Jack* and *Cornish kae* as well as *chuff, chalk, chawk, killigrew, Hermit crow, Market Jew crow*. In Cornish its name is *palores* which literally means a 'female digger' (c.f. *Cornish bal maiden*). **2** Just as the *Norfolk dumplings* or people of Norfolk are also called *Norfolk turkeys*, so Cornish people have been called

Cornish Choughs as a mild / friendly insult. Payton records that in the Civil War, the Cornishmen's Irish allies (whom the Cornish dubbed 'Irish kernes' – from Ir. *ceithearn* – mercenary warriors) retaliated by calling the Cornishmen *Cornish Choughs* (Payton 1996:164). The collective noun is a *chatter* of choughs (Hendrickson 1983:57).

Cornish chow Another name for the *Cornish chough* (q.v.).

Cornish Christmas bush Nance refers to the '*Cornish Christmas bush*' which was "made of crossed hoops to which leaves of evergreen were tied" (1963:51). It is sometimes called just *Cornish bush* (q.v.). Nance also informs us about the *talking bush* which was "a holly-bush lashed at the mast head of a ship when in harbour on Christmas Eve" (ibid. p.157). See *Cornish bush*.

Cornish Christmas cake Unlike the English Christmas cake, it has a lot of whiskey and orange juice (for recipe see internet page http://www.cornish-ancestors.co.uk/clul/Recipes/recipes.htm ; see also C.W. 36, 2003/4, p.51). The Cornish *Twelfth Cake* (eaten on 6th Jan.) was more interesting since it contained a sixpence (its finder would have enough money for the next year), a ring (the finder would marry within the year) and a thimble (the finder would "die an old maid") (see Hunt 1881, 2nd, p.388). An old Cornish superstition dictated that it was unlucky to eat Christmas cake before Christmas (Day 2003:384).

Cornish Christmas pudding Like a normal Christmas pudding except that it has port wine and almonds (for ref. see *Cornish Christmas Cake*). A Cornish superstition states that "the more you taste of various Christmas puddings, the greater will be the number of happy days during the following year" (C.W. 40, 2004, p.11).

Cornish Christmas tree As holly was called (O.C. XI,12, 1997, p.6). It was often called *penn'orths of Christmas* (Courney 1890:7) and was sold by gypsy women. In Cornish dialect holly is *holm*, *pricklyum* (Hawke 1989:29) or *prickly Christmas* (Gendall & Gendall 1991:4) and in the Cornish language it is *kelyn(en)* (cf. W. *celyn* and Bret. *kelenn*). If there was no holly they would take a branch of *Cornish furze* (q.v.) and stick red berries and red ribbons on it (Gendall & Gendall 1991:2–3). "At Christmas Cornish miners hung a holly bush on the pit headgear" (Day 2000:180) and fishermen hung holly on the mast. The Cornish also believed it was unlucky to burn holly (C.W. 40, 2004, p.11). See *Cornish bush* for other Christmas entries. See also *Cornish kellywyck*.

Cornish church 1 An architecturally distinct church in Cornwall that was "long and low, and built of granite with a grey slate roof. Both aisles usually run the full length of the nave and chancel, often incorporates earlier transepts, and … exhibiting three parallel pitched roofs terminating generally in a western tower"

(Daniell 1988:24). **2** The 'Cornish' Church or rather the *Church of Cornwall*. An autonomous Anglican body proposed by some Cornish people that would be analogous with the Church in Wales (see C.W. .38, 2004, central page). In Cornish the term *eglos Kernow* is used (Jenkin 1984:51). The word *eglos* (cf. W. *eglwys* and Bret. *iliz*) is derived from the Greek *ekklesia* (church – i.e. 'that which is called out'). Hence our word 'ecclesiastical'.

Cornish churchtown John uses this term as a category of Cornish town centered around a church and the name of which is dedicated to a particular saint (1981:3). Examples include St. Austell, St. Ives and St. Germans. Yet in Cornish dialect the word *churchtown* often refers to just a small hamlet or "group of houses surrounding a church" (Phillipps 1993:25). In Cornish the word is *treveglos* (pl. *trevow eglos*).

'Cornish' chute Or rather *'Cousin Jack chute'*. So called as it began in Dolcoath and was then adopted worldwide. In Cornwall this mine chute is called a *mill* (Buckley 1989:19).

Cornish cider One popular form of cider is *scrumpy* and *pimpey* was a weak cider made of apple, cheese and water (Jago 1882:234). Moreover, just as a worm is put in a bottle of tequila, so on the Lizard a frog (i.e. a *quilken*) was put into a cask of cider to purify it (see Caine and Gorton 2001:34). Cider has also been used in some traditional Cornish drinks e.g. *burndockle* which was hot cider, sugar and eggs (Ivey 1976:11) and similar to the Cornish *eggyot* (q.v.). One cure for a cold was to drink *Sampson* – a punch of cider, brandy, water and sugar (*Sampson with his hair on* had a double measure of brandy). In the *Letterpouch* dance at Christmas, a jug of cider was balanced on the head (Gendall & Gendall 1991:8).

Cornish Cinderella There was a real person dubbed the *'Cornish Cinderella'*, Thomasine Bonaventura (from inside flap of Tangye's book 1978: this epithet is also recorded on pp 110 & 120). Thomasina was a shepherdess born in St. Mary Wike (now Week St. Mary) in early C15th. She married a merchant who took her to London, then when widowed married an even richer husband. Finally her third husband was John Percival, Lord Mayor of London. On his death she returned to Cornwall and helped the poor (see Courtney 1890:110) and died in 1512. See *'Cornish' Dick Whittington* and *Cornish shepherdess*. See also *Cornish Rumpelstiltskin*.

Cornish cinnamon cake A cake made with egg whites, flour, butter and cinnamon (for ref. see *Cornish burnt cream*).

Cornish claw As the Cornish peninsula has been described (by du Maurier 1967:15) since Cornwall appears to 'reach' or 'grab' into the Atlantic in the same way that the 'leg' or 'boot' of Italy is said to stride into the Mediterranean.

Cornish clay (Corn. *pry gwyn* – i.e. 'white clay') China clay. It has many industrial uses.

Cornish clayworker A Cornishman who worked in the *Cornish clay* industry (Arthur uses this term 1955:15). *Clay maidens* were the women who worked there (cf. *Cornish bal maidens*).

Cornish cliff castles As Payton refers to the *Cornish castles* (q.v.) on the coast (1996:55). Botallack Mine, St. Just would be an example. Actually in Cornish dialect the word *cliff* means "all the ground between the shore and cultivated land. The cliff proper … is called the edge of the cliff, the *cleeves*, or the *carns*" (Bottrell 1873:156).

Cornish cloak Alford refers to the red '*Cornish cloaks*' which drove the French from the coast (1978:37). Thus the *Cornish hobby horse* (q.v.) was born. In a similar Welsh legend an invading force of Napoleon's ships was repelled in 1797 by mistaking Jemima Nicholas and women dressed in red for troops. According to Cunnack the Cornish story refers to a possible C14th (not Napoleonic) French invasion (1975).

Cornish cloam oven As the clay oven of Cornwall have been called (Rawe 1986: 101). The word *cloam/clome* means earthenware. Hence *cloamers* were marbles (Jago 1882:136–137; also called *clayers*, see Merton 2003:61, as opposed to the glass *alleys*). The adjective is *cloamin* and there was even a *cloam egg* – a clay egg which helped the brooding hen lay (Phillipps 1993:25).

Cornish cloth Label for an inferior type of cloth locally made from *Cornish hair*. The presence of old fulling mills testifies to its manufacture (James Whetter uses the term in *Cornwall in the 13th Century*, 1998 – cited O.C. XIII, 4, spring 2005, p.50).

Cornish clotted cream As *Cornish cream* (q.v.) is sometimes called (e.g. by Pascoe 1995). It is also called *clouted cream* (Hawke 1975:12; Kittow, p.29).

'Cornish' cloud ships C. Spooner mentions phantom ships called *cloud ships* over Cornish seas which were the sign of storms (*Folklore* 72, 1961, 323–329). A similar supernatural phenomenon haunting Cornish ships was *Jack Harry's Lights* – phantom lights in the form of a sunken vessel that presaged a storm (Courtney 1880:30; Jago 1882:195). See *Cornish black ships*.

Cornish clusters As groups of Cornish communities in different parts of the world (e.g. by Lay in C.S. 2nd, Vol. 3, 1995, p.33 in C.W. 10, 1996, p.32) See *Cornishtown*.

Cornish coastal coach Baron describes 'the Pioneer' as 'the *Cornish coastal coach*' (1934:268). See *Cornish Riviera*.

Cornish coat of arms A name sometimes used (e.g. by Marin 1951:11) for the *Cornish Arms* (q.v.).

Cornish Cobb A variety of *Cornish Game* (see internet species list http://www.emea.eu.int/pdfs/vet/phvwp/055303en.pdf).

Cornish cobbles Square paving stones used in *Cornish paving* (q.v.).

Cornish cob cottage A unique type of vernacular architecture described by Rawe: "Most of the original *Cornish cob cottages*, apart from those in north Cornwall and on Bodmin Moor, were thatched; they were low-built – a single floor only, with perhaps a loft – and the eaves would come well down to protect the walls; where possible, they would be built into the lee of a hill slope for shelter. Some have rubble or even slate walls at one end, the weather side" (1986:176). In Cornish it is called *chy pryen*.

Cornish cockerel A *Cornish Game* cock (used in C.W. 22, p.21). In Cornwall a cock is called a *stag*. This is related to the English expression *stag main* (a cock fighting tournament). A fighting cock was called a *chanticleer* (Hawke 1975:10). See *Cornish killick*.

Cornish coffee Or *Cornish mead coffee*. Like Irish coffee but with mead not whiskey.

Cornish coinage towns Towns where the tin was tested. These towns were Helston, Liskeard, Lostwithiel, Penzance and Truro. The large blocks of tin sent for coins was called *coining tin*.

Cornish colours Black and gold (the phrase is used by Tremain 1992:20 and Payton 1993:225). These are the colours of the *Cornish rugby shirt* (q.v.) but the colours of the *Cornish flag* (q.v.) are black and white.

Cornish column A column (or whole page) in Cornish in an otherwise English-language publication. For instance, since 1991 *The West Morning News* has provided a *Cornish Column* (*An Goloven Gernewek*) for its Cornish-speaking readers.

Cornish Come Motion As Jenkin (1945:167) records the old spelling of the *Cornish Commotion* (q.v.).

'Cornish' common spotted orchid Or rather the *Common spotted orchid, Cornish form* (*dactylorhiza fuchsii ssp. Cornubiensis*) which has a dark pinkish shade.

Cornish Commotion This term is recorded by Carew (1602:131 – and later by other wirters like Jenkin 1945:166–7) for the commotion in 1549. This episode ensued as a result of Edward VI's rejection of the Cornish people's petition to have the old service in the *Cornish language* (q.v.) instead of the New Prayer Book. A good Cornish dialect word for 'commotion' is *crant* (James 1979:3). See

Cornish Prayer Book Rebellion.

Cornish community nicknames Jan Gendall's term for a particular category of nicknames that are common in Cornwall (and Scilly) for 'rival' neighbouring communities since in the past even someone form the next village was a foreigner (Bird 1988:140) or rather a *furriner*. Examples of such nicknames are St. Ives Hakes, Bodmin Shoemakers and Polperro Stinkers. (see Gendall 1995).

Cornish compliment A gift of no real value to the giver (Marten 1992:21). Even though this jocular expression is popular in Devon! It may well be Cornish in origin and corresponds exactly in meaning with the Cornish phrase *Cornishman's gift* for which see appendix 2. By contrast, an *Irish compliment* is a back-handed compliment (Edwards 2004:44) and a *Yorkshire compliment* is similarly a useless gift.

Cornish Connection A Cornish society overseas.

Cornish Constitutional Convention Founded by Dick Cole, Bert Biscoe and Stephen Horscroft after the failure of the *Cornish Millennium Convention*. Its inaugural meeting at County Hall, Truro, July 2000 expressed commitment to attaining a Cornish Assembly (see Deacon et al 2003:107).

Cornish contingent As Jenkin (1945:128) refers to the body of *Cornish archers* (q.v.) present at the battle of Agincourt (1415).

Cornish conversation (Corn. *keskows Kernewek*) Conversational practice in the *Cornish language* which has been held in certain pubs (C.W. 6, 1995, p.10).

Cornish Convocation A synonym of the *Cornish Stannary Parliament* (Rawe 1986:155) particularly in its reconvened form since 1972. Prior to that it had last met in 1752.

Cornish cooking range Another name for the *Cornish range* (q.v.).

Cornish cooking stove As the *Cornish slab is sometimes called* (see Ivey 1976:61 and Venable 1993:70). See *Cornish range*.

Cornish copper mining, the Father of John Coster (for his epithet see the internet site: http://ourworld.compuserve.com/homepages/jonrees/corbookC.htm). Cornwall has been called *The Copper Kingdom* (Rawe 1986:157) and *The Land of Copper*.

Cornish corner John Rowe mentions the phrase '*Cornish corner*' to refer to a hillside graveyard for Cornish miners in the old Nevadan mining city or Virginian city (*Folk Life*, Vol. 3, 1965, p.34). Many of those buried there had died from tuberculosis.

Cornish Cornwall The phrase is used by analogy to D.P. Moran's "Irish Ireland" (Edwards 2004:92) and refers to those Celtic Cornish (i.e. non-English) aspects of Cornwall and Cornish culture (the phrase appears e.g. in C.W. 37, 2003, p.27).

'Cornish' corpse bird Nance records the term *tebel edhen* as "bird of evil omen" (1978:298). It is to be compared with the Welsh *aderyn corff* or 'corpse bird' (sometimes associated with the owl) whose presence near a house was a death omen.

Cornish cost-book system This refers to the system by which the name of each *Cornish adventurer* (q.v.) was recorded in a *cost book* that also calculated his profits or liabilities (Payton uses the term prefixing the word 'Cornish' [1996:229 and 1999:167 and 245]). The mine company was organized with a warden and warden's court similar to the *Cornish stannaries* (C.S. Vol. 4, 1996, p.122).

Cornish cottage (Corn. *pennti kernewek*) As *Cornish Grand Bard* Rod Lyon refers to the traditional C18th Cornish home with small windows and a *talfat* or loft (C.W. 40, 2004, p.63).

Cornish county arms Another name for the *Cornish Arms* (q.v.).

Cornish cousin Term applied to a fellow Cornishman. According to Carew "all Cornish gentlemen are cousins" (1602:75). No relation to a *Welsh cousin* which refers to a distant relative (Edwards 1998:38). See *Cornish cousin Jack.*

Cornish cousin Jack 1 Or just *Cousin Jack* (yet often the word 'Cornish' is prefixed – see Nance 1956:59 and O.C. Vol. 4, 1996, p.113). This refers to a fellow Cornishman, especially outside Cornwall or overseas. According to John Rowe this nickname was used in America since "if a Cornish miner were asked if he knew a likely man to fill a job he would immediately say that he would send home for his *Cousin Jack*" (*Folk Life*, Vol. 3, 1965, p.26). See *Cornish grapevine*. In Devon Cornishmen are known as *Cousin Jackers* (Marten 1992:8). In Australian slang a *Cousin Jack* is "usually portrayed as stupid" (Davey and Seal 2003:77) and this may well derive from the oxymorous 'foolsh wisdom' of the stereotype Cornish miner in a form of *Cornish joke*. **2** *Cousin-Jacky* (or *Zacky*) was also "a local term of contempt" (Jago 1882:144 and 315) and meant a foolish person or coward (Courtney 1880:15). **3** In Cornish smugglers' slang *Cousin Jacky* was cognac (Vivian 1969:26). Not to be confused with a *Cornish Jack* (q.v.). **4** Cousin Jack was also the name for a *Cornish pasty* among Cornish miners in Australia (Jauncey 2004:94). By contrast, Cornish miners in America called the *Cornish pasty* a '*Cousin Jack pasty*' (Cassidy 1985:805).

Cornish cousin Jennie See *Cornish Jenny.*

'Cornish' Cousin John The Cornishman has been called a *Cousin John* as well as a

Cousin Jack (Payton 1999:279). Courtney recorded this form as *Cousin Jan* (1880:14).

Cornish coven As opposed to witches' covens after the Sabbat ceremony which "elsewhere ended in orgy and wild revelry" (MacLeay 1977:20), "the *Cornish covens* finished the night by departing *en masse* with their toads, cats and so forth for Wales where they stole milk from cattle and helped themselves to milk" (ibid. pp.20–1). See *Cornish witch*.

Cornish Cox The apple variety *Cornish Mother* has also been called the *Cornish Cox* (see internet page http://www.cornwall/gov.uk/Environment/trees/ab-de03t.htm).

Cornish crabber Type of boat. See *Cornish lugger* and *Cornish shrimper*.

Cornish crab lobster pot A basket shaped lobster trap (Harris 1983:50).

Cornish crake A name for *Cornish English* or *Cornish Dialect*, especially *Cornish American*. Angus Murdoch writes "*Cornish crake* is founded on the English language, but with such picturesque adaptations that it sounds like a foreign tongue" (*Boom Copper: The Story of the First U.S. Mining Boom*, Hancock, Michigan, 1943, rep. 2001, p.202 – cited in C.S. 2nd, 12, 2004, p.111). *Crake* means to croak or quaver (Jago 1882:145), a harsh cry (Thomas 1895:77) and also to complain (Ivey 1980:17). In Hiberno-English *crake* or *craik* also means to complain (Share 1997:61) and is possibly related to Ir. *craic* – 'crack' or chat.

Cornish Cracker A hybrid of rhododendron sometimes called *Damaris Cornish Cracker*. It has yellow flowers and is in bloom from April to May. The word 'rhododendron' is derived from the Greek words *rhodos* and *dendron* meaning 'rose tree'. Several varieties can be grown early in Cornwall because of the mild climate. See *Cornish Cross*, *Cornish Loderi* and *Cornish Red*.

Cornish cream (Corn. *dehen kernewek*) Clotted cream (for which see *Cornish scalded cream*). Baker informs us that "a Cornish girl who on May Monday could find a lady fern frond long enough to cover a cream scalding pan received a dish of cream for the luck she had brought to the dairy" (1996:59). This dish was called a *shern* (Thomas 1895:120–1). A lump of cream is a *dab* or a *dollop* (Hawke 1975:16 and 17). **2** A variety or cultivar of *Cornish Heather* (*erica vagans*) (see C.S. 1st, Vol. 10, 1982, p.12). See *Cornish Gold*, *Cornish Lime* and *Cornish White*. **3** Tom Jago from Camelford (the creator of Bailey's Irish Cream) "said that he might well work on a Jago's *Cornish Cream* in the future" (C.W. 38, 2004, p.9).

Cornish cream tea *Cornish tea* (q.v.) accompanied by a *Cornish pasty* such as the *Cornish split* spread with jam and *Cornish clotted cream*.

Cornish cream to a Cornish cat, as good as As the dialect verse of Bernard

Moore (S.S. Hunt) was described (see Best in the section 'The Arts', question 10).

Cornish crest As the *Cornish arms* (q.v.) is sometimes called (e.g. in C.T. 3, No.2, Christmas, 1996, p.36).

Cornish cricket, the home of As Bodmin has been called due to the fact that in the late C18th, as it was a garrison town, the military would play cricket (Ian Clarke records this toponym – C.S.2nd, 12, 2004, p.188). Cf. *Cornish golf, home of* and *Cornish hurling, home of*.

Cornish crock An earthenware cooking utensil (Heard 1984:131).

Cornish Crockpot Another name for *Crockpot Cornish* (see appendix 1).

Cornish cross 1 A Celtic style stone cross typical of the type found in Cornwall. See *Cornish wheel*. **2** *Cornish Cross* is also a rhododendron hybrid of which two forms exist: *Penjerrick* and *South Lodge*. Both sub-varieties are rose pink and bloom form April to May. See *Cornish Cracker*. **3** A cross breed of a *Cornish hen* (e.g. *Cornish Rock*) or a *Cornish Rex*.

Cornish crossed Rex A cat that is a cross between a *Cornish Rex* and another breed (especially another rex like the Devon Rex).

Cornish Crow A translation of the Welsh name for the *Cornish Chough* (*brân Gernyw* – i.e. 'crow of Cornwall'). Interestingly Underwood also calls it "the red-legged *Cornish Crow*" (1983). In *Cornish dialect* the word *crow* means a type of hut – as in *piskies' crows* (beehive huts believed to be inhabited by the *Cornish piskies*) and a *pig's crow* (i.e. a pigsty) (see Jones 1996:11). A *night-crow* was a child who stayed up late (Thomas 1895:108). The Cornish word for 'crow' is *bran* (pl. *bryny* – cf. Bret. *bran*, pl. *brini*;Van. *bran*, pl. *brenni* and W. *brân*, pl. *brain*).

Cornish crowd As the old fiddle is called that is carved on the bench end at Altarnun (http://www.bagpipeworld.co.uk/Reconstructions/Cornish3.htm). On Sunday nearest 28th April at Towednack church a *crowder* met everyone outside (Courtney 1890:28). A large *Cornish pasty* (q.v.) was described as being "as long as John Bedella's fiddle" (Phillipps 1993:63).

Cornish crowdy crawn Sometimes the tambourine-like *crowdy crawn* is preceded by the word 'Cornish', so as to distinguish it from the Irish *bodhrán* (see internet site http://www.heirloommusic.com/celticcornernotes.html). See *Cornish bodhrán*.

Cornish crown, jewel in the 1 So Padstow has been described (C.W. 32,2002/3, p.54). **2** St. Michael's Mount (for which see *Cornish Mount, the*) has been called "the jewel in Cornwall's crown" (in the brochure *The National Trust Devon & Cornwall: Visitors' Guide*, 1992).

Cornish crown jewels New design which incorporates the Prince of Wales' feathers (the Prince of Wales is also the Duke of Cornwall) and Prince Charles' zodiac symbol (as shown in *Cornish Goldsmiths*).

Cornish crowsheaf Sometimes the word 'Cornish' precedes the crowsheaf (O.C. 4, p.391). This is the top sheaf of an *arrish mow* (pile of sheaves stacked before rain) and was found in an enclosure called a *mowhay*. According to Stevens there was a *hand mow* (with 50–60 sheaves) and a *knee mow* (with about 100 sheaves) (1977:267). The word *mow* is usually pronounced as Chairman Mao and not as in lawnmower. It is not to be confused with the dialect word *mo* meaning cow, the Cornish *mo* (the dark before dawn) and the word for swine as in the St. Ives *Fair Mo* on the last Saturday in November ('Pig Fair' – from the Corn. *mogh*, cf. W. *moch*, Bret. *moc'h* and Ir. *muc*).

Cornish crusher Brown and Acton explain that "the crushing rolls of a *'Cornish crusher'* were used to break down softer ores such as copper or lead. They were usually driven by a waterwheel or clutched to a whim engine. Other types of crusher such as jaw and cone crushers are present-day devices for reducing rock to a predetermined size" (1994:133).

Cornish crystal 1 An alternative name for the *Cornish diamond* (q.v.). Salmon mentions a Dr. Borlase rector of Ludgvan who "corresponded with Pope, sending him *Cornish crystals* for his grotto" (1903:170). Cf. *Cornish diamond*. **2** An *Gwrys Kenmewek* – Award in the *Cornish eisteddfod* competions for *Cornish language* prose (for *Cornish language* verse the award is the Mordon-Caradar Rosebowl).

Cornish cunning folk Term applied to a special category of *Cornish witches* who would do ill-wishing, (O.C., Vol.XIII, No.2, spring 2004, p.20). The word 'cunning' literally means 'knowing' (from O.E. *cunnung* or knowledge and the verb *cunnan* to know; cf. Ger. *kennen* to know) and Hunt calls the *Cornish charmer* (q.v.) a *"knowing man"* (1881, 1st, 211).

Cornish curl James Jewell has called the *crimping* (i.e. twisted pastry edge) on the *Cornish pasty* the *'Cornish Curl'*(e.g. in *Landmark* autumn/winter 1996, Vol.39, No. 3,4, p.23 – pub. Waukesha County Historical Soc., Inc., Wisconsin).

Cornish cut, the Also called the *burnt cut*. A method of using explosives in Cornish mines with hard rock by drilling many holes (see Earl 1978:181). See *Cornish powder*.

Cornish cycle With reference to the *Cornish engine* "the so-called *Cornish cycle* was similar to the single-acting principle established by Watt, with steam acting on top of the piston but using the steam expansively, thus producing enormous fuel savings" (Crowley 1976:22). In the *Cornish cycle* an engine could be made rotative (see *Cornish rotative beam engine*).

Cornish cyder Spelling sometimes used for *Cornish cider* (q.v.). *Cyder* was the original Cornish spelling (see Nance 1978).

Cornish dance night Term used by Neil Davey to translate both the *ceilidh-troyl* (from the Irish/Gaelic *ceilidh* and Corn. *troyl*) and the *noze looan* ('happy night') (C.W. 38, 2004, p.31). This is an evening with traditional Cornish music and dancing as well as perhaps some storytelling.

'Cornish' Danna There is a species of flower called *Danna cornubiensis*. It is identified with the flower *Physospermo cornubiensis*.

Cornish Daw An old name for the *Cornish Chough* used by John Taylor (the Water Poet) in his travels through Cornwall in 1649 (cited by Michael Tangye in O.C. XII, 3, 1998, p.29). Perhaps the name derives from the confusion of the Cornish word *choca* or *chogha* which could mean jackdaw as well as chough (see Nance 1978). Other related dialect names for this bird are *chank daw* and *cliff daw* (C.W. 28, 2002:54).

Cornish dawe An older spelling of *Cornish daw* (O.C.X.5., autumn, 1987, p.248).

Cornish Declaration Group Shortlived group that distributed declarations entitled 'One and All' demanding devolution and opposing overdevelopment (Deacon et al 2003:84).

Cornish denomination, the Methodism has been described as "the dominant *Cornish denomination*" (Deacon et al 2003:8). See *Cornish Amphitheatre, John Wesley's*.

Cornish Development Agency There is a campaign in Cornwall for such a body that would be analogous with the Welsh Development Agency. The Cornish also call for a *Cornish Assembly* and a *Cornish University* which awards all its own degrees.

Cornish Devil As Trevithick's *Puffin' Devil* is also called (C.W. 34, 2003, p.36).

Cornish dialect or *Cornish English*. The English spoken in Cornwall with a distinct accent and a rich vocabulary much of which is derived from the *Cornish Language* (q.v.). The various regions of Cornwall have their own sub-dialects with some different words. The Cornish word for dialect is *ranyeth* (literally 'part language').

Cornish diamond The phrase is usually seen in the plural and *Cornish diamonds* are rock crystals or quartz. The name is mentioned by a few writers (Tregarthen 1940:172 In folklore *little standings* (i.e. fairies) "were covered with trinkets, such as knee and shoe buckles of silver and gold, glistening with *Cornish diamonds*"

(Bottrell 1873:85). In *Cornish dialect* the word for these stones is *morion* (Hawke 1975:38), *spaars* (Treenoodle 1846:102) or *spar-stone* (Courtney 1890:53). In 1602 Carew referred to them as just "diamonds" and implied that they were real (p.18) yet a real diamond is *adamant*. The term is similar to the *Welsh diamond* (Edwards 1998:42) and the *Irish diamond* (Edwards 2004:53).

Cornish diaspora Graham Sandercock defines *Cornish diaspora* as "the spread of Cornish people throughout the world" (C.W. 8, 1996, p.14). Yet the term also refers to those Cornish people themselves who live abroad. In many cases they are descendants of those Cornish miners who emigrated to places like Australia and North and South America to provide their necessary skills. Another term for them is *Cornish Overseas* and Claire Barden–Dan calls them "the *Cornish outside Cornwall*" (C.W. 14, 1997, p.30). See *Cornish Gathering*.

'Cornish' Dick Whittington Courtney dubs Thomasine Bonaventure (for whom see *Cornish Cinderella*) as "the *Cornish female Whittington*" (1890:110). Dick Whittington was a poor boy whose cat rescued the King of Barbary from mice. He was rewarded and also became Lord Mayor of London.

Cornish difference A new phrase made popular by certain academics (e.g. Payton and Deacon in Payton, ed. 1993:275 and Laviolette in C.S. 11, 2003, p.162 and p.176) and refers to that which is culturally distinct about Cornwall. The aspect of *Cornish difference* is emphasized as just one argument to justify some form of autonomous recognition such as a *Cornish Assembly* or a *Cornish Development Agency*. It is synonymous with what Bernard Deacon terms '*Cornish distinctiveness*' (ibid. p.317) and with *Cornish exceptionalism* (q.v.).

Cornish doll Just as there are Welsh dolls and Irish dolls dressed in their traditional costumes, collectors can also buy a *Cornish doll* (e.g. made by Cherakyn Dolls, Camborne) dressed in *Cornish tartan* (q.v.) and with different models like the *Cornish bal maiden* (q.v.) and tin miner. In Cornish 'doll' is *jowanna* and *popet* (cf. Fr. *poupée*). In Madron Well little girls still baptise their dolls (Jenkin 1984:21).

Cornish Domesday Van der Geest refers to the "*Cornish Domesday*" (*The Celtic History Review*, Vol.2, issue 4, summer, 1997, p.3). By this he means the Cornish place names, especially those beginning with *Tre-* and *Tin-* in the Domesday records. The Domesday Book was compiled in 1086.

Cornish double acting steam engine A *Cornish engine* with double beat valves and condenser, built by Harvey's of Hayle in 1840 with a 24 inch bore (C.W. 1, 1994).

Cornish double jacking Mining term mentioned (e.g. in C.W.W. 1994, 11, p.27).

This refers to the pair work in which one Cornishman would hold and rotate a steel drill while his partner would use an eight pound hammer to hit the drill.

Cornish double pipes As Julian Goodacre refers to the *Cornish bagpipe* (q.v.) since there are two chanters (for ref. see *Cornish Pipes in C*).

Cornish double plural In *Cornish dialect* the tendency to use a plural with some words already ending in 's'. For instance, Ivey speaks of *bottomses* (low ground) and *downses* (high moorlands) (1980:9 and 21). See also *Cornish stampses*. This grammatical feature is also extended to Cornish words e.g. *meryan/muryan* is already the plural form of the Cornish word for 'ants' (also believed to be the souls of children who died unbaptised) and the singular form was *muryanen*. However, Cornish people often talk of 'muryans'.

Cornish dough cake A tea-time cake that is spread with butter. It is one of the cakes made by W.T. Warren & Sons.

Cornish dragon Unlike the Welsh Dragon (which symbolizes the victory of Wales over the white dragon – i.e. England), the dragon is depicted negatively in Cornwall. For instance, St. Petroc (see *Cornish saints, father of*) "whispered a prayer into the ear of a *Cornish dragon*, after which it swam to new lands". Another Cornish saint Sampson also banished dragons (see the internet article *The Dragon in Folkore and Legend*). *Cornish cunning folk* would sometimes dispense *dragon's blood* which was "believed to be effective ingredient in charms for provoking live" (*Folklore* 116, April 2005, p.86). See *Cornish palm*.

Cornish draught engine Term used by Orchard (1990:13) for which see *Cornish engine*.

Cornish droll 1 A *droll* was a teller of stories or *whiddles*. Often the word 'Cornish' is prefixed. He would wander around and also accompany himself on the fiddle. Unlike the Irish *seanchaí* the *Cornish droll* gradually disappeared and so Henry Quick wrote "The *Cornish drolls* are dead each one" (cited by Hawke 1973:10). **2** The story itself, as used by Sarah L. Enys in her book *The Cornish Drolls*. In fact in Cornish the word *drolla* (pl. *drollys*) meant a "tale, story, play with folk-tale plot" (Nance 1978).

Cornish droll-teller A synonym (used by some writers e.g. Stevens, p.20) for the *Cornish droll*.

'Cornish' Duchy The Duchy of Cornwall. The Duke of Cornwall (apart from the name of a Cornish cooking apple) is the title (along with Prince of Wales) of the heir to the English throne. Historically the Duke was not just a *duk* but also a *hembrynkyas-lu* or leader of the army (Nance 1978:54 – cf. *Cornish Captain*).

Cornish duck The *Cornish pilchard* (q.v.) (Partridge 1937:212). A synonym is the

Mevagissey duck (Heard 1984:21 and Stevens, pp.12–13). On similar lines, one Cornish phrase for a lot of noise was "like a duck in a *bussa*" (C.W. 23, 2001, p.11). This expression also combines the duck with the pilchard since the *bussa* was an earthenware pot for storing pilchards. Similarly in Cornwall a *poor man's goose* was liver and potatoes "equal in taste to goose" (Walker 1994:22). The substitution of poultry names for fish is common – e.g. the *Bombay duck* (dried fish in an Indian restaurant). This corresponds to the *Irish goose* which is codfish (Edwards 2004:78), the *Norfolk/Yarmouth capon* which is a red herring (Partridge 1937:1060), a *Taunton turkey* or salt herring (Green 1998:275), an *Alaska turkey* which is a salmon (Green, ibid. p.12) and a *Billingsgate pheasant* which is a herring (Green, ibid. p.90). This confusion may stem from the fact that the barnacle goose was thought to have been a 'fish' or sea creature (Brewer 1870). Moreover, "the Cornish thought puffins tasted of fish, and ate them during Lent" (Day 2003:216). Similarly, "in Cornwall, the blue tit ... was believed to be a bird by day and a toad by night" (Day ibid. p.198).

Cornish Dumnonia Term used by Payton (1996:68) for the region of the South West inhabited by the Celts (and, just as Wales' border once extended a little beyond the English-Welsh border, so the territory of the Cornish Celts transcended the Tamar). Cornish even has names for some of these formerly Celtic places of the West Country like *Keresk* (Exeter). Indeed apart from *Dewnans*, the other name for Devon is *Pow Densher* ('County of the Devonshire people'). This name is interesting since, as distinct from *Pow Saws* ('Shire/land of the Englishmen', i.e. England), it may suggest that Devon was once regarded as a part of Cornwall, not of England. Today the term *Devonwall* (a portmanteau term of Devon and Cornwall) refers to a similar area but connoting that Cornwall is subsumed by Devon.

Cornish dwarf A supposed prehistoric supernatural race analogous with the *Cornish knockers* and *Cornish piskies*. According to the J.R.I.C. "Like all existing pigmy races, the *Cornish dwarfs* were hunters alone, and on being driven to the woods and the morasses ... the pigmies also dug hollows underground and in banks and dwelt there" (Vol. 15, 1902–03, 297). The Cornish word for 'dwarf' is *cor* and this prefix can be seen in the word *corgi* (i.e. W. 'dwarf-dog' – the word would be exactly the same in Cornish). In Cornwall St. Neot is "the pygmy saint" (see Best, in the section 'History', question 1).

Cornishe An old spelling of *Cornish*.

Cornish eagle Stevens writes "I often watch the buzzard, the so-called *Cornish eagle* ... as he soars effortlessly in the summer thermals" (C.W. 38, 2004, p.67). The Cornish word for 'eagle' *er* (c.f. W. *eryr* and Bret. *erer*) is a cognate of the English word 'eyrie' (an eagle's nest). In Cornish dialect 'buzzard' is *kit* (Hawke 1989:22) and in Cornish it is *bargos* (cf. W.*barcut* – kite; cf. Bret. *barged*) which is connected with the verb *bargesy* – 'to hover'. See *Cornish Pheasant*.

Cornish earldom Although Cornwall is often known as a duchy (*ducheth*), at one time Cornwall was known as the *Cornish earldom* (see Deane and Shaw 1975: 21). In Cornish this was a *conteth* (earldom or county), the land of a *yurl* (earl).

Cornish Early Gentian (*Gentianella angelica*) A type of plant that has produced a subspecies *Cornubiensis* unique to Cornwall and is to be found on the sand dunes of the north coast (see C.S. 2nd, Vol. 3, 1995, p.153).

Cornish Early Red A variety of rhododendron also called *Cornish Red* (q.v.).

Cornish ecclesiastical capital Once the title of Padstow since St. Petroc (see *Cornish saints, father of*) founded a monastery there in C6th.

Cornish eggyot This drink often appears preceded by the word 'Cornish' (see Rothwell 1989) and the name is a contraction of *eggy-hot*. It is taken to prevent colds and is made from hot beer, eggs and sugar and was once popular on Christmas Eve.

Cornish Eisteddfod (Corn. *Esethvos Kernow*). The Cornish form of the Welsh *eisteddfod* (literally 'session' derived from the W. verb *eistedd* to sit). It is held on St. Piran's Day (March 5th) under the auspices of the *Cornish Gorsedd* (q.v.). The first *Cornish Eisteddfod* was inaugurated on 1st September 1928 at Boscawen Un by Archdruid Pedrog of Wales.

'Cornish' Elgin marbles Donald Rowe (brother of comedian Jethro) was "caught red-handed returning rocks – taken thirty years ago to use as moulds for clay bowls – to his beach at Cot Valley near St. Just. Donald … decided to return 'Cornwall's equivalent of the Elgin Marbles' after a public outcry erupted over the removal of several others for an art installation on Morecombe town's promenade" (C.T. March, 1999, p.77). The actual (so-called) Elgin Marbles were the marble reliefs stolen from the Parthenon of the Acropolis (c.1799–1803) by the Scotsman Lord Elgin.

Cornish Elm (*ulmus cornubiensis*) (Corn. *elowen*, pl. *elow*; an *elowek* is an elm grove). It is distinct from the slightly larger English Elm and called by Couch the "narrow-leaved elm" (1871:74–5). Nicholls describes it as "Cornwall's native tree" and says that its wood was used to make *Cornish gigs* (1986:7). In *Cornish dialect* it is called *elmin tree* (Thomas 1895:83) or *elin tree* (Ivey 1976:24) or *ellem* (Hawke 1975:19) and *ellum* (Hawke 1989:29). Dutch elm disease destroyed many specimens. On *Dipping Day* (May 1st) anyone not carrying either a branch of *Cornish Elm* or whitethorn (both called 'May') would be *dipped*, i.e. drenched with a bucket of water (Couch 1871:75).

'Cornish' Elysium S.P.B Mais (author of the new *Cornish Riviera* guide) wrote in 1928 "we had to have a name for this Elysium, so we called it the *Cornish Riviera*" (cited in C.S. 2nd, 7, 1999, p.101). Elysium was the blessed abode of the dead in Greek mythology.

Cornish emblem Term used by some (e.g. Pearce 2000:47) for the *Cornish arms* (q.v.).

Cornish Emigrant's Song, the A song by Hawker about Cornish workers migrating to America (cited by Payton 1999:73).

Cornish enclaves Areas where communities of *Cornish Cousin Jacks* (q.v.) are to be found in U.S.A. such as Tangher Island in Chesaspeake Bay (C.W.W. 1995, 16, p.49).

Cornish engine In the mines and water works this was a single-acting pumping engine. The steam raises a heavy pump rod or plunger and forces the water to come up. The term *Cornish engine* is also loosely applied to include the double acting *Cornish rotative beam engine* (Brown and Acton 1994:132).

Cornish engineer 1 Maker of a *Cornish engine* (q.v.) such as "the *Cornish engineers* who were developing their own engines and trying to acquire patents for them" (O.C. X, 12, 1991, p.590). **2** In mining jargon an 'engineer' was "the superintendent of machinery" as opposed to the *engine man* who attended to and worked the machine (Orchard 1990:19), not to be confused with the *man-engine* (see *Cornish man engine*) which was used to lift and lower the men underground.

Cornish engine house Also called a *Cornish castle*, a tower which housed the *Cornish engine* (q.v.). It was often made of stone with a distinct chimney at the side. In dialect it is called an *inyun house* (Clemo, p.130). Jones recalls that "On St. John's Day Cornish miners place a green bough on the shears of the engine houses in commemoration of his preaching in the wilderness" (1997b:12).

Cornish English 1 As the *Cornish dialect* (q.v.) is sometimes called (C.S. Vol. 4, 1996, p.69). As Jenkin says, *Cornish English* was originally called 'naughty English" (i.e. imperfect English) (Jenkin cites Andrew Borde in 1542 – see 1984:25). Alan M. Kent has also coined the term 'Cornu-English' for this dialect (C.S. 2nd, 10, 2002, pp.215 and 221). See *Anglo-Cornish* in appendix 1. **2** Carew used the term *Cornish English* for those people in Cornwall who were *Anglo-Cornish* as opposed to pure Cornish or Cornish–speaking (1602:43). See *Cornish Saxon*.

Cornish ensign Like the *Cornish flag* (q.v.) but in the left hand corner, instead of a black background there is the Union Jack. See *Cornish arms*, *Cornish maritime ensign* and *Cornish red ensign*.

Cornish enthusiasts Kennedy's translation of the Cornish word *kernewegoryon*

(C.S. 2nd, 10. 2002, p.287). The word literally means a 'Cornish speaker'.

Cornisher A neologism meaning 'more Cornish' (see the internet page http://search.yahoo.com/search?p=+cornisher&UTF-8&+FP-tab-web-t&fl+0&x+w). See *Cornishest*.

Cornishery Alternative spelling of *Cornishry* (q.v.).

Cornishest The superlative form of the word 'Cornish', i.e. 'the most Cornish'. For reference and the comparative form see *Cornisher*. Cf. *Cornishmost*.

'Cornish' Eton Helston Grammar School in Wendron Street was once known as the "*Eton of Cornwall*" (Jenkin 1945:230 and 454). Charles Kingsley was a pupil there.

Cornish exceptionalism A new phrase coined by Mark Sandford to show that, unlike the case of other counties, Cornwall's distinct heritage constitutes an exception and "that Cornwall was sufficiently 'different' to warrant … an assembly" (C.S. 11, 2003, pp.44 & 50). See *Cornish difference*.

Cornish exoticism Term used by Jonathan Howlett to refer to the projection of mystery when portraying Cornwall, as typified in P.B. Mais' book *The Cornish Riviera* (C.S. 2nd, 12, 2004, p.47).

Cornish Express engine A train (see O.C. Vol. VI, No. 9, autumn 1965, p.384).

Cornish fairies 1 As Jones calls the *Cornish piskies* (q.v. *Cornish piskey*) (1996:5). In Cornish the word 'fairy' is *spyrys* (pl. *spyryjyon*) or an *bobel vyghan* (i.e. 'the little people'). **2** Barber and Riches describe the *muryans* as "*Cornish fairies*, originally larger than humans, which (in expiation of some unspecified crime) were condemned to diminish each year until they became ants and then died" (1971:108) *See Cornish double plural*. Other fairies in Cornwall include the *spriggans* which also live in the smine. See also *Cornish browney*, *Cornish knocker* and *Cornish piskey*. In Cornish dialect *fairy* means a weasel. See *Cornish knocker*.

Cornish fairings Cornish sweets (Walker 1994:42). They were usually crunchy biscuits with a ginger taste that were bought from *standings* (stalls) at hiring fairs (hence the name). They are sometimes called *ginger fairings* (Kittow, p.7).

Cornish fair traders A *fair trader* or *free trader* (Jago 1882:108) was a smuggler. Often it is preceded by the word 'Cornish' (e.g. by Bottrell 1873:120 and Tregarthen 1940:203). Also called a *free trader* (see Jago 1882:108 in the entry 'anker'). The *Cornish fair trader* was sometimes in need of a *troacher* (i.e. hawker of smuggled goods – see Courtney 1890:61) and would use *ankers* (four gallon kegs) to carry the *custom* or "raw smuggled spirits" (Hawke 1975:15b), especially *moonshine* (smuggled brandy). Smugglers would add *shrub* (a herb)to rum to hide the salt water taste. Tobacco seized by the *revenue men* was bunt at a furnace in Falmouth called the *King's/Queen's Pipe*. One who brought news about smugglers would be given a *kimbly* (a gift of cake also given at a wedding or christening – see Jago, ibid. p.201). Another name for a smuggler was a *truckler* (Hawke 1975:65) – possibly derived from the *truckle* (small wheel) of the *Cornish wheelbarrow* (q.v.) carrying the contraband.

'Cornish' Falstaff, the Anthony Payne was called "the Falstaff of the West" (Stevens p.36) for whom see the *Cornish Giant*. Sir John Falstaff was the jovial and corpulent old knight in Shakespeare's *The Merry Wives of Windsor*.

Cornish Farmyard Traditional Cornish song like *Old MacDonald had a Farm* (O.C. June 1990:21).

Cornish farthing 1 A farthing *Cornish token* (most tokens in Cornwall were fathings except a few which had the word 'Halfpenny' on them – see Mayne & Williams 1985:22). See *Cornish halfpenny*. **2** Area of land for which see *Cornish ferling*.

Cornish fashion 1 Term applied to the old West Cornish style of jumper with a 'V' neck that showed the Guernsey-frock underneath (Nance 1963:99). **2** Refers to the term is used by Padai Dwyer (*The Celtic Pen*, issue II, winter 1996, pp.21–5).

'Cornish' fathom (Corn. *gourhes*, pl. *–ow*) The 'fathom' of Cornish fishermen was 5ft and not the usual 6ft (Nance 1963:76).

Cornish Faust As Jan Tregeagle has been called (C.W. 9, 1996, p.35). Faust was the hero of Marlowe's *Tragical History of Dr. Faustus* (c.1592). Faustus was a magician who sold his soul to the Devil. For Tregeagle see *Cornish Bluebeard*.

'Cornish' feast bun Merrick describes the large *Cornish saffron bun* as "the feast bun of Cornwall" (1998:24) since it was eaten at feasts, especially at St. Peterstide (29th June) in Porthleven.

Cornish ferling Smirke referred to the '*Cornish ferling*' as "a fourth part of a *Cornish acre*" (q.v.) (R.I.C. Report 1862, pages 29, 36 and 37). It is usually called a *farthing* but Smirke also called it a *fourthling* (ibid. p.32). It is derived from O.E. *feorðling* or fourth.

'Cornish' Fern There is a light green variety of fern called *Polypodium cornubiensis*.

Cornish festival, the world's largest The festival *Kenewek Lowender* (i.e. 'Cornish Happiness' – in Cornish syntax the order of the words should be reversed) which always attracts the *Cornish diaspora*. This is a biennial festival in mid-May in S.

Australia (see *Cornish Towns*). In Australia it is called the '*Cornish Festival*' and, apart from Cornish food, music and games, recent additions to the festival include fireworks and a vintage car display (see Davey and Seal 2003:169–170).

Cornish Feta Cornish version of the Greek *feta* cheese (made from either goats' or ewes' milk – from Gk. *féta* meaning 'slice'). For other cheeses see *Cornish Blue*.

Cornish fiction See *Cornish novel*.

Cornish fig A raisin (O.C., Vol. XI, No.11, 1996, p.530). For an actual fig the phrases *broad fig* or *dote fig* were used (Hawke 1975: 7 and 17 – Treenoodle spelt it *doat fig* 1846:92) By contrast a *split fig* is a miserly person "who would cut a raisin in two rather than give overweight" (Jago 1882:274). In Cornish *fygesen* is a fig and *fygesen an howl* (i.e. 'fig of the sun') is a raisin. There is also a *fig pasty* (with raisins – Merton 2003:21).

Cornish fisherman's toast "Here's health to the Pope, death to our best friends, an may our streets run with blood". Here the reference to the Pope is an allusion to the Spaniards and the 'best friends' are the pilchards.

Cornish fish jouster The *fish-jouster* was a woman who sold fish. Often the term is preceded by the word 'Cornish' (e.g. O.C. Vol. XII, No.2, spring 1998, pp.33–5). Courtney mentions the word *jowst* as meaning to "fall from a donkey's back" (1880:31) and it therefore conveys the idea of a load (carried on the back). Thus she was also called a *back jouster* (Hawke 1975:3). She had a *cowal* (fish basket – yet this basket was also carried on the head – as distinct from the *flasket* or clothes basket and the *maund* or food hamper – Phillipps 1993:30 and 41). The *jouster* was also called a *jowder* or *chowder* (Jago 1882:196), a *fouster* (Hawke 1975:21) and also a *fish fag* (Hawke, ibid.). In Cornish she was called either a *gwrek an puskes* (fish wife) or *gwerthores puskes* (fish-seller).

Cornish fish stew A fish stew using many herbs (see Bissell 1996:36–7)

Cornish fix The therapeutic need (especially of someone living in a city) for the tranquility of Cornwall – "the isolation and the need for that *Cornish fix* is felt less by the young leaving the Duchy" (C.W. 14, 1997, p.30).

Cornish flag (*An Baner Kernow*) Also called St. Piran's flag. A white cross on a black background symbolizing the *white tin* (smelted tin) and the *black tin* (unsmelted tin ore). In 1847 Cornish quarrymen from Wadebridge marched against corn exports when food costs were high "with a red flag – the symbol of spilt blood – and a pasty on a pole" (see Deacon et all 2003:8–9. See *Cornish arms* and *Cornish ensign*.

Cornish flag of independence See also *Cornish Independence flag*.

Cornish folk football Term used by D.A. Reid for a traditional form of football in which the gentry participated (cited by Andy Seward in C.S. 5, 1997:167). Elsewhere this was not the norm. By contrast, in *Cornish hurling* (q.v.) the gentry might only organize or patronise the sport e.g. by providing the ball.

Cornish folk music, the queen of Epithet given to Brenda Wooton the famous Cornish folk singer (see http://www.ionamusic.com/rootnote.htm).

Cornish Fool, the sobriquet of Dick Hampton also called 'Foolish Dick', Methodist preacher at the time of the Great Revival 1814 (C.T. 11, June 1995, p.51).

Cornish Foot, the A reference to the Cornish military regiment in existence in the Civil War under Sir Bevill Grenville (Payton 1996:159).

Cornish foreshore rights The rights that belong to the Duchy of Cornwall not the monarch in connection with the Cornish foreshore (O.C. Vol. VI, No.3, 1962, p.100).

Cornish foreigners Ellis writes that the Saxons called Cornwall "the land of the *Kern-weahlas* or *Cornish foreigners* sometimes called the land of the '*West Welsh*' " (1985:134). It seems clear that while the suffix – *wall* may indeed be a cognate of the word 'Welsh' (from Saxon *welisc* or foreigner), the prefix *Corn-* in the name 'Cornwall' derives from the word 'horn' as in the *Corn Gwlas* or 'Horn of the Nation' (in Cornish 'horn' is *kern* – cf. Gk. *keras* – hence *Kernow* i.e. Cornwall). It is from an association of (goat) horns with cuckolding e.g. that one archaic slang word for cuckolded was *cornuted* (Partridge 1937:212) (c.f. It. *cornuto*). Thus the slang phrase *to send a man into Cornwall without a boat* (meaning to cuckold him – see Partridge ibid, 212–3), was not coined as an insult to the virtuous Cornish ladies, but rather form a pun on the words 'corn' and 'horn'.

Cornish '45 The 1549 rising has been described (e.g. by A.L. Rowse and Mark Stoyles) as "Cornwall's equivalent of the Scottish '45' " (cited by Payton C.S. Vol. 11, 2003, 13). The allusion here is to the unsuccessful Jacobite rising in Scotland in 1745.

Cornish Forty Niners Those Cornish miners who went to California in the gold rush of 1849 (W.B. 19th Jan., 1849 cited by Barton, 1971:166).

Cornish Fowl Another term for the *Cornish Game* (q.v.) (*The Encyclopedia Americana* 1943, Vol. 22, p.465).

Cornish frock A knit frock (C.W. 2, 1994, 32). Fishermen used to wear a *duck frock* which was a woven cotton overall over the *Guernsey frock* to protect it (Nance 1963).

Cornish fruit loaf The recipe for this rich loaf involves soaking the fruit and sugar overnight in tea. Hence it is also called *tea loaf* (see C.W. 1995, 16, p.47 and Pascoe 1995).

Cornish Fumitory (*fumaria occidentalis*) A rare variety of plant.

Cornish fun, king of Jago referred to J.T. Tregellan (for whom see the *Cornish Mathews*) as "The very master of *Cornish dialect* and the *king of Cornish fun*" (O.C. Vol.XII, No.3, autumn 1998, p.15). See *Cornish Mathews*.

'Cornish' fungus 1 *Melastiza cornubiensis* **2** *Cheilymenia cornubiensis*.

Cornish Furry dance Often the word 'Cornish' is prefixed to the furry dance (e.g. by Day 2000:87). The *Furry dance* (from Lat. *feria* or holiday) is also called *Flora Dance* (from 'flower') or *Faddy dance* (perhaps from the *Fading* dance). It is performed on the 8th May (or Saturday before if it falls on a Sunday or Monday).This date is the Apparition of St. Michael. According to Cunnack the dance symbolizes not only a triumph of spring over winter but also the battle between St. Michael and the Devil for Helston (1975:5). Lach-Szyrma observed that it resembles "continental processional May dances" rather than the Maypole dance (see JRIC 8, 1883–5, p.265). There are in fact a number of dances performed in the day and the *Hal an Tow* song is sung.

Cornish fury, the The Cornish leaders An Gof and Flamank (Payton uses the phrase in C.S. 2nd 1, 1993, p.5).

Cornish furze Or *Cornish fuzz*. Gorse which is also called *wing* (Ivey 1976:75). It was mentioned in contrast with French furze (W.B., 13 July, 1838, cited by Barton 1971:48–9). It was cut into fagots for fuel. The phrase is also mentioned by Wright as synonymous with the dwarf furze or *Ulex nanus* (1898–1905, Vol. 6, p.74). In Cornish the word is *ethyn(en)* (cf. W. *eithin*) and in dialect furze twigs are called *bruss* or *browse* (Phillipps 1993:22). On May day a piece of *Cornish furze* was hung on the door (Courtney 1890:29). See *Cornish Christmas tree*.

Cornish fuzz Will Coleman and Nigel Pengelly point out "we even have our own species: *ulex gallii*, the *Western gorse* or *Cornish fuzz*, lower and more compact than its cousin *ulex europaeus*, it forms wonderful gold cushions mingled with the purple of bell heather" (C.W. 34, 2003, p.22). The form *fuzz* sometimes appears as *vuzz* (Phillipps 1996) and also *fursse* (Ivey 1976:27). Moreover, the dialect word *fuzzies* refers to charred furze twigs (Clemo p.102).

Cornish Gaelic An incorrect name for the *Cornish language*. While Cornish is indeed a Celtic Language, it belongs to the Brythonic branch of Celtic (together with Welsh and Breton). The word Gaelic (in Corn. *Gwydhalek*) would be appropriate for the languages of the Goedelic Celtic branch (i.e. Scottish Gaelic in particular, but also Irish and Manx). On an internet site the Cornish translation of Trelawny (see *Cornish national anthem*) is glossed as '*Cornish Gaelic*' (see http://sniff.numachi,com/~rickheit/dtrad/pages/tiTRELAWNY.html).

Cornish gallon See *Cornish metric gallon*.

Cornish Game A breed of poultry developed in Cornwall. It derives from the interbreeding of Asils (or Asells) and Malays with Old English breeds. *Cornish hens* (q.v.) have similar sturdy bodies to cocks. Often it is cross-bred with the White Plymouth Rock (see *Rock Cornish* – appendix 1). A *mabyer* is a young (Cornish) hen and a *stag* is a cock. An itinerant poultry dealer was a *regrator* (Thomas 1895:116). *Pip* is a disease among hens and a *voryer* was a fowls'/hens' path (Jago 1882).

Cornish Gannet A species of bird mentioned in a list of Cornish birds by P.A.S. Pool (C.S. 1st, Vol. 3, 1975, p.44). In Cornish it is called *sethor* (literally 'archer') – a name which could derive from their fishing abilities since, as Jean Lawman observes, "gannets may put on a diving display if they locate a fish shoal" (C.W. 39, 2004, p.25).

Cornish gansey A *Cornish Guernsey* (q.v.). This dialect spelling is used by Kernow Knitwear.

Cornish Garden Cooker A variety of apple ripe in September and October. It is cultivated in Porthallow vineyard. See *Cornish Aromatic* for other apple varieties.

Cornish garter A silk garter of Cornish tartan edged with lacework. It is worn by the bride in a traditional Cornish wedding (see http://www.thecornishstore.com/shop).

'Cornish' gateway town Launceston has been called 'Cornwall's gateway town' (C.T. April, 1998, p.50).

Cornish gathering A large meeting or festival usually for *Cornish diaspora* (q.v.).

Cornish geese dancing Also called *geeze/giz dancing*. The word is probably derived from the Cornish *gys* meaning 'guise'. For this custom see *Cornish guisers*.

Cornish gentian (*Gentianella anglica ssp.cornubiensis*). A wild flowering plant (for information see Project Report 51, *Plantlife 'Back from the Brink' Project* Natural History Museum, London 1995, p.22). It is also called *early gentian*.

Cornish ghost town, California's The town of Bodie. Cornish miners went there for gold in 1860s and 1870s. There was a population of 10,000 and there were sixty saloons yet by the 1940s there were no inhabitants (C.W. 33, 2003, p.5).

Cornish ghost-dog The *Shony* is described as the *"Cornish ghost-dog* whose appearance heralded a storm" (Barber and Riches 1971:134). For other supernatural dogs in Cornish folklore see *'Cornish' wild hunt.*

Cornish Giant 1 A variety of apple which is also called *Lawry's Cornish Giant* or *Collogett pippin* (Spier 1996:32). It is a very large pale yellowish green with red stripes and is good for cider or cooking. See *Cornish Aromatic* for other apple varieties. **2** There have been many giants in Cornish folklore but the epithet the *Cornish Giant* was applied to Anthony Payne (the *Falstaff of the West*) (Bird 1989: 56–7). He stood 7ft. 4 inches tall and fought for the *Cornish Royalists* under Sir Beville Grenville in the Civil War **3** The same epithet has also been applied to Richard Trevithick (1771–1833) e.g. by Jenkin (1984:64) and in his biography by L.T.C. Rolt *The Cornish Giant* (pub. Lutterworth, 1960) because of his 'giant' status in the world of industry but also because of his great physique. *Trevithick Day* is held in Camborne on the last Saturday in April.

Cornish giant legends A category of Cornish legends (so termed by Deane and Shaw 1975:18). Such stories are myths like the giant Gogmagog who wrestled with Corineus (according to Geoffrey of Monmouth, even the name 'Cornwall' was fictitiously derived form the giant Corineus). Cornish giants played *bob and buttons* (the *bob* was the Mount and the *mit* was Trecobben Hill from where throw was made – see Hunt 1881, 1st, p.51) and there are places associated with giant legends like the Giant's Hedge near Lerryn built by Jack the Giant (Westwood 1992:24). Another place is Ralph's Cupboard, a cleft in the rocks near Portreath where the giant Ralph or Wrath would trap boats and eat people (Westwood, ibid. pp.48–9). In Mawgan the villagers used *sprouse* (light hay) to cover traps for giants in the churchyard since they came to steal the corpses (Westwood ibid. p.37). This is similar to the *kergrim* or ghoul seen in Cornish graveyards (Underwood 1983:38 – q.v. *Cornish Tenny Tiny*). Giants are also featured in dialect expressions such as "an artful maid is stronger than Bolster (a giant)" (Hawke 1973:35). Because of all the giants Cornwall has been called 'Land of Giants' (Clies Stevens in C.W. 40, 2004, p.74).

Cornish gift See *Cornishman's gift* (appendix 2).

Cornish gig A type of boat for rowing or sailing which was traditionally made from the *Cornish Elm* (q.v.). It is longer and lighter than a *Cornish lugger* and since the mid C19th had two masts not three.The gigs vary from different areas e.g. Penzance and Newlyn have different mizzens. Gig racing has become a very popular sport during the summer months, with the World Gig Championships being held in the Isles of Scilly in early May.

Cornish Gill-flower Alternative spelling of *Cornish gilliflower.*

Cornish Gilliflower A very late variety of dessert apple. It is a dull red and russet colour. It was also called *Jelly-flower*. See *Cornish Aromatic*.

Cornish Gillyflower Alternative spelling of *Cornish Gilliflower*.

Cornish gingerbreads As Pascoe (1995) refers to *Cornish fairings* (q.v.). Day informs us that in Penzance gingerbread cakes were raffled in a game called *lilly-bangers* which used cup and dice (2000:67).

'Cornish' Girard, The Or rather 'Girard of Cornwall' (Girardus Cornubiensis). Author (fl.1350) whose works include *De Gestis Britorum* and *De Gestis Regum West-Saxonum*.

Cornish goad A measurement of nine feet. The *goa(r)d* originally referred to the pole of this length (Thomas 1895:89). Yet according to Jago *goad* meant "half a square yard of land" (1882:178). See *Cornish yard*. A *landyard* was 18 ft. (Hawke 1975:33). The term originated from the Corn. *garthow* or *pyger*. The goad (from O.E. *gad* – an arrow/spear head) was a sharp stick used to drive oxen (hence 'to goad' meaning to incite). By extension, the length of the stick was used as a unit of measurement.

Cornish god of fire The Celtic god Lugh. So called since *Calan Est* or *De Halan Est* is *Lunasa*, *Lughnasadh* according to the internet site "Pagan Cornish".

'Cornish' Godfrey Or rather 'Godfrey of Cornwall'. C14th Carmelite divine and author educated at Oxford and Paris.

Cornish Gold 1 *Argyrantheum Cornish Gold* is a variety of perennial. **2** *Cornish clay* has sometimes been called, like platinum, 'white gold' (see, for instance, *White Gold from Cornwall and Devon* by Charles Thurlow). See *'Cornish' white gold*. **3** A variety of Cornish heather (see http://www.userszetnet.co.uk/heather/namesc.html). The phrase *Cornish Gold* has also been used as the title of a book about farm life in Cornwall by Mary French (1979). Moreover, "in Cornwall gold was a cure-all, and if rubbed on a wound it would stop bleeding" (Day 2003:134). See *Cornish cream, Cornish Heath* for other heather varieties. See *Cornish kings, the gold of*.

'Cornish' golden age Tim Saunders talks of "The last golden age" to describe the heroic episode of the Cornish Rebellion (q.v.) (*Planet* 30, Jan. 1976, p.33).

Cornish golf, home of As Tregennna is described (C.W. 32, 2002/3, p.5). Charles Frean introduced golf to Tregenna in 1888. There is still a golf course at the Tregenna Castle Hotel. See *Cornish cricket, home of*.

Cornish gook Sometimes this kind of bonnet called a *gook* is preceded by the word 'Cornish' (e.g. see Wakelin 1994:29) and with good reason since the Devon *gook* refers to what the Cornish would call an *arrish mow* – i.e. a temporary hay rick built in bad weather (Downes 1986:59). Jago described the *gowk* as "like a Quaker's bonnet ... with a 'curtain' behind" (1882:180). The word *gook* is related to the Cornish words *cugh* or *cugol* as in *cugol barth* or bard's hood. It was worn by the *Cornish bal maiden* (q.v.) and was similar to the Breton *coife.*It is also known as a *goop* "now popular as sun hats" (Ince 2001:21). The word *gook* is not to be confused with the *Cornish dialect* word *kook* which was a game of throwing quoits (C.T. Vol. 3, No. 1, 1996, p.3).

Cornish Goonhilly A small breed of wild horse in Cornwall which was also called the *Cornish horse* or *Cornish pony*. Some sources believe that it became extinct as late as the 1920s (C.T. Vol. 2, No. 9,1996, p.30). Its name derives from the area of the Lizard where it roamed freely, feeding on the *Cornish heath*.

Cornish goose dancers For the goose dancers or, as Couch called them, *goosey-dancers* (1871:80) see *Cornish guisers*.

Cornish gorse See *Cornish furze*.

Cornish Gorsedd (Corn. *Gorseth Kernow*). The Cornish form of the *Gorsedd* (Welsh spelling) or meeting of bards that is opened by the *Cornish Grand Bard* on the first Saturday in September. It is also called *Gorseth Byrth Kernow* or the *Gorsedd* of the Bards of Cornwall (c.f. W. *beirdd* – poets). It began in 1928 whereas the Breton *Goursez* began in 1900 (see Bowen 1991:377 and 410). See *Cornish Eisteddfod*.

Cornish Gorsedd motto *An Gwyr erbyn an Bys* (The Truth against the World). In the *Cornish Gorsedd* ceremony another motto *Kernow bys vyken* (Cornwall for ever) is shouted by all after the national anthem.

Cornish Gorseth See *Cornish Gorsedd*.

Cornish Gorsett Less common spelling of the Corn. *Gorseth* (see O.C. Vol. X, No. 3, autumn 1986, p.155). See *Cornish Gorsedd*.

Cornish Grace Written by William Bullock with the words "We love the place, O God". It was translated into Cornish by Henry Jenner as "Ny gar an le, a Dhew" and set to music by Kenneth Pelmear. It is used at the opening or closing of ceremonies.

Cornish Grand Bard The highest *Cornish bard* (q.v.) in the *Cornish Gorsedd* (q.v.). In Cornish he is called *Barth Mur*. There is also a deputy Grand Bard (*cannas Barth Mur.*) as well as a former Grand Bard (*kyns Barth Mur*). He is the equivalent of the Welsh Archdruid (W. *archdderwydd*, Corn. *arghdrewyth*).

'Cornish' Grand Canyon Also called *Cornwall Grand Canyon*. A 500ft hole in ground made by Delabole slate (see C.T. 8, March 1995).

Cornish Grandies Cornish nobles. Sir Bevill Grenville wrote in a letter that "All our *Cornish Grandies* were present at the battle with the Scotch General Ruthen..." (cited by Tangye 1978:77). The reference made is to the defeat of Lord Ruthren's force by the king's army at Liskeard in 1643.

Cornish granite The local coarse-grained granite of Cornwall which the Cornish also call *moorstone* (See C.S. 1st, Vol. 3, 1975, p.44). *'Cornish granite'* was used to build the Strand Bridge in London (see W.B. 17 Dec. 1813). *Rab* is granite rabble (from Corn. *rabmen* – the suffix *men* means 'stone') and *growder* is decomposed granite whereas *pooled granite* is split by wedges (Jago). This is also derived from Cornish (*men-growyn*). *Kennack granite* is named after a place near the Lizard. *Luxulyanite* a variety of speckled granite found ar Luxulyan (Bird 1988:63) whereas *Manaccanite* or *Gregorite* were names for Titanium – discovered by Rev. William Gregor (see Bird ibid. p.63). See *Cornish diamond*.

Cornish grapevine Term used for the system of contacts and acquaintances with which Cornishmen would help a fellow *Cornish cousin Jack* (q.v.) to find work. "The extremely effective *'Cornish grapevine'* brought many Cornishmen to the Californian mining districts" (C.W. 7, 1995/6, p.9).

Cornish grate unlike an ordinary grate this was like a piece of furniture. Dulcie Wing recounts theat "the room had a lovely *Cornish grate*, with cupboards each side, the glass fronted one containing the best china" (C.T. 10, May 1995, p.37).

Cornish Graveyard, the There is a *Cornish graveyard* at Keweenaw in Michigan. Moreover, "*Cornish Graveyard*" was also a poem by D.M. Thomas (Payton 1993: 301). See *Cornish corner*.

Cornish Green or *Green Cornishware* or *Cornish Green and White*. A recent form of crockery which is a variation of the original *Cornish Blue*. *Cornish Green* crockery has green and white stripes. See also *Cornish Yellow*.

Cornish greenstone Term used with reference to the tomb of Thomas Vivian, prior of Bodmin in Bodmin parish church (O.C. Vol. IX, No. 8, spring 1983). By coincidence, a green stone called malachite is to be found in Cornwall. *Cornish serpentine* (q.v.) can also be greenish.

Cornish Gretna Green As David Wright refers to Temple which he also calls *Cornwall's Gretna Green* and even as *England's Gretna Green* (C.T. June 1999, pp.1 and 20). This town was a tryst for eloping couples who could be married easily there. Gretna Green is a village on the Scottish border where from 1754–1940 young English people could go to get married without their parents' consent.

Cornish grey granite As Ferris (p.8) refers to *Cornish granite* (q.v.).

Cornish griglan bizom As the *Cornish broom* (*bizom, besom, bassam* or *bazaam*) of heather or *grig(lans)* has been called (Nance 1956:43), as opposed to the *caihar* broom of coconut fibre (Hawke 1989:21). It is derived from the Cornish word for heather *gruk* (*gruglon* is a heather bush). It was often sold by *Diddikies* (i.e. Gypsies) and is not used by a *Cornish witch* (q.v.).

Cornish guardian of the bees Thus Briggs describes the *browney* (1976:45). The *browney* is a creature akin to the *Cornish piskey* (q.v.) who can make bees settle. The bee is called a *dumble drain* (Hawke 1989:30) whereas the *apple bee* is a wasp and a swarm is a *glez* (Jago 1882:187) or *hez* (fro. Corn. *hes* and related to the *huer's* cry *hevva !* when a 'swarm' of fish was sighted). A hive is a *bee butt* (Ivey 1976:4 and 6) or a *cowel gwenyn* in Cornish (i.e. 'bee basket'). The hive was moved and covered with a black cloth when someone died (Couch 1871:84) yet if the bees are moved on Good Friday they will die (Hawke 1973:15). Indeed to sell bees is unlucky since a swarm in May heralds the birth of a lamb (Dean and Shaw 1975). The Cornish rubbed elderflowers on a hive to stop the bees leaving and if they saw a swarm near the house they would claim it by covering it with a handkerchief (Day 2003:232). Moreover, in Cornwall the *half-crease* system applied to bees which were "frequently lent and the honey divided" (Thomas 1895:91). See *Cornish mead.*

Cornish Guernsey Thick fisherman's pullover. There are different styles e.g. Newlyn, Lizard and Polperro, all of which have different stitch patterns. A *collaminks* was the Newlyn fisherman's jumper whereas a *dopper* was worn by Mousehole fishermen. Another name was a *say shimmy* (Nance 1963).

Cornish guinea fowl As the *Cornish Game* (q.v.) is sometimes called.

Cornish guise dancing Performance of *Cornish guisers* (q.v.).

Cornish guisers As the *Goose Dancers* or *Geese dancers* are sometimes called (e.g. by Day 2000:36). The *goose dancers* or as Courtney calls them *Giz' dancers* (1880:24) were mummers who performed plays at the Christmas season. They had no association with geese and their name is derived from their dis*guise*. Hence the Cornish saying "as good as a Christmas play" (Hawke 1989).

Cornish guizers Alternative spelling of *Cornish guisers.*

Cornish guttural 'gh' As Richard Gendall refers to a unique letter in the *Cornish language* (O.C. Vol. VII, NO.4, spring 1969, p.170). The sound is something similar to a 'g' pronounced guttually as the letter 'ch' (also heard in Welsh) but for the exact sound one should listen to a Cornish speaker.

Cornish Gwary Mur Alternative name for the *Cornish miracle play* (q.v.) used by some (e.g. in C.W. 19, 1996, p.29). from this word we have *gwaryer* (pl.-*yoryon*) or player. In Cornish the play was called *Gwary myr/merkyl* (i.e. 'play of appearance/miracle'). Bottrell recorded the word *guare* (see *Cornish hurling motto*) which was called by boys in the game of quoits (1873:156).

Cornish Habbard A variety of *Cornish Game* (q.v.) (for ref. see *Cornish Cobb*).

Cornish hagiography The study of Cornish saints and their legends (C.S. 2nd, 2, 1994, p.133). The word 'hagiography' is derived from the Greek words *hagios* (holy, saint) and *graphē* (writing). Yet in Modern Greek the same word (pronounced *ayiographia*) has come to mean mainly iconography (i.e. the painting of icons).

Cornish hair Poor quality wool from the distinct breed of *Cornish sheep* (q.v.) which was exported without any duty (Carew 1602:39). Carew attributes the condition of this wool not to the breed but to the fact that "the shire, through want of good manurance, lay waste and open" (ibid. p.39). By contrast *piskey wool* is very soft, white and silky (Tregarthen 1940:67). The confusion of hair with wool is etymological. In O.E. the word *hære* meant "sackcloth of hair" (Hall 1894:165) and suggests wool. Moreover the association between hair and wool is also shown in modern Gk. in which *malliá* is hair and *malli* is wool. See *Cornish cloth*.

Cornish halfpenny In C18th there were various copper halfpennies which were really tokens minted by private companies (see Mayne & Williams 1985:42–7, cf. *Cornish ounce*). A halfpenny was called a *ha'pmy* (Hawke 1975:27 – cf. Dev. *apmee*) or *ha'penny* (Phillipps 1993:15) while a *happard* was a halfpenny worth of something (Thomas 1895:92), as was a *(h)aa'path* (which also meant a daft person – Ivey 1980:32). In Cornish a halfpenny was *demma* (i.e. 'dime'). Hawke says that a friend who gave someone a knife was given a halfpenny so as not to cut the friendship (1973:33). See *Cornish penny*.

Cornish Hallowe'en 1 As Deane and Shaw refer to the Cornish festival of Allantide (1975:37) which was rich in very distinct customs. In Cornish the name is *Gol/Nos Calan Gwaf* (Feast/Night of the first day of winter) and derives from the Celtic new year. Children were given Allen apples and girls placed them under pillows to dream of their future spouse (Wright 1986:35). Wedding cake and myrtle were put under the pillow for the same purpose (Hawke 1973:22 and 24). Moreover, at All Hallow's Eve another way to inspire a dream was to place shoes in a 'T' shape (Hawke ibid. 24). In Newlyn a cross was made with candles at each of the four points and apples were hung from this (Courtney 1890:3). Moreover, another *Cornish Halloween* custom was to eat a large apple under a tree to cure a cold (Hawke 1989:15). **2** Midsummer's Day, about which Couch wrote "What Hallowe'en is to the Scotch, this day is to us" (1871:75).

Cornish hard rock miners Term used for the Cornish tinners since the mines often had hard rock (C.W. 29, 2002, p.28). Jenkin calls them "Cornish hard rock men" (1984:32).

Cornish haywain A type of harvest cart in E. Cornwall and Devon with low sides and fixed ladders ar each ends (Smith 1988). See *Cornish wain*.

Cornish Heath (*Erica vagans*) An endemic variety of heath which can be found on the Lizard. It is also called *Goonyhill* (C.S. 1st, Vol. 10, 1982, p.6). In Cornish it is *kykesow* which survived in dialect as *kekezza* (Thomas 1895:98), whereas ordinary heather is *gruk*.

Cornish Heaven As Morvah has been called:

"A paradise, another Eden
    A *Cornish Heaven* was Morvah then …" (Tuck 1988:43).

Although the name Morvah seems to derive from *mor* (sea) and the suffix *-va* (which indicates a place) hence a 'sea place', it is believed to be named after an unknown saint.

Cornish heavy cake Rich cake made with yeast (Walker 1994:32). It is often pronounced *'evvy cake*.

Cornish heavy cream cake Courtney's term for *Cornish heavy cake* (q.v.) which has always been served with tea (1890:38). In dialect it is known as *fuggan*.

Cornish hedge As Paul and Rodney Phillips point out "The ideal *Cornish hedge* comprises two parallel granite walls with a packed fill of earth between them" (O.C. XIII.2, 2004, p.41) and a *Cornish shovel* is used to dig the foundation (ibid. p.42). The Cornish usually call it just *adge* (Hawke 1975:1) while a normal hedge is called a *fence* (JRIC, 8, 1979, p.120). The confusion may derive from the ambiguity of the Cornish word *ke* (pl.*-ow*) which means "hedge, fence, low wall of earth and stone" (Nance 1978:257). Even dialect expressions like "sun cracking the hedges" (Hawke 1973:12) for hot weather suggests earth and stone.The base stone of the *Cornish hedge* is called the *grounder*. A gap in a broken down hedge was called a *clut*, a *freath* or a *gurgo* (which was also a low hedge) whereas an actual drain hole at the bottom is a *rabbit box* (Nicholls 1986:26). The word *freath* may relate to the *frith* or wattled hedge or gate (Jago 1882:171 and in L.C. – it seems a cognate of the Welsh *ffridd/ffrith* or mountain pasture [where perhaps there would be walls/hedges to contain the sheep]). A *butt-gap* was a hedge of pitched turf (Jago 1882:126) and a *cock-hedge* was a "quickset hedge" (Thomas 1895:75). A trench at the foot of a hedge is a *greep* (Thomas 1895:90) or *gripe* (Ivey 1980).

Cornish hedged field A field surrounded by *Cornish hedges* (C.T. 10, May 1995, p.37). In Cornish the adjective 'hedged' is *keek* and *keas* is the verb 'to hedge'. A field so enclosed would be called *kew* in Cornish (cf. W. *cae*) as opposed to a *mes* (cf.W. *maes*, Bret.*maez*) or open field. Cornish also has the word *park* for field or enclosure (cf. Bret. *park*, Ir. *páirc*).

Cornish hedger One who make a *Cornish hedge*. There is a Guild of *Cornish Hedgers*. One dialect saying is to "eat like a hadger (hedger)" (Phillipps 1993:63). A *Cornish hedger* also knows about *casting* or hedge repairing (O.C. X, 2, spring 1986).

Cornish hedging The making of a *Cornish hedge* (term used e.g. in C.T. 5, 1994). The rows of stones would slant alternately and this pattern was called *kersey* or *Jack and Jill* (Nicholls 1986:11).

Cornish hellan The '*Cornish hellan*' is a type of roofing slate (C.T. 8, 1995, p.15). This is clearly related to the *Cornish dialect* word *helling* which is "roofing stone and in West Cornwall a roof " (Phillipps 1993:34). Carew referred to the blue *heling stones* (superior to the 'sageleaf' coloured or common grey tiles) which he derived from *hele* to 'cover over' (1602:18). See *Cornish Blue*.

'Cornish' helmet A Cornish miner's helmet. The statue of the *Cornish miner* (q.v.) is described as wearing "his *Cornish style helmet*, complete with candle" (*C.W.W.* Kynyaf 1995, nyver 16, p.11).

Cornish hen A *Cornish bantam*. In Cornish the word 'hen' is *yar* (cf. W. *iâr*) and the *pen yar* (i.e. the 'hen's head') is the *neck* (last sheaf) which is cut at Harvest (see *Cornish witch*). In the *Colperra* rhyme (on Shrove Tuesday – *Nicky nan night*) the words 'hen cock, han cock' are said. According to Cornish superstition, "whistling girls and crowing hens are sure to come to no good end" (C.W. 39, 2004, p.11). See *Cornish Game*.

Cornish hen pheasant Recipe for pheasant which includes stuffing the bird with cream cheese and apple and wrapping it in bacon (Butcher & Annand 1994:80).

Cornish Herb and Garlic A type of Cornish cheese. See *Cornish Blue* for other cheeses.

Cornish herb pie Recipe given by Bissell (1996:30–1) for a pie or pasty with vegetable. Just as the French word *herbe* does not mean herb but grass, so the *Cornish dialect herb*(*y*) means not herb but green vegetables – hence *herb pasty*. Conversely, the dialect word *grass* (as in *grass pasty* – for which see *Cornish pasty*) does mean herbs or greens.

Cornish heroic metre Andrew Hawke's term to describe the poetic style of the

Cornish Ordinalia (C.S. 1st, Vol. 6, 1978, p.49).

Cornish high tea A full *Cornish cream tea* (q.v.) including *Cornish heavy cake* (Jenkin 1945).

Cornish high-backed settle Unique old piece of Cornish furniture, usually of oak. It resembled a bench with a high back (Rawe records the term 1984:89).

Cornish highwayman Les Merton tells us of the unknown *"Cornish Highwayman"* called Deck Turpin who "used to give everyone he robbed one of his mother's pasties" (2003:42).

Cornish Hill Another recent name for St. Just Hill, the site of a former Cornish settlement at Dayles Ford in Victoria, Australia which is in danger of urban development (C.W. 5, 1995, p.34).

Cornish hobby horse 1 Peter Thurston's book was entitled *The Cornish Obby Oss* (1912). This term applies to both the *Old Blue Oss* are the *Old Red Oss* which feature in the May Day celebrations in Padstow. Each 'horse' is just a man under a sheet and accompanied by the *teaser* dancing in front of him with a mask and club. **2** There was also the Christmas time hobby horse (Corn. *pen glas*) the head of which was a real horse's skull on a pole covered by a sheet and similar to the Welsh *Mari Lwyd* (both Corn. *glas* [the word *glas* also exists in Welsh] and W. *llwyd* mean 'grey'). In L.C. the name is *pedn glaze* (Gendall & Gendall 1991) and in dialect the word *pedn-pral* was a horse's head (Thomas 1895:110 – no relation to a *pedn-paley* or tom-tit – see Jago 1882:231).

Cornish hoggan The *Cornish pasty* (q.v.). Jago said it was a pork pasty (1882:188).

Cornish Hog's Pudding "The *Cornish Hog's Pudding* is not made elsewhere" (C.W. 10, 1996, p.10). The mixture for this pudding is put into the skins (called *ox middles*) and come cured from Brazil. By contrast, pigs' intestines are used for smaller sausages.

Cornish Holocaust, the The Cornish Prayer Book Rebellion of 1549 in which priests were martyred and 11% of the Cornish population was killed, i.e. "half the able-bodied male population". The term is used by both Kenneth MacKinnon (C.S. 2nd, 2004, p.269) and Tim James (C.W. 40, 2004, p.25). The word 'holocaust' is mainly associated with the Nazi genocide of the Jews in W.W.2 and means literally 'totally burnt' (Gk. *holos* all and *kaustos* burnt).

Cornish homecoming festival As *Dhwelans* is described (C.W. 37, 2004, p.12). This is the festival held for those Cornish who return home from overseas.

Cornish Home Rule Cornish autonomy with a *Cornish Assembly* (q.v.). Whetter shows a cartoon of a Cornish marriage guidance counsellor who tells the couple: "That was great – you're Welsh, your husband's Scottish and I'm Cornish. And we all finished up agreeing about Home Rule" (1977:135).

Cornish Honeypin A variety of dessert apple which apple growers describe as "2nd early" (see Spiers 1996:58). See *Cornish Aromatic*.

Cornish honey-pin Hyphenated spelling of *Cornish Honey Pin* (used by Wright 1986:34).

Cornish honorary banner A flag mentioned not as synonymous with, but in contradistinction with the *Cornish banner* (i.e. *Cornish flag*). Though it is not described, from the context one might infer that it is, like the *Cornish ensign* (q.v.), a variation of the Cornish flag, perhaps with a crest (for this term see O.C. X, 7, 1988, p.336).

Cornish hornpipe A dance and the music for that dance.

Cornish horse As the small breed of *Goonhillies* (also called *Canelys*) once common on the *Cornish moors* has been called (Rawe 1986:99). The phrase "three on a horse like going to Morvah fair" could not have applied to the small local horse – yet centuries ago the *Cornish horse* was used to carry sand (Carew 6002:40). In Cornish miners' jargon the *horse* was a type of rope attached to the *kibble* (iron bucket) (see Orchard 1990:41) as well as a fault in the rock or *lode* (Hawke 1975:29) while a horse is a *hoise(y)* (Ivey 1976:34) or *oss* (Hawke ibid. p.41). Horses are called by the Cornish with *kep- kep- kep!* and a *munger* is a straw horse collar. Moreover, *Tom* was the name of the horse *piskey-ridden* by the *night-riders*. However, the *Flying Hoss* was a throw in *Cornish wrestling* (q.v.) (Davey 1983:11) also called the *flying mare*. No relation to *Cornish mule* (q.v.).

Cornish horse omnibus Early form of transport e.g. Martin's 'bus' from Looe to Menheniot (O.C. VI, 5, 1963, p.225). There was also Kit Treen' *kittereen* or "primitive omnibus" between Penzance and Truro (Jago1882:202). See *Cornish van*.

Cornish horse whim A *Cornish whim* (q.v.) worked by one or two horses. In Cornish mines it was used to wind small shafts. (C.W. 23, 2000, p.26).

Cornish Host (Corn. *An lu kernewek*) The army of Cornishmen led by Michael Joseph and Thomas Flamank.The word 'host' is often capitalized (e.g. Williams 1987:63).

Cornish hot cakes Potato cakes with sultanas (Waller 1994:44).

Cornish hug A hold in *Cornish wrestling*. It has been described as "a peculiar grip used by *Cornish wrestlers*" (Wright 1898–1905, Vol. 1, p.734). It is also used by several Cornish writers Courtney (1890:37) and Jenkin (1945:459). It is not one of the terms used by *Cornish wrestlers* today. No relation to a *Welshman's hug* which is an itch (Edwards 1998:88).

Cornish hugg Alternative spelling of *Cornish hug*.

Cornish huggan Rothwell refers to the '*Cornish huggan*' which she believes, "must have been the forerunner of the pasty" (1989). It is described as a piece of unleavened dough with pieces of pork inside.

Cornish hugge An old spelling of *Cornish hug* (q.v.).

'Cornish' hundred 1 With reference to the variable 'long hundred' used by fishermen, Smylie writes "In Cornwall it (i.e. the hundred) is 132 fish – 33 warps of four fish" (1998:115). Moreover, the '*long hundred*' was "8 times120+5 for good measure" (O.C., Vol. XIII, No. 1, autumn 2003, p.13). **2** In Cornwall the term 'hundred' (Corn. *keverang*) was also used as a land measurement. This is probably related to the W. *cyfran* or 'gavelkind' (literally 'portion' or 'share') since this amount of land may have been the equal inheritance of each son. The word 'Cornish' is often prefixed (see C.S. 1st, Vol. 3, 1975 p.47).

Cornish hunting tartan As opposed to *Cornish national tartan*, this is the other motif for the *Cornish kilt* and has a characteristic dark green background.

Cornish hurler (Corn. *hurlyas*) A player of *Cornish hurling* (q.v.). The word *hurlers* in *Cornish dialect* also means small sparks, which were sometimes indicative of a storm (Courtney 1890:136) as well as a screen or griddle for sifting corn (Thomas 1895:95). The Hurlers are also a circle of stones on Craddock Moor – once men who were literally 'petrified' (like Lot's wife) since they violated the Sabbath by hurling. There are many parallel tales such as the stone women of Moelfre, Wales who had been winnowing on Sunday.

Cornish hurling (Corn. *hurlya*) Traditional Cornish sport which is played on Feast Monday (after Sunday nearest to 3rd February) at St. Ives (on the sands) and on Shrove Tuesday and the following Saturday at St. Columb (in the streets and fields). Two teams – the 'Town' and 'Country' play with a small ball (see *Cornish hurling ball*). The word 'Cornish' often precedes the word 'hurling' (e.g. in Bowles 1945:121) and by Andy Seward (C.S. 2nd, 5, 1997, p.167). It is not to be confused with the Irish *hurling* or *hurley* (played with a stick) yet *Cornish hurling* is said once to have resembled hockey. See *Cornish cricket, home of*.

'Cornish hurling', home of St. Columb has been dubbed the "home to the Cornish sport of hurling" (C.W. 27, 2001, p.6). See *Cornish cricket, home of*.

Cornish hurling ball The silver ball used in *Cornish hurling* (O.C. June 1990:37).

In Cornish the hurling ball is called *pel arghans* (i.e. 'silver ball'). It is also referred to by the terms *town ball* and *country ball* (Jenkin 1945:465). Moreover, the phrase 'drinking the silver ball' means drinking cocoa if one is a teetotaler (Jenkin, ibid, p.465). Rawe believes that a gold ball was originally used (1986:117). If so Greenaway's theory seems more plausible – that the ball represented the sun in a hurling match that symbolised the battle between winter and summer (cited by Jenkin, ibid. p.465 n.1). It is the mayor of St. Ives who tosses the ball up to start play.

Cornish hurling motto The motto sometimes written on the *Cornish hurling ball* (*Gwary whek yu gwary tek* – 'Fair play is good play'). It is also used for *Cornish* wrestling (q.v.) See *Cornish motto*.

Cornish Hybrid Heath (*Erica williamsii Druce*) A hybrid of *Cornish Heath* and cross-leaved heath (C.S. 10, 1982, p.7).

Cornish Hybro A variety of *Cornish Game* (q.v.) (for ref. see *Cornish Cobb*).

Cornishify To make Cornish cf. Scotchify. See *Cornishise*.

Cornish imps As Payton calls the *buccas* (1996:26). See *Cornish bucca*.

Cornish Independence Flag Phil Rendle refers to this flag designed in 1927 which is a *Cornish flag* (q.v.) or Cross of St. Piran with a hand holding a red sword in the centre (O.C. XII, 3, 1998, p.24 and p.26). It is also called the *Cornish Flag of Independence* (ibid. p.26).

Cornish Independence Party Shortlived political party of 1950 which sought economic reform (see Deacon et al 2003:31).

'Cornish' Independent A Cornish candidate in a general election not belonging to any British party. John Carah Roberts who contested Camborne in 1929 (with 6.3% of the votes) was called a '*Cousin Jack Independent*' (Deacon et al 2003:21).

Cornish Indian game As *Cornish game* is sometimes called due to its Asian provenance (Davidson 1999:378).

Cornishiness The quality of being *Cornishy* (as distinct from *Cornish*).

Cornish-Irish Feud As John Rowe refers to the feud between Cornish miners and their Irish colleagues in Butte, America (*Folk Life*, Vol. 3, 1965, p.36).

Cornish Iron Man As the 9 ft. high sculpture by Den Hornick is called. It is made out old items of industrial waste (C.W. 14, 1997, p.17). It can be seen in the National Trust garden at Trelissick, Feock near Truro. It is also referred to as the *Cornish Man of Iron*.

Cornishise To make Cornish (e.g. used in C.W. 1, June 1994). In Cornish the verb *kernewekhe* means to make or become Cornish.

Cornish isle, sweet thrushes of our As the *Cornish bal maidens* (q.v.) were described in the *Cornubian*, 7 Jan. 1887 (cited by Sharon P. Schwartz in C.S. 2nd, 6, 1998, p.16).

Cornishism A Cornish turn of phrase or colloquialism (Heard 1984:66).

Cornishize Alternative spelling of *Cornishise*.

Cornish Jack 1 No relation to the *Cornish Cousin Jack* (q.v.) as this is another name for the *Cornish Chough* (see Swainson 1886:74 and Wright 1898–1905, Vol. 1, p.734). **2** A type of fish (see http://www.highiq.net/Text/fish.txt).

Cornish jackwain A variey of cart with four wheels and low sides (or without sides) which was drawn by a horse (see Smith 1988). See *Cornish wain*.

Cornish Jennie/Jenny A Cornish lady, especially one living overseas. The female equivalent of a *Cornish Cousin Jack* (q.v.). The synonym *Cousin Jenny* is perhaps more common (but for the word 'Cornish' is sometimes prefixed see C.W. 7, 1995/6). The plural is *Cornish* or *Cousin Jennys*, not 'Jennies' (O.C. Vol. X, No. 7, 1988, p.314). Another form was Cousin Jinny (Jauncey 2004:94). In West America the term 'Cousin Jenny' was applied by all (not just Cornish people) to any Cornishwoman in the same way that the nickname 'Cousin Anne' was applied to a Welshwoman (See Cassidy 1985:805). In Australian slang a Cousin Jenny does not always refer to simply a Cornishwoman *per se* but to the wife of a *Cousin Jack* (Davey and Seal 2003:78). A *jennyquick* was a goffering iron (Thomas 1895:96) and a *popping jenny* was a hand lamp with red and green light (Nance 1963).

Cornish Jews In 1867 Max Müller cited a M. Esquiros "a believer in *Cornish Jews*" (p.486). The phrase *Cornish Jews* refers not to the historical Jewish community in Cornwall (see Pearse and Fry 2000) but to the Jews of Cornish legend who had once worked the mines. This is conveyed in the Cornish term for an ancient tin work – *whel Yedhewon* (i.e. 'Jews' mine'). The *Cornish knockers* (q.v.) are often described as "the souls of Jews … sent to work as slaves in the tin mines" (Hawke 1975:32). Hence Couch referred to these old works as *Jew's offcasts* (1602:19–20), also called *Jews' pieces* (Jago 1882:195–6), *Jew's whidn* or *Jew's works* (recorded by Venetia Newall in Pearce & Fry, eds. 2000:16). Other mining terms include *Jew's bowels* (bits of tin in disused mines) and *Jew's leavings* (tin and mixed refuse) and *Jew's tin* (larger blocks of tin) and a Jews' house (old tin smelting house) (Pearce and Fry ibid. 16). Other Cornish expressions include *Jews' ears* (a fungus) and *Jews' fish* (halibut) (Jago 1882:195–6) whereas a *Jew's eye* is something of little value. Moreover, *Jew* was the name of the black field beetle which would be pressed with the words 'Jew, Jew, spit blood' (Jago, ibid. 321). Many tenuous connections with Jews are from false etymologies eg. Market Jew and *Jew-whydn* (the former a corruption of Marazion and the latter from *Chew widden* or 'White Thursday' when black tin was first smelted white).

'Cornish' John Or rather 'John of Cornwall' (Johannes Cornubiensis). C12th theologian who studied in Paris. Although described as a *Bas-Breton* (i.e. low-Breton) he was born in St. Germans.

Cornish joke A joke in which the hero (perhaps a stereotype *Cornish tinner*) displays the oxymoron of "foolish wisdom"(see *The Celtic Chronicles*, May/June 1995, p.3). The *Cornish joke* often involve the use of a *double entendre*, such as employing a *Cornish dialect* term which has a different meaning in standard English. Moreover, malapropism or ambiguity deriving from Cornish pronunciation are also hallmarks of the *Cornish joke*. For instance, Bottrell mentioned two English visitors who enquired about 'caves' and ancient huts. The Cornishwoman wondered why he wanted 'caaves' (i.e. calves) and replied "You don't seem much like butchers". When she understood her mistake, she at least tried to direct them to the ancient huts and added "Oh Lord, you're looking for the *crellas*" (1873:157). As for the caves, the gentlemen would have been understood on that count as well if they had asked about the *fogous*.

'Cornish' Judas *Jack o'Lent*. A ragged effigy similar to Guy Fawkes yet formerly made at the beginning of Lent. *Jack o'Lent* was dragged through the streets, hanged, shot and then burnt. Couch identified it with Judas (1871:74). Deane and Shaw maintain that "the Cornish image was said locally to represent Judas Iscariot" (1975:166). Day makes the same analogy between *Jack o'Lent* and Judas (2003:53). The comparison is a pertinent one since in several countries e.g. Spain, Portugal, Mexico, and Greece an effigy of Judas is burnt at Easter.

Cornish jugular Expression used by Payton to refer to the Cornish people's religion (1996:165). The instance cited is the Parliamentarians' persecution of priests in several parishes after the English Civil War. This was tantamount to an indirect attack on the Cornish people themselves and their religious freedom.

Cornish jury A jury biased in favour of the defendant (perhaps as the jurors were his fellow accomplices). According to the old saying "a *Cornish jury* will never convict a smuggler" (Vivian 1969:20; Jenkin 1945:15). The Cornish word for 'jury' is *an deudhek den* (i.e. 'the twelve men').

Cornish Kae A synonym of the *Cornish Chough*.

Cornish Kea A type of plum that can be used to make wine, jam and chutney. The trees grow around Kea, near Truro.

Cornish kellywyck Special walking stick made by Den Tuthill of Redruth (see Williams 1982:93). "The Cornish believed that if they made a walking stick out of holly they would get rheumastism" (unless they had a rowan twig in their pocket) (Day 2003:380–381). No relation to *kiddliwink* which was a beer house.

Cornish kennel stone See *Cornish kinning stone*.

Cornish kettle With reference to the *kettle loaf*, Martin tells us that "the name stems from the *Cornish kettle* or cover, which used to be placed over the dough as it baked on a griddle within the *Cornish peat* or wood fire" (1993:27).

Cornish kibble Metal bucket that was attached to rope to pull up ores. for the mine. The word 'Cornish' is sometimes prefixed (e.g. by Payton 1996:239). The form *kibbal* also exists (Jago 1882:200) and there is even the adjective *kibbled* to describe maize chopped (for the bucket – see Phillipps 1993:38). The word is derived from Corn. *kybel* (pl. *kybellow*) which, according to Nance meant a well-bucket as well as a tub or mine bucket (1978). The similarity of *kybel* to the Modern Gk. *kouvás* and Tk. *kova* (in both cases 'bucket') is probably coincidental. The *kibble* was replaced by the *skip*. See *Cornish bucket*.

Cornish killick A *killick* (derived from the Cornish word *culyek* or 'cock', cf. W. *ceiliog*; Bret. *kilhog* and Van. *kilhgog*) is an anchor. As Nance informs us, "the *Cornish killick*, once doubtless four-armed, was latterly a two-armed affair … made of wood and stone" (1963:102). It is distinct from the *raft bag* or canvas anchor (Nance ibid. 134) and the *jinny-lin* or iron anchor (Nance ibid. 198).

Cornish kilt There have been *Cornish kilts* and patterns of *Cornish tartan* for a few decades now (see C.S. 1st, Vol. 6, 1978, p.46) and recently some patterns ('setts') of *Cornish tartan* (q.v.) have become established. It is even accompanied by a *Cornish sporran* (q.v.). In contrast with the *Cornish bagpipes* (q.v.), the *Cornish kilt* seems to be an invented custom however, as Woodhouse observes, the garment of the *Cornish piper* (q.v.) on the bench end at Altarnun "with a lot of imagination … could be a *Cornish kilt*" (1994:52). It does indeed resemble a kilt, but a pleated kilt like the Greek *foustanélla* rather than a Celtic kilt.

Cornish kilted The adjective of *Cornish kilt*. It could apply to a person wearing one. Corvovi Creations advertise that they make "*Cornish kilted* outfits".

Cornish kilt pin A pin to fasten a *Cornish kilt* (q.v.). Several such pins are available e.g. with the St. Mylor Cross, the Sancreed Cross (with four Stafford knots), the Lanivet pin (Lanivet was a popular site of pilgrimage) and recently a kilt pin which is shaped like a sword combined with the wheel Cross of St. Columb.

Cornish King A variety of potato. In Redruth *kings* meant donkeys (Jago 1882:202). Indeed the donkey is also called a *Redruth king* since a Redruth man once crowned a donkey to mock George IV (Gendall 1995:12). Other names for the donkey are *Jerusalem pony, moke, mawgust, neddy* and *neggur* (Hawke 1989:30) while in Cornish it is *asen* (a cognate of the word 'ass'). Other 'Cornish kings' include 'The King's son' (Billy Bray – for whom see the *Cornish tin mining evangelist*), the "King of Fowey in a quiet way" ('Q' – see C.W. 39, 2004, p.59 – for whom see the *Cornish Literary Giant*), and the 'King of Prussia' (sailor and *Cornish fair trader* John Carter, b.1770 since his idol was Frederrick the Great – see Jenkin 1984:60). The 'King of Mid-Cornwall' was J.T. Treffry who who built the giant breakwater at Par (Rawe 1986:92). The 'Silver King' was John Gundry (Payton 1999:115) and there is also a "King of the piskies" (Couch 1871:61). See also *Cornish fun, king of*.

Cornish kings, the gold of So gorse has been called (C.W. 37, 2004, p.29). See *Cornish Gold*.

Cornish kings, the seven The kings who with Arthur beat the Danes at the battle of Vellandruchar (Deane and Shaw 1975:29 and Westwood 1992).

Cornish kinning stone As Day records "Cornish *kinning*, or *kennel, stones* were crystalline holed stones worn round the neck, especially to cure eye complaints" (2003:113). Another Cornish cure for eye disease was to apply club moss, especially if it were on the third day of the moon (Day ibid., p.175). Moreover "in Cornwall, the crowfoot ... known as the kenning herb or kennel herb" was also believed to cure eye disease (Day ibid. p.238). Yet another cure was to rub a *ram* (i.e. tom) cat's taol on the eye. A *kennin* (Jago 1882:199) or *kennel* (Thomas 1895:98) is a sty on the eye.

Cornish kitchen 1 A synonym of the *Cornish range* (q.v.). **2** A type of blue striped chinaware also called *Cornish Blue* and *Cornish China* (Davey 1983:77). Possibly it was so named because of its association with the following: **3** The name of a broadside ballad that mentions the aforementioned blue and white crockery:

> "In a Cornish kitchen with the log fire glow on the wall
> And the nickety nack of the grandfather clock, the blue and white
> china and all…"

Cornish kitchen range Another way of referring to a *Cornish range* (James 1979:49).

Cornish Kiwi A New Zealander of Cornish extraction (Sue Bradbury uses the term in C.W. 36, 2003/2004, p.38). The word *kiwi* is Maori for a species of flightless bird. By extension, a *kiwi* is also a person who comes from New Zealand, a variety of fruit from there as well as a New Zealand dollar or New Zealand English. See *Cornish All Blacks*.

Cornish knight's fee Four *Cornish acres* (q.v.).

Cornish knocker Often the word 'Cornish' is prefixed (e.g. by Edwards 1976:73) for **1** the small goblin that dwells in the tin mines (Hunt 2nd, 1881:348). The knockers are believed to be the souls of Jews condemned to work the mines since they had crucified Christ. So as not to disturb them miners would not whistle underground (Hawke 1973:17). Perhaps the name *knocker* is related to the term *knacked bal* (mine that has stopped working – also called *scat bal*) which Ivey gives as *knocked* (1976:38) and indeed the *knocker* is also called *knacker* (Hawke 1975:32). With the word 'Cornish', it is more easily distinguished from the *Kentish knocker* which refers to a smuggler (cf. *Cornish fair trader*). Other Cornish names for the knockers are *nickers* (see Hawke 1975:40) and in West Cornwall they are called *nuggies* (Curnow 2002:17). The *bucca*, *gathorn* and *spriggans* were also Cornish spirits who haunted mines (Jago 1882:175) and counterparts of the German *Kobolt*. Miners would leave a *didjan* (small piece of *croust* – i.e.lunch) for the *knockers*. Moreover, just as the *knockers's* tapping would indicate the position of a lode, so a similar Cornish sprite called the *cooper* would hammer beneath a cellar when there was a catch of pilchards (Nance 1963:64). **2** There is also a beer called *Cornish Knocker* brewed by Skinners, Truro. See *Cornish Blonde*.

Cornish lace The lace was a land measure which in Cornwall was 18 ft square but the imperial measure was 16½ ft (Nance 1956:106). In *Cornish dialect* the verb *lace* means beat or punish (J.R.I.C. Vol. 1, Part 3, 1864–65, p.50).

Cornish lace agate A form of agate (a semi-precious stone).

Cornish lady Spelt with two words, unlike *Cornishwoman*. Not to be confused with the '*Lady of Cornwall*' who is chosen annually to offer a swathe of corn to the *Cornish Grand Bard* (q.v.) at the *Cornish Gorsedd* (q.v.).

Cornish land rod As the *lorgh* has been described (Nance 1978:265). This was half a lace or 9 ft. The word *lorgh* also meant a walking stick and it was also a staff which (together with the *scryp* or wallet) was carried by a pilgrim.

Cornish lane A proverbial narrow lane. Westwood, for example, alludes to the very narrow "*Cornish lanes*" (1992:66). The phrase is also mentioned in Payton (1993) with reference to Carbis Bay, Mullion. Such lanes are called *gurgoes* (Jago 1882:184 – not to be confused with *gurgo* – a low hedge). There is also a *drang* which is "a narrow lane between two walls" (Phillipps 1993:27).

Cornish language The Cornish language or *Kernewek* (*Kernuack* in L.C.) is a Brythonic Celtic language very similar to Welsh and Breton. Apart from sharing similar vocabulary, these languages also have common grammatical features like mutations (see *Cornish mutations*). Cornish was spoken throughout Cornwall in the Tudor period and gradually the language was spoken only in the western region. Even decades before the death of Dolly Pentreath (see *Cornish speaker*, *last*) in 1777 the number of Cornish speakers had already dwindled considerably. While historians attribute the death of Cornish to the lack of a *Cornish Bible* (q.v.) and *Cornish Prayer Book* (see *Cornish Prayer Book Rebellion*), its slow death may still have been inevitable. Even if Cornish had still managed to survive until the time of Wesley, the otherwise praiseworthy movement of Methodism may (as in the Isle of Man) have proved an inadvertent threat to the language by evangelizing solely through the medium of English. Moreover, had a hypothetical minority of speakers still managed to preserve Cornish until the Victorian era then children who spoke Cornish in school would certainly have been punished with an instrument similar to the 'Welsh Not' in Wales. For a few century now Cornish has been revieved – speakers of *Unified Cornish* (and K.K.) chose to revive the purer medieval/Tudor form whereas speakers of *Late Cornish* see the revival as a continuation of Cornish as it would have been spoken by its last speakers.

Cornish Language Board (Kesva an Taves Kernewek) Founded in 1967 to take over responsibility from the Gorsedd and the Federation of Old Cornwall Societies for promoting the revived Cornish Language (q.v.). It holds its own series of examinations at four grades. Originally the Cornish it promoted was Nance's Unified Cornish (q.v.) however in 1987 it decided to adopt the new spelling system of Ken George known as Common Cornish (q.v.) or 'Kernewek Kemmyn'.

Cornish Language Council (*Cossell an Tavaz Cornoack*). The board that represents the *Late Cornish*.

Cornish Language Day (Deth a Gernewek) A special day devoted to speaking the Cornish language. Historically it might have been arranged by the Old Cornwall Societies (see C.S. 6, 1978, p.49) but in modern times more often by the 'Fellowship' or 'Agan Tavas'.

Cornish Language Fellowship (*Kowethas an Yeth Kernewek*) Founded in 1979 to promote the use of Cornish.

Cornish language group for children As *Dalleth* (Corn. 'Beginning') has been described (C.W.W. 1993, 10, p.24). It is the equivalent of the Breton group *Diwan*.

Cornish language revival, father of the Henry Jenner. This epithet is recorded by Ellis (1985:156). Jenner was an author and active member of the *Cornish Revival*. He has also been called the *Father of the Cornish Revivalist Movement* (C.S. 7, p.96). So related is the name Jenner with Cornwall that in Scouse slang one name for a Cornishman is a *Jenner/Janner* (see the internet site Merseytalk 9).

Cornish language weekend (*pennseythun Gernewek*) A weekend spent at a retreat with other learners and speakers of Cornish during which time only Cornish is spoken (C.S. 6, 1978:49). In *Unified Cornish* weekend would be *penseythen* (*pen* head + *seythen* week)

Cornish language Will o' the Wisp As Matthew Spriggs calls Rev. Joseph Sherwood (C.S. 2nd, 6, 1998, p.46 passim). This appellation is perhaps due to the fact that his main Cornish writings are not extant so nothing more than a 'glimmer' of his work still remains. The Will o'the Wisp is what the Cornish would call the *Jack o'lantern* which is the *ignis fatuus* (see *Cornish piskies, queen of the*). In Cornish it is called *tan nos* (i.e. 'fire of night').

'Cornish' lantern The correct form is *Cousin Jack lantern* which refers to "an improvised lamp made by placing a candle in a can of grease" (Monteleone 1949:59). The phrase probably derives from the Cornish people's use of a *croggan* or limpet shell (see *Cornish Bluebeard*) in which a candle was often placed (Nance 1963:68). It may also be an allusion to the candle placed in the *Cornish miner's helmet*.

Cornish Large Black A breed of pig (Mason 1951:157 & 167). See also *Cornish White*, *Lop-eared* and *German 'Cornish'* in appendix 2.

'Cornish' last Normally a *last* of fish is 123,000 or 124,000 in Wales but in Cornwall it was 132,000 according to Smylie (1998: 115). See *'Cornish' hundred*.

'Cornish' Latifolia Or *Latifolia (Cornish type)* (*Latifolia var. cornubiensis*) A unique variety of plant.

'Cornish' Laureate Or rather 'Laureate of Cornwall'. An unnamed official poet who was called to recite verses on the occasion of inspecting troops collected from press gangs (W.B., 5th June 1812). The word 'laureate' is derived from the 'laurel' with which he was crowned.

Cornish leechdoms fragments of superstitions related to remedies or prescriptions communicated by T. Quiller Couch (see Hazlitt 1905: 145–6).

Cornish lemon drizzle cake Cake made with lemon juice, grated lemon rind and icing sugar (Butcher and Annand 1994:49–50).

Cornish Liberalism, the Mecca of As Gary Tregidga describes Pencrebar, home of the Liberal politician Isaac Foot (C.S. 2nd, 8, 2000, p.166).

Cornish liberation, swan song of Term used by Garry Tregidga to refer to Acland's decision in 1920 to stand down in the following election when the Labour party also wanted this vote (C.S. 2nd, 7, 1999, p.80).

Cornish-like That which seems Cornish (O.C. Vol. VI, No.5, autumn 1963).

Cornish Lime A variety of *Cornish heather* (for ref. see *Cornish Gold*) See *Cornish Cream for* other heather varieties.

Cornish Lions There is an allusion to *Cornish Regiment* (q.v.) as "The *Cornish Lions* led by donkeys" in W.W.I. (C.W. 28, 2002, p.25).

Cornish litany in this deliverance was requested for "ghoulies, ghosties, long-leggity beasties: things that go bump in the night" (see Best).

Cornish literary giant Sir Arthur T. Quiller Couch (1863–1944) (for this epithet see C.W. 1, 1994, p.9). He was a scholar of both Oxford and Cambridge and a prolific author as well as editor of the *Cornish Magazine*.

Cornish little trees " Sometimes washed on the beach … are the *Cornish 'Little trees'*, a deep water coral with the branches like a miniature tree and has special powers according to an old legend. It is said that your house will never burn down if you keep a 'Little Tree' in it (Rendell 1983:80). Courtney calls them *ladies' trees* and recalls that they were hung specifically in the chimney (1890:170).

Cornish loan words The term applies to *Cornish dialect* words or words from other West country dialects that are derived from the *Cornish language* (Wakelin 1994: 28–30). Wakelin gives an example of the dialect word *clunk* meaning to swallow which is derived from the Corn. *collenky* (which Nance suggests is from *cowl* – completely, fully and *lenky* – swallow; c.f. W. *llyncu*) therefore to swallow entirely. Some standard English words are also *Cornish loan words* e.g. 'gull' (Corn. *gwylan*, pl. *gulla*), 'morgay' (Corn. *mor* sea + *ky* dog), 'porbeagle' (for which see *'Cornish' shark*) and 'wrasse' (Corn. *gwragh* which also means 'hag' – see *Cornish witch*). However, the word 'penguin' (despite what many Cornish or Welsh people would like to believe) does not really derive from the Cornish/Welsh words *pen* (head) and *gwyn* (white) (cf. Bret. *penn* + *gwenn*). Most probably it is from the Lat. *pinguis* – fat or from '*pin-wing*' (*Chambers C20th Dictionary*).

'Cornish' lobster The Latin names for the Norway lobster or Dublin (Bay) prawn are *Astacus/Homarus/Nephrops norvegicus* and also *Nephropsis cornubiensis*.

Cornish local preacher Martin writes with reference to what he considers a Cornish stock character, "the *Cornish local preacher* – perhaps the best representative of his race – has his counterpart in the Welsh evangelist" (1951:14). See *Cornish tin mining evangelist*.

Cornish Loderi A variety of rhododendron. It is crossed with *Snow Queen* to produce the hybrid *Nimbus*. See *Cornish Cracker*.

Cornish Logan Rock A moving rock. The phrase is used by Courtney (1890:77 and 145) and by Tregarthen (1940:77). In 1824 Lt. Goldsmith (nephew of

Oliver) displaced the 70 ton Logan Stone at Land's End (see Brewer 1870). According to Gendall (with reference to the St. Levan witches) "one became a witch by touching the *laggan* stone nine times at midnight" (1995:6).

Cornish log and stone cottages Cottages built by immigrant Cornish miners in Mineral Point, Wisconsin (the term is used by Judy Locy in C.W.W. 1993, 10, p.2).

'Cornish' London In C18th and C19th Truro "was regarded as the London of Cornwall" (Stevens, p.39). In Cornish London is *Loundres* (see *Cornish March*). Some Cornish people still use the word *Londoner* (and *Cockney*) to mean someone "from anywhere East of Exeter" (see the internet page on *Cornish Dialect & Idiosyncracies* – http://members.aol.com/ ht a/alisonams/cornwall2.htm). See *Cornish capital*.

Cornish long-handled shovel As the *Cornish shovel* (q.v.) is sometimes called (Ivey 1976:60; Phillips 1986:118 and O.C. Vol. XI, No. 9,1995, p.447).

Cornish longs How Kent contemplates "the next step" of Cornish language films (C.S. 11, 2003, p.153) See *Cornish shorts.*

Cornish Longstem A variety of apple. It is a small dark green and yellowish cooking apple that was late and was often pickled. (Spiers 1996:63). See *Cornish Aromatic.*

'Cornish' Lourdes Bird says that Madron's Well "was a kind of mini-Lourdes" (1988:63). Here handkerchiefs have always been left for "the water spirit". The well, like the baptistery was dedicated to the Celtic saint Madron whose feast day was on 17th May. Lourdes, France has been a place of pilgrimage since Bernadette Soubirous had visions of the Virgin Mary there in 1858. See *Cornish well.*

Cornish Lugger Type of small fishing vessel. A mackerel driver is the largest lugger (for a six or seven member crew) whereas a pilchard driver had a crew of four or five men. Some Cornish towns like St. Ives and Newlyn have different luggers.The name is derived from the 'dipping lug' (i.e. mainsail) as *Cornish luggers* had a foresail and mizzen sail (C.W. 32, 2002/3, p.15). The word 'Cornish' is often prefixed (e.g. by Nance 1963:94, 98 and 132).

Cornishly In a Cornish manner.

Cornish macaroon A kind of Cornish sweet cake made by W.T. Warren & Son, Penzance.

Cornish Made Words stamped on goods that are made by small businesses in Cornwall, many of which use the Made in Cornwall trademark.

Cornish Mafia We may have heard of the so-called *Welsh Mafia* (the *Taffia* – see Edwards 1998:86) and the *Irish Mafia* (the *Murphia* – see Edwards 2004:108) but there is also a 'Cornish Mafia'. The term was coined by Angus Calder (cited by Payton 1996:225) with reference to those influential Cornishmen at the time of Walpole. There is also a black souvenir Mafia T-shirt with white letters (see http://www.thecornishstore/shopp).

Cornish Maid An engine built in 1919 for steam threshing and owned by the Parsons (see O.C. Vol. X, No. 10, spring, 1990, p.477). See *Cornishman*.

Cornish Mail A train service. See the *Cornishman*.

Cornish mainland 1 Sometimes this term (or its form *Cornish main-land*) is used to refer to Cornwall with the implication that the Isles of Scilly are Cornish (e.g. Deane and Shaw 1975:41 and C.S. 11, 1983:51). **2** Rowse uses the word 'mainland' to refer to England beyond Cornwall, wishing "that we could loosen our subjection to the mainland" (1986:298).

Cornish main-land Hyphenated spelling of *Cornish mainland* (e.g. in C.S. 11, 1983, p.51).

Cornish malaise This phrase referes to the apparently Cornish stereotype traits of "anger and ambition" (C.W. 1996, 17, p.9). The word *malaise* is, of course, the French word for 'sickness'. See *Cornishman's disease* in appendix 2.

Cornish Mallow (*lavatera cretica*) A purple flower also found in the Mediterranean and, as its Latin name suggests, is also called Cretan mallow.

Cornishman 1 A man born in Cornwall or of Cornish descent (spelt as one word, not Cornish man). In Cornish *kernow* means 'Cornishman' or 'Cornwall'. This confusion with the word *kernow* may explain for the name *Cornwaller* for a Cornishman (Hunt 1881:79). **2** The fastest express train from Paddington launched by 3521 locomotives. See *Cornish Mail*. **3** *The Cornishman* was also the epithet of the Cornish world heavyweight boxing champion Bob Fitzsimmons who beat Gentleman Jim Corbett in 1897 (Payton 1999:327). **4** The *Cornishman* was also a 6 hp Marshall traction engine for steam threshing which was exhibited by Frank Garland at the Royal Cornwall Show, Falmouth in 1896 (O.C. X, 10, 1990, p.473). The first threshing machine was invented by Richard Trevithick in 1812. See *Cornish Maid*.

Cornishman, Gluvias the (W. *Glywys Cernyw*) As the Welsh called St. Gluvias, the patron saint of the parish church of Penryn (Salmon 1903:207).

Cornishman, honorary A category of Cornishman (see C.S. 2nd, 10, 2002, p.236, n.89) which is analogous to *Cornish by adoption* (q.v.).

Cornishman, Scotchman and Australian The meaning of the initials of the C.S.A. mine in Queensland, Australia.It was called C.S.A. as it was owned by proprietors of these nationalities (see Payton 1999:300).

Cornish man engine A machine first implemented in 1842 which was powered by a water wheel and could lower men to mine levels and raise them to the surface. By the following year (i.e. 1843) the depth to which this new machine could be lowered had increased from 27 fathoms to 280 fathoms (see O.C. VII, 11, 1972, pp.502–506).

Cornishman for a Cornish Seat, a Roseveare's campaign slogan in Bodmin in the 1950s (cited in C.S. 2nd, 8, 2000, p.172).

Cornish Man of Iron See *Cornish Iron Man.*

Cornishman, Tin miner, King's son and Epithet of Billy Bray for whom see *Cornish tin mining evangelist, the.*

Cornishman's For phrases with the word *Cornishman's* see appendix 2.

Cornish marble Pressed slate used in monuments (Bird 1989:21 and Payton 1996:10).

Cornish March, the Great As the 500th anniversary march to London was called in honour of the heroes who went to London for the original *Cornish March* in 1497 (C.W. 13, 1997, p.33). In June1997 in the quincentenary *Keskerdh Kernow* (the Corn. *keskerdh* connotes 'walking together') marchers walked 320 miles from St. Keverne to London. See *Cornish Rebellion.* There was also a musical composition called the *Old Cornish March* (Deane and Shaw 1975:11)

'Cornish' Mardi Gras Or rather *"The Mardi Gras of Cornwall".* As *Mazey Day* of the *Golowan* Festival has been described (C.W. 35, 2003, p.18). (The *Golowan* festival is St. John's Day for which see *Cornish midsummer fires*). *Mazey Day* is not to be confused with *Mazed Monday* (the Monday after the Saturday payday when the miner was still suffering from a hangover from the *kiddleywink* or unlicensed pub – also called *'Bad Monday'* – Deane & Shaw 1975:73). The phrase *Mardi Gras* (Fr. 'Fat Tuesday') is applied to the great carnival day just before Lent e.g. in New Orleans. and the actual Cornish equivalent of this was *Nicky nan night* (or *Hall Monday*), the day before Shrove Tuesday when boys would knock doors asking for pancakes and play tricks.

Cornish Maritime Ensign The ensign seen on the Enterprise boats between Truro and Falmouth. It comprises a *Cornish flag* (q.v.) of St. Piran, i.e. a large white cross on a black background. However, in the top left hand quarter there is a Union Jack and in the bottom left hand quarter there are fifteen bezants on a black background. The remaining two quarters are black (C.W. 1994, 12, p.39).

Cornish Marlgrass A distinct variety of wild grass (Encycl. 10. 469.c).

Cornish Mathews With reference to the versatile London comedian Charles Mathews (fl. Early C19th), "John Tabois Tregellas was … a man who pursued a great variety of interests, but his fame rests on his lectures and stories in the *Cornish Dialect*, earning him the name 'The *Cornish Mathews*'" (O.C. XII, 3, 1998, p.18 – this epithet is also used on pages 15 and 21).

Cornish maypole The *Cornish maypole* was slightly distinct with strings of eggs painted and with ribbons. (W.B., 12 May 1870). What was also interesting about the *Cornish maypole* was that some villages had the custom of 'borrowing' it from the neighbouring village (Deane and Shaw 1975) and some *Cornish maypoles* have been at least 30m tall.

Cornish mead A liquor made from honey and heather. On St. Bartholomew's Day (24th August – he is patron saint of bees and honey) "the monks of Gulval bless *Cornish mead*" (Day 2000:143) … says that there are two strengths of Cornish mead: mead wine and liqueur mead and that "the association between mead and marriage goes back to pagan times when the custom was for the happy couple to drink honey wine at their wedding and for a month afterwards, from which we derive the word 'Honeymoon'" (C.T. August, 1998, p.16). In Cornish 'mead' is called *metheglin* or *medheklyn* while *bragas* (bragget) is a mixture of mead and ale. There is even *Cornish mead* ice cream.

'Cornish' mease In Cornwall a mease meant 505 herring, whereas the Scottish /Irish/Manx and Welsh mease was 500 fish (see Nance 1963:113). A *cran* was 800 herring (Jago 1882:146).

Cornish meat pie As the *Cornish pasty* has also been called.

Cornish Memorialists (C.S. 1st, 1973, Vol. 1: p.62). See *Cornish Sea Fencibles*.

Cornish memory game And also called *Cornwall Memory Game* played with a box of photographic reminders based on Pelmanism (C.W. 16,1998, p.19).

Cornishmen (Corn. *Kernowyon*) Plural of *Cornishman* and also spelt as one word.

Cornish men an tol See *Cornish tol-men*.

Cornish menhir Courtney alludes to "*Cornish menhirs* and barrows" (1890:103). A menhir is a tall standing stone and in the Brythonic Celtic languages the word means literally 'long stone' (or rather 'stone long') (thus also called *long stone* – Jago 1882:211 and Ivey 1980). In *Unified Cornish* it is either *menhyr* (*men-* stone + *hyr* – long) or *hyrven* and in K.K it is *menhir* (cf. Bret. and W. *maen hir*). See *Cornish barrow*.

'**Cornishmen's' tails** Cornishmen are said to be born with tails which drop off when they cross the Tamar (Courtney 1890:157).

Cornish mermaids One internet site refers to the *merrymaids* (see *Cornish merry maid*) as *Cornish Mermaids* (http://www.scubanaked.com/images/mermaid02.html). Hunt compares the 'Cornish mermaids' with the *Nixies* in their capacity to seduce and drown their lovers (1881, 2nd, p.472). Day records that "*Cornish mermaids* filled up harbours with sand if offended and ... also took 'idiot children' under their protection" (2003:99). In Cornish the mermaid is called *morvoren* (*mor* sea + mutation of *moren* girl – hence the prefix *mor-* is a cognate of *mer-* in mermaid, cf. Fr. *mer* – sea). In Cornwall a *mermaid's comb* was a shark's jaw (see *Cornish shark*). A man from Cury who had helped a mermaid was given one so he could comb waves seeking the mermaid's help (Westwood 1992:17–8). Moreover, *mermaids' purses* (or *pisky purses*) are are the brown purse-shaped egg cases of the ray or dog-fish (Nance 1963:114). The Merry maids are not to be confused with the Merry Maidens – a stone circle (of *Dawns Men* – dancing stones) near Lamorna.

Cornish merry maid As Hunt (1873, 1st, p.149) refers to the *Cornish mermaid* (q.v.).

Cornish metal men The Roundheads or Parliamentarians in the Civil War referred to the Cornish as uncivilised "*Cornish mettal-men*" as they worked in the mines (cited by Payton 1996:164).

Cornish Metaphysician Samuel Drew (1765–1833) of St. Austell. He was a *buddle boy* (boy who washed ore at a tin mine), smuggler (see *Cornish fair trader*) and cobbler and became an editor, historian and theologian (see Best in section 'Men and Women', question 6).

Cornish Methodism, Mecca of As Jenkin calls Gwennap Pit (1945:164) (q.v.).

Cornish Methodism, open air cathedral of Gwennap Pit where Wesley preached (Payton 1996:212). Here on spring Bank Holiday the annual Methodist Service is held. See previous entry and also *Cornish Amphitheatre, John Wesley's*.

Cornish Methodist Schism The break away of the *Bryanites* (see *Cornish Bible Christians*) with the main body of *Candrums/Ranters/Roaring Methodies* (i.e. Methodists).

Cornish metric gallon Rev. Brian Coombes postulates "a '*Cornish metric gallon*' of 5kg". He informs us that "a gallon of 10 lb. was formerly used as far east as Port Isaac, Pelynt and St. Tudy" for apples and potatoes and there was also "a special 'apple gallon' of 7lbs." (O.C. XII, 11, 2002, p.8).

'**Cornish' Metropolis** Plymouth even since the last century has called itself "the Metropolis of Cornwall" (cited in C.S. 2nd, 10, 2001, p.176). The word 'metropolis' literally means 'mother city' (from Gk. *mētēr* mother and *polis* city – hence our word 'police'). See *Cornish Capital*.

Cornish midsummer fires As Hunt (1881, 1st, p.206) refers to the fires burnt on St. John's Day (*Golowan* or *Gol Jowan*). In Cornish the term *tansys Golowan* literally means 'fire of St. John' since they were burnt on the eve of the birthday of St. John the Baptist (i.e. 23rd June). Significantly this date coincided with the summer solstice (the fires symbolizing the sun). Herbs were thrown onto the fires; sometimes to avert witches, people would hold hands in a circle around the fires (Courtney 1890:40). As well as fires, barrels of tar were lit (elsewhere in Britain tar barrels have also been lit with New Year fires or even on Guy Fawkes' night – resembling the conspirators' barrels of gunpowder). Because of the fires, this night was called *tar-barrel night* (Bowley 1945:125). Day adds that for the same reason the Cornish would dance around the fires and jump over them when they were lower (2000:106). In several countries such as Greece, young people also jump over fires on St. John's Eve. The Cornish light bonfires again on the eve of St.Peter and Paul (28th June).

Cornish mile In C16th Cornwall and Scilly "a mile was then the equivalent of one and a half miles today" (Bowley 1945:50 n.). An exact equivalent is not always recorded. Carew, for instance, merely stated that "*Cornish miles* are much longer than those about London" (1602:62).See *Cornish acre*.

Cornish mill In contradistinction with the tall three-storey mills of south England, Benneys refers to "the typical low two-floored *Cornish mill*" (1972:91 & 93). See *Cornish water mill*.

Cornish Millennium Convention Launched in 1998 to oppose the closure of South Crofty Mine etc. It produced the document *Into the Millennium or into Oblivion* (see Deacon et al 2003:99).

Cornish mine captain Form used by some (e.g. Deane and Shaw 1975:63 ; C.S. 9, p.116) for the *Cornish captain* (q.v.).

Cornish mine chimney The chimney tower of a mine (C.W. 32, 2003/4, p.20).

Cornish miner engineer One whose work combines the role of both a *Cornish miner* an a *Cornish engineer* (C.W. 20, 1997, p.22).

Cornish mine fairy Day's term (2003:63) for the *Cornish knocker* (q.v.).

Cornish mine goblins See *Cornish knockers*.

Cornish mine manager The *Cornish mine captain* (O.C. June 1990:18). See *Cornish captain*.

Cornish Mine Punch A punch of rum, brandy, lemon juice, boiling water and sugar (for ref. see *Cornish Christmas Cake*). It seems a variation of the old Cornish drink *shenagrum* (of rum, sugar lemon and hot beer – Jago 1882:262).

Cornish Miner, The The name of a monument dedicated to the Cornish miner that was unveiled in 1996 in Bendigo, Australia (C.W. 9, p.12).

Cornish miner, the converted Epithet which Thomas Shaw gives to Billy Bray in the internet site "St. Billy of Baldhu". See *Cornish tin mining evangelist*.

Cornish miner homes A row of restored buildings in Mineral Pont, Wisconsin that belonged to Cornish miners (C.W.W. 12, 1994, p.25).

Cornish Miner Poet Epithet of W. Francis of Gwennap (O.C. VII, 11, 1972, p.506). **Cornish miner's brooch** A brooch made of Cornish tin with the design of a *Cornish pick*, a *Cornish shovel* and the *Cornish coat of arms*. It is made by the Piran Pewter Company who also make a *Cornish Celtic cross* brooch.

Cornish mine spirits As Briggs (1976:254) calls the *Cornish knockers* (q.v.).

Cornish miners, patron saint of As St. Piran is sometimes called (e.g. by Day 2000:60). See *Cornish patron saint*.

Cornish miners, village of The settlement of 900 Cornish miners in Burnley, Lancashire. The Cornishmen had gone to replace the locked-out colliers (W.B. 20 Oct. 1873). Cornish miners have justifiably enjoyed the reputation of being the most skilled miners in the world, sadly Cornish miners were quite often used as strike breakers, both in the British Isles and overseas.

Cornish miner's helmet The *Cornish helmet* (q.v.) that was worn by miners (e.g. in C.T. April 1998, p.52). Jenkin describes a miner's hat with a candle stuck in the front (1984:32).

Cornish miners' saint As St. Piran has been called (C.W. 19, 1998/99, p.4). See *Cornish patron saint*.

Cornish Mines, Queen of As Dolcoath has been called (C.T. 12, p.43). This mine closed in 1921 was 3,500ft deep.

Cornish mining pick Mentioned by John Rowe as a distinct type of pick used for *Biddick diggings* in mines (*Folk Life*, Vol. 3, 1965, p.28). See *Cornish pick*.

Cornish mining ton Term used by Orchard (1990:38) for the *Cornish ton* (q.v.).

Cornish Minister Or Minister of Cornwall. A proposed cabinet minister who would be responsible exclusively for Cornish affairs and analogous perhaps with the Welsh or Scottish Secretaries. Some Cornish people would like to see the appointment of such a position (see Payton 1993:240–242).

Cornish miracle plays Religious dramas called in Corn. *Gwary merakl* or *Gwary mur*. The word 'Cornish' is often prefixed (e.g. Jenkin 1945:128). They were called 'miracle' plays since in the course of the performance the Virgin Mary or the saints would often intervene miraculously (hence elsewhere similar plays were called *'saints' plays'*). These plays were usually performed in a *Cornish round* (q.v.). In dialect the expression 'a regular *miracle play*' has come to mean a farce (Ivey 1976:44).

Cornish mist Or *mizzle* – a portmanteau of mist and drizzle (e.g. see C.W. 1, June 1994, p.13) similar to Scotch mist (which the Cornish call *Scotch dew* – Hawke 1975:51). *Skew* was a "thick drizzling rain" (Jago 1882:265), also called *skiff* (Nance 1963:148) and *damping* is another Cornish word for this "misty rain" (Ivey 1976:20). Moreover, *slag* means a "heavy driving mist" (Stevens 1977:268) and *strunty* also meant misty or foggy (Jago 1882:283) while *cortilly* weather was also foggy or misty (Ivey 1976:17). *Hag* also means mist and *luer* is a "night mist" (Ivey, ibid. p.42), probably related to *lew* – a mist in valleys or creeks portending rain (Nance 1963:108). A *tew* is Cornish for a thick imprenetrable fog (Nance 1978:299) and *mussiky* is also thick fog (Hawke 1975:39) while *morlew* is Cornish for a sea-mist (Nance 1978). *Newl* (cf.W. *niwl*) is another Cornish word for mist which has connotations of haze (Nance 1978). See *Cornish weather*.

Cornish mock mayor Deane and Shaw refer to the '*Cornish Mock Mayor*' who is still elected in many villages (1975:178). He is sometimes paraded in a *fish-jowster's* cart or thrown into a stream or rubbish tip. In Lanner, for instance, on Boxing Day the miners elected a mock mayor who drank from the *Cuckle's Cup* (Bird 1988:55). Similar festivities centered around a 'mock prince' on Easter Sunday at Polperro (Deane and Shaw 1975:167).

Cornish mole, the first As Courtney refers to Lady Alice of Coombe (1890:110-111). The word 'mole' is *goth* in Cornish and *wont* in Cornish dialect.

Cornish Moneywort (*Sibthorpia europaea*) Small plant found in the summer usually near streams and moist woods in Cornwall and parts of south England. It has clusters of small round leaves (that resemble coins – hence its name) and tiny white flowers. Martin calls it "one of the plants of fairy origin" (1951:39).

Cornish Money-wort Hyphenated spelling of *Cornish Moneywort* (Martin 1951:179).

Cornish monoglot Someone who can only speak Cornish. A few centuries ago this term would have applied to many Cornish people, especially in the west if they did not have much contact with outsiders. Today the term can be applied only to infants whose parents have learnt Cornish. Such children would probably go to the *Dalleth* nursery and hence would learn English later.

'Cornish' Montanist, the As Jim Hall calls Maximilla in the *Origo Mundi* (C.S. 2nd, 7, 1999, p.165). Maximilla was stoned to death for heresy as she called God Christ and refererred to the Trinity. Montanus lived in C2nd and declared that the Holy Spirit would be giving new revelations through himself and his two prophetesses Priscilla and Maximilla.

'Cornish' Montpellier Penzance has been described as 'the Montpellier of England' (Rawe 1986:101). Montpellier in France was a fashionable C19th resort.

Cornish moors The moors of Cornwall, e.g. Bodmin (the term is used by several writers eg. Tregarthen 1940:115; Rawe 1986:40). Martin says that sometimes "visitors to the *Cornish moors* have declared themselves '*piskey-led*' or '*pixy-mazed*'" (1951: 17). In Cornish 'moor' is translated *gunran* (the barren part of a parish) or usually *ros* (whence the dialect word *rose*). A *moor cross* is "a Celtic cross used as a sign post" (Tregarthen 1940:6) and *moorstone* is granite (see *Cornish granite*).

Cornishmost The most Cornish. Another Cornish superlative is "a *bettermost* class of people" to refer to the upper middle class (Phillipps 1993:21). See entry below. C.f. *Cornishest*.

Cornishmost town in Cornwall, the Baron described St. Just as "the westernmost town in England and the *Cornishmost* town in Cornwall" (1934:261).

Cornish Mother Or Mother apple. A red flushed sweet dessert apple. The word 'Cornish' has been prefixed since 1884 to distinguish it from the American Mother (see Spiers 1996:63).

Cornish motto *Kernow bys vyken* (Cornwall for Ever). Coined by analogy to the Welsh *Cymru am byth* and the Irish *Erin go bragh*. The motto on the *Cornish arms* which is *Onen hag oll* (One and All). See *Cornish arms* for the origin of this motto. There have also been other *Cornish mottos* like Jenner's *Bedheugh byntha Kernewek!* (Be forever Cornish!) and *Kernow kensa* (Cornwall first). See also *Cornish hurling motto*.

Cornish Mount, the 1 As Thurston C. Peter referred to St. Michael's Mount (J.R.I.C. Vol. 14, 1900–01, p.223; see also Penn 1906:10 and Cunnack 1975:13 who also cite this epithet). Often it is called simply 'The Mount' (e.g. by Trevail 1990:23). Its name in Cornish is *Carreg-luz-en-kuz,* with reference to the petrified forest at its base (Hunt 1st, 1881). This idiosyncratic spelling seems to contain the words *carrek* (K.K. *karrack*) or rock, *los* or grey, *yn* (meaning in) and *cos* (K.K. *koes*) denoting wood or forest. Bird spells it *Carrek Luz en Couze* which she translates as 'the Hoar Rock in the Wood' (1989:107). Probably it is similar to the place name

Carnglooze which, according to Holmes, is derived from *carrek-los* or 'grey rock' (1983:14). In Cornish dialect it is *Dinsul* (Thomas 1895:80).The large granite crag in Mount's Bay with the C14th castle which at low tide can be reached by causeway. Blind people would climb St. Michaels's Mount to be cured (Day 2003:338) and if newly-weds went to the Mount "the one who was the first to sit on the stone seat in the castle" would be the dominant partner – as would the partner who drank first from St. Keyne's well, near Looe (Day ibid. p.342). **2** By extension the Cornish Mount was also a token (see Mayne and Williams 1985:80).

'Cornish' Mount Ararat Mount Ararat is the name if the hill on which Sir James Tillie was buried (in 1714) seated upright in his tower in the hope that after death he would be resurrected. This tower is called Pentillie Castle, south of St. Mellion, three miles from Callington. Eventually Sir James was buried within the tower (see White 1994:15 and Westwood 1992:44). Mt. Ararat, located in East Turkey is where Noah's ark was believed to have became lodged after the Flood. See *Cornish Noah's Ark*.

Cornish mouse trap As the Parliamentarians referred to Cornwall where they had suffered defeat at the hands of the *Cornish Royalists* (q.v.) (Payton 1996:162).

Cornish Movement 1 As Whetter calls *Mebyon Kernow* (1977:70). Group formed in Redruth in 1951 with the aim of promoting Cornish interests and securing a *Cornish Asssembly* (q.v.).The term literally means 'Sons of Cornwall' (c.f. W. *meibion*). Some members later formed the *Cornish Nationalist Party* (q.v.). **2** The *Cornish Movement* was a new orgaisation proposed by Pedyr Prior in 1990 which would have a more flexible membership than *Mebyon Kernow* (see Deacon et al 2003:91).

Cornish mule 1 A cocktail of rum, vodka, lime juice, orange juice and pineapple juice (see The Virtual Bar.com internet site). **2** The Cornish word for 'mule' is *mul* and at one time many mules in Cornwall must have been a unique crossbreed from the special *Cornish horse* (q.v.). A *mule* was the offspring of a male donkey and a mare (Jago 1882:223) whereas a *moil/moyle* was from a female donkey and a stallion (Hawke 1975:38). Moreover, a *pair* of mules was fifty mules used to carry tin (Hawke ibid. 42).

Cornish music Term used by Neil Davey (brother of Merv – see *Cornish piper*) to refer to: **1** Traditional Cornish music with *Cornish bagpipe*. and **2** Brass band music (C.W. 38, 2004, p.27 & p.28). Yet there is also a strong tradition, as in Wales, of male voice choirs in Cornwall.

Cornish mutations The changes that occur at the beginning of words due to certain grammatical rules. They are the equivalent of the Welsh *treigladau* and Breton *kemmadurioù*. For instance, the word *car* (friend) becomes *ow har* (my friend) and *y* *gar* (his friend). Similarly the word *tre* (town) becomes *an dre* (the town).

Cornish mynolla Nance refers to the *Cornish mynolla* which was "a piece of granite hollowed out" (1963:113) and a primitive form of the *mean-ollas* or *menolas* which was "a square box filled with stones and clay, used by fishermen in their boats before the invention of stoves" (ibid. p.112).

Cornish mystery cycle Cycle of *Cornish* mystery plays, especially the three plays of the *Cornish Ordinalia* (q.v.).

Cornish mystery play A name comparable in meaning with the Fr. *mystère* and Ger. *Mysterienspiel* for which see *Cornish miracle play*.

'Cornish' Nash Or rather *Cornwall Nash* Cocktail of white rum, gin, triple sec, grapefruit juice and cherry brandy. See *Cornish mule*.

Cornish National Anthem 1 *The Song of The Western Men* by Rev. Robert Stephen Hawker with the words:

> "And Shall Trelawny die?
> Then twenty thousand Cornishmen
> Will know the reason why…"

The song was based on the imprisonment of Bishop John Trelawny (1650–1721) in the Tower of London in 1688 since (along with seven other bishops) he had refused to sign James II's decree that would have brought back Roman Catholicism. When William III came to the throne Trelawny became Bishop of Exeter and then Winchester. **2** Moreover, Payton says that 'Lead Kindly Light' "was also for a time a *Cornish national anthem*"(1999:284).

Cornish National colours See *Cornish colours*.

Cornish National Day Many Cornish people would like to see St. Piran's Day (5th March) in honour of the *Cornish patron saint* (q.v) declared as an official public holiday comparable with St. Patrick's Day in Ireland. Another important 'national' (rather than folk) day in Cornwall is 27th June (the anniversary of the execution of the leaders of the *Cornish Rebellion*).

'Cornish' National dish As the *Cornish pasty* (q.v.) has been called (Deane and Shaw 1975:56). In Carew's day a *dish* was a gallon of tin (a *foot* was two *dishes* and half was a *topliff* – 1602:27). Moreover, the Cornish also drink a *dish* of *Cornish tea* (q.v.).

Cornish National dress tartan See *Cornish national tartan*.

'Cornish' national drink *metheglin* or mead (see *Cornish mead*). It is described by

Best as 'Cornwall's National Drink'.

Cornish national flag See *Cornish flag.*

Cornish nationalism, the flower of As *Mebyon Kernow* has been described. Yet the full quote is more poignant: "As Eastern Europe celebrates the springtime of nationalist movements, *the flower of Cornish nationalism – Mebyon Kernow –* may be wilting and could fold and die" (Western Morning News, April 20, 1990 – cited by Deacon et al 2003:90).

Cornish Nationalist Movement Deane and Shaw define the '*Cornish national movement*' as applying to *Mebyon Kernow* (1975:64). Deacon et al also use this phrase (2003:vi). According to Thomas Hardy "there is little likelihood that a *Cornish Nationalist Movement* will ever be set afoot" (O.C. 2nd, 8, 1980, p.38).

Cornish Nationalist Party (C.N.P.) Party founded in 1969 by Leonard C. Trelease with some of the disillusioned members of *Mebyon Kernow* (see *Cornish Movement*). Its main aim is to establish a *Cornish Assembly* (q.v.).

Cornish National tartan This *sett* (Scots word for a tartan pattern) was designed by Morton Nance "the red represents the *Cornish Chough*; the silver thread signifies the tin that, together with the black, makes St. Piran's cross. The strip of bardic blue is symbolic of the sea" (C.W. 37, 2004, p.29). Laviolette suggests that the red not only symbolizes the *Cornish Chough* but rather the blood of those heroes slain in the *Cornish Rebellion.* Moreover, he adds a fifth colour – gold which represents the gorse (C.S. 11, 2003, p.155). See *Cornish hunting tartan.*

Cornish nation-ists Term used by Bert Biscoe in prefence to (and perhaps to avoid any negative extremist connotations of) the term 'Cornish nationalists' (C.W.W. 1995,14, p.5).

Cornish Needle, the A large *menhir* in a field at Lezerea Farm, Burran, Wendron near the Helston-Redruth road (C.T. 6, Dec.1994, p.48). See *Cornish pebble.*

'Cornish' Neptune See *Cornish Sea, Neptune of the.*

Cornishness The quality of being Cornish or of that which is Cornish.

'Cornish' Nessie From the cliffs above Mawnan "there have been a number of sightings of the local sea monster, a dinosaur-like creature with a long neck, small head and hump, and known as *Morgawr*" (Bird 1988:67, C.T. 1, July 1994, p.29). The name *Morgawr* means 'Sea giant' (Corn. *mor* sea + mutated form of *cawr* giant). The "Falmouth Bay's Monster" has also been sighted off the coast of Portscatho (Bird ibid. p.114).

'Cornish' Newspaper War Or rather 'Cornwall's Newspaper War'. Term that describes the rivalry between the more conservative *Royal Cornwall Gazette* and the slightly more liberal *West Briton* in the early C19th (term is coined by Brian Elvins in C.S. 9, 2001, p.145).

Cornish Nickey Largest fishing vessel used by Manx fishermen with four sails and which could do 10 knots. It was so called after the Cornish name Nicholas (see *Manx Sea Fishing 1600–1900's Resources Book*, Manx Heritage Foundation, 1991:23).

Cornish Nightingale Fanny Moody of Redruth (1866–1945), *prima donna* of international fame who sang with the Royal Italian Opera Company. The *Welsh Nightingale* was Edith Wynne (Edwards 1998:102) and the *Swedish Nightingale* was Jenny Lind (Brewer 1870).

Cornish nitro An explosive used in mining (Earl 1978:178). See *Cornish Cut*.

'Cornish' Noah's Ark With reference to the King Harry Ferry, first built 1889, Patricia Schama tells us that "the engine house looked rather like a shed and so the boat was known locally as 'Noah's Ark'" (C.T. May, 1999, p.48). There is an inn at Lelant called Noah's Ark. See *Cornish Mount Ararat*.

Cornish novel Term used (e.g. by Payton 1996:285) for a genre of novel that is set in Cornwall. The Cornish novel was made popular by Daphne du Maurier but with many new proponents.

Cornish oats A Cornish variety of oats as distinct from *lea* oats (mentioned at the turn of the century by James Stevens, 1977:113,150 and 189) which were called *pillas*. In Cornish it is *kerghen* (pl. *kergh*) (cf. Bret. *kerc'h*, W. *ceirch*, Gaelic *corca* and Ir. *coirce*).

Cornish Obby Oss See *Cornish hobby horse*.

Cornish Old Smokey Type of cheese (see internet site of Shell Bay Seafood Restaurant). See *Cornish Herb and Garlic*, *Cornish Pepper* and *Cornish Yarg*.

Cornish Olympians, The Epithet applied to those Cornish athletes who won medals at the Olympics, notably Thomas J.Hicks who won the marathon in St. Louis in 1904 and Frederick Holman who in 1908 won the 200m. breastsroke (C.W. 8,1996, p.7).

Cornish on the prairie, The Epithet of the Cornish South Dakotans (C.W. 8, 1996, p.15). They have a society called Little Cornwall on the Prairie.

Cornish Open Gorsedd See *Cornish Gorsedd*.

Cornish open stope Payton says that "in the mines … extractive work was according to the well-tried *Cornish open stope* type, employing either overhand or underhand stoping" (1999:306).

'Cornish' Orchid There is a variety of orchid called *Orchis cornubiensis Pugsley*.

Cornish Ordinalia A *Cornish mystery cycle* of three *Cornish miracle plays* recounting man's fall and redemption (c.C14th). The first play is entitled *Origo Mundi* (Origin of the World) telling the story of Adam's fall. The second play is *Passio Christi* – (the Passion of Christ) and the third is *Resurrectio Domini* (Resurection of the Lord) which would have been played over the course of three days. See *Cornish round theatre*. The official directing the *Cornish mystery plays* (q.v.) was called an *ordenary* (Nance 1978:276). These three plays were successfully presented together at St. Just in August 2004.

Cornish ore bucket As the *Cornish kibble* (q.v.) has been called (see internet site www.stagestheatre.com/es/SundayGoldstudyguide.pdf).

Cornish organ The bellows (Jago 1882: 143). In *Cornish dialect* (q.v.) this is called *billis, billez* or *billees* (Jago, ibid. p.116) and even the *Cornish double plural* (q.v.) form *billises* (Phillipps 1993:10 – cf. Dev. *bellerziz* Downes 1986:84) whereas in the *Cornish language* (q.v.) it is *megynnow* (cf. Bret. and W. *megin*). Moreover, the word *organ* (or also *orgal*) in *Cornish dialect* meant the plant 'penny royal' (Courtney 1880:40). Yet in Cornish dialect 'to bellow' would be *belve* (Phillipps 1993:21). In Cornwall "it is unlucky to put the bellows on the table" (Hawke 1973:13). For other tools see *Cornish pick*, *Cornish shovel*, and *Cornish wheelbarrow*.

'Cornish' ounce In normal English usage an ounce was a sixteenth of a pound. However, in Cornwall, according to Couch, the word 'ounce' was used to refer to a sixteenth part of a *sean* of fish (1871:48) and, as Hawke says, a "16th part of any property" (Hawke 1975:41). In Cornish an ounce is *uns* (pl. *–yow*). The Druid halfpenny (see *Cornish half penny*) issued in 1791 was called "half an ounce" (Mayne & Williams 1985:46). See *Cornish pound*.

Cornish out-door sound As Woodhouse refers to the *Cornish bagpipes* (q.v.) (1994:58).

Cornish oven 1 The *clome ob'n* or clay oven (Butcher and Annand 1994:112). **2** It is also used as a synonym of the *Cornish range* (Merton 2003:62).

Cornish owlman A new species of Cornish mythical being from Mawnan. It is a "flying man-like owl thing from England" (see internet site http://lurkanica.com/Monsters/cornish-owlman.htm). It is "like a feathered birdman with an owl-like face, red glowing eyes, grey feathers and black claws" (Day 2003:92). Cf. *Cornish corpse bird.*

Cornish paasty Jenkin uses the spelling *'paasty'* to convey the *Cornish dialect* pronunciation (1945:364). See *Cornish pasty.*

Cornish Palm Type of palm tree, also called the Torbay Palm (*Cordyline australis*) which is from New Zealand. Possibly this was the palm tree from which a red gum exuded that was used to make *'dragon's blood'* medicine (Hawke 1973:32).

Cornish paradox 1 Term used by Ivey and Payton to describe the contradictory stance of some marked by "the insistence that Cornwall is part of England but the belief the Cornish are 'not really English'" (C.S. 2nd, 2, 1994 p.156). **2** Alan Kent writes also refers to "…the *Cornish paradox*: how on one side there is a heavy realism and down-to-earthness. On the other hand there is the mystical" (C.W. 1994, 11).

Cornish parkin Oatmeal cake made with ginger and treacle (Rothwell 1989 and Waller 1994:36)

Cornish parliament See *Cornish Assembly* and *Cornish Stannar.*

'Cornish' parstee Jauncey provides the spelling 'parstee' for the *Cornish pasty* (2004:92).

Cornish Party, the 1 Before the emergence of the *Cornish National Party* the title of the *'Cornish Party'* was traditionally given to the Liberals (Payton 1996:293) also called "the Party of Cornwall" (C.S. 2nd, 10, 2002, p.194). **2** As Whetter dubs *Mebyon Kernow* (1977:79) See *Cornish Movement.*

Cornish passion play See *Cornish Ordinalia.*

Cornish passport There has even been a *Cornish Passport* with the words *Cernow* and *Tremencummyas* (Nance did not provide the word 'passport' but in K.K. it is *tremengummyas* – from *tremen* passing + *cummyas* licence/permit). It has been issued by the Cornish Passport Office in Lostwithiel (C.W. 2,1994, p.31). Payton mentions the story of three Cornish people who travelled to five European countries in 1992 using their *Cornish passports!* (1993:246).

Cornish pastay Phonetic spelling of *Cornish pasty* (q.v.) (used e.g. by Merton 2003:62).

Cornish pastez Dialect plural of *Cornish pasty* (q.v.) (Curnow 2002:36).

Cornish pastie An alternative spelling of *Cornish pasty* (see *The Cornish Magazine*, Vol. 1, 1898, 48–50 and Merrick 1995:32).

Cornish pasty 1 A kind of pie called a *(h)oggy* in dialect and shaped like a large

Brazil nut (indeed that is why a Brazil nut is called a *pasty nut* in Cornwall – see Curnow 2002:18). Indeed because of its shape, an orange segment has also been called a *pasty* (Hawke 1975:42) and a *pasty board* is cardboard (Jenkin 1945:425).The pinched pastry that gives the pasty its distinctive appearance is called *crimping*. There are a variety of fillings but the classic is meat, swede, onion and potatoes. There was even a *'mouse pasty'* with which children were threatened if they wet the bed (Courtney 1890:162) – perhaps derived from an actual superstitious practice wherby such a child was thought cured if fed "roasted mice" (Hawke 1973:29). This is similar to the threat of a *sparble-pasty/pie* which was a kick (Thomas 1895:124), a *chack pie* or scolding (Nance 1956:104) or the *sherd pasty* (with *sherds* or *gays* i.e. broken pieces of china – once made by Elizabeth Dunstan alias Lizzie Sherdy – Deane and Shaw 1975:55). The varieties of pasty include *bits pasty* (with herbs – Merton 2003:22), *apple n'hinge pasty* (lungs and heart), *nattlin pasty* (pig's entrails), *muggety pasty* (calf's/sheep's entrails), *sour sab pasty* (with sorrel), *taddago pasty* (with *veers* – prematurely born suckling pig), *grass pasty* (meat and herbs – Phillips 1993:3 – the inclusion of meat may be due to the ambiguity of the dialect word *meat* which means simply 'food', ibid. 41), *windy pasty* (empty pasty baked, then split and spread with jam – Wright, p.161), a *lammy pasty* (with still born lambs – Deane and Shaw 1975:56), a *likkey pasty* (leeks and bacon), *love apple pasty* (with tomatoes – Merton 2003:24), *thrashan pasty* (a large one for harvesters – Merton ibid.30) and a *neaps pasty* (with turnips). A *corner pasty* was not a type but the end piece kept for later (Phillipps 1993:26). Moreover, miners would leave the ends or *didjans* (small pieces) of their pasties for the *knockers* (Merrick 1995:9) and fishermen who brought pasties to sea would not have a good catch (ibid. p.11). **2** In rhyming slang *Cornish pasty* (mispronounced 'peysty' with the 'a' as in 'paste') is applied to a young lady who is rather attractive (i.e. 'tasty') and, in keeping with rhyming slang (where the second element is usually dropped) the admirer may just remark "that girl is a bit *Cornish*" (see Puxley 2003:115). By contrast, if someone wants to refer to a *Cornish pasty* in rhyming slang then they must call it a *'cheap and nasty'* (Ayto 2002:142). In Cornish slang a pasty might be called a *mouth organ* (Merton 2003:26). **3** In English slang *Cornish pasties* are "a particular style of men's shoes with a moulded sole considered unfashionable" (see internet page http://www.probertencyclopaedia.com/ZC.HTM).

Cornish pasty debate Term to describe the perpetual controversy as to what a true *Cornish pasty* should be, as regards filling, etc (C.T. 2, 8, March 1996, p.48).

'Cornish' pasty girls The pasty girls were school-girls chosen each week to warm the children's pasties beside the classroom fire (Wright 1986:12). In the same way the *kiddle boys* warmed up the men's pasties at the clay works.

Cornish pasty mix Ready ingredients for a *Cornish pasty* (q.v.) which can be bought (Merrick 1995:22).

'Cornish' pasty paste Wright mentions the ready made *pasty paste* for the pastry which is shortcrust and has less fat (1986:12).

Cornish pasty tea *Cornish tea* (q.v.) with a *Cornish pasty* (q.v.)(see O.C. X. 9, 1989, p.418). On the point of *Cornish tea* and sugar, Jenkins maintains that "the true Cornishman does not take sugar with his tea, except when eating pasties" (1984:71).

Cornish Patch F. Audrey Hosier with reference to the steep and rocky Saltash passage on the Tamar writes "Until 1894 the last half mile of the approach from Plymouth was in the *Cornish Patch*" (O.C. IX. 12, 1985, p.581).

Cornish Path-moss (*Ditrichum cornubicum*) A rare type of plant that used to be found near Lanner but now the only location in the world where it grows is around Phoenix Mine near Liskeard (C.S. 2nd, Vol. 3, 1995, p.167).

Cornish patron saint St. Piran was a Celtic saint who came from across the Irish Sea and who is believed to have discovered tin. Hence the *Cornish flag* (q.v.) which indicates the cross of white tin is also called St. Piran's flag. However, (like Ireland's trio of main saints: Patrick, Columb and Brigid) "some research suggests that Cornwall has three patron saints", i.e Piran, Michael (see *Cornish Mount*) and Petroc (see *Cornish ecclesiastical capital* and *Cornish saints, father of*) (C.W. 35, 2003, p.56). Moreover, St. Piran also shares St. Patrick's association with drink. Thus in dialect a drunkard is still called a *peraner*. There are so many saints in Cornwall that, like Ireland, Cornwall has been called 'Land of the Saints' (C.S. 2nd, 12, 2004, p.5).

Cornish patron saint of tinners Epithet of St. Piran (q.v.). See *Cornish patron saint*.

Cornish paving A distinct style of paving (e.g. with *Cornish cobbles*) which involves using stones of different sizes (see http://www.formpave.co.uk/prod_cornish.html). A paved road was called a *caunse* (Bottrell 1873:52).

Cornish peasant Condescending term (used by an Englishman) for the typical Cornishman. Jenkin referes to "what English visitors are pleased to call a '*Cornish peasant*' adds enormously to its value and interest" (Jenkin 1945: 260). Despite the pejorative connotations the word 'peasant' has acquired, etymologically the word simply means a farmer (from O.Fr. *paisant* who worked the land cf. Fr. *pays*).

Cornish peat A form of peat which in Cornish dialect is called *dells* (Hawke 1975:16).

Cornish peath One of Carey Morris' paintings was entitled *A Cornish Peath* (1905) featuring women drawing a bucket of water from a *peath* (well) (see *Cambria*, July/Aug, 1999, Vol.2, No.5, pp.26–8). *Peath* is an alternative spelling of *peeth* (from Corn. *pyth* well) for which see *Cornish well*.

Cornish Pebble On May 22nd people "to cure sciatica and rheumatism crawl under the *Cornish Pebble*, a large stone balanced on two others, at Perranarworthal, near Falmouth." (Day 2000:90). This cure may derive from the semantics of the Cornish word *leghow* (pl.) meaning 'flat stones' or 'slabs' which also happens to mean 'rickets' (Nance 1978: 264). In *Cornish dialect* the word *'pebble'* means stone (Courtney 1890:34) whereas a pebble is called a *tottie* (Tregarthen 1940:7), a *bullie* (Phillipps 1993:22), a *pobble* (Courtney 1880:44) or *bobble* (Jago 1882:240(cf. Dev. *popple* – yet *bobble* also meant a "ground swell" (Thomas 1895:70). These dialect words are from Corn. *bulyen*. In Cornwall some people used to rub pebbles on warts for a cure (Hawke 1973:30). See *Cornish tol men*.

Cornish peller Day prefixes the word 'Cornish' to the *peller* (2003:129) for which see *Cornish charmer*.

Cornish peninsula 1 Name sometimes preferred to Cornwall (e.g. several times by Manuel Alberro in C.S. 2nd, 9, 2001, pp.15, 16, 22, 24 and 30 as well as by Patrick Laviolette in C.S. 2nd 11, 2003, pp.142, 143 and 165). The word 'peninsula' literally means 'almost an island' (Lat. *paene* almost + *insula* island) and the Cornish word *gorenys* shares this meaning (*gor* prefix indic. 'over' or 'above' + *enys* island ; cf. W. *gorynys*). **2** The phrase *Cornish peninsula* could also refer to a specific peninsula within Cornwall, e.g. the Lizard.

Cornish penny Token paid to miners and "exchanged for goods at the company shop" (O.C. Vol. XII, No.9, pp.55–6). One description of counterfeit tokens mentioned "copper penny pieces, having on one side the device of a steam-engine-house, and the figures 1811, with the words '*Cornish Penny*' in the margin, and on the other side the device of a fish between blocks of tin and cakes of copper " (W.B. 19 Feb. 1813). In dialect a *penn'orth* or *pennard* is a pennyworth and *pennyleggan* is penniless (Thomas 1895:111) and a *penny short* means daft (Ivey 1980:50 – cf. *haa'path* i.e. halfpenny [worth] a daft person – see *Cornish half penny*). Moreover, a *penny-cake* was the leaves of the navel-wort – "children pluck and string them to resemble a pile of pennies" (Jago 1882:231). However, *penny-meen ways* (i.e. criss-crossed – Hawke 1975:43) has no relation to the word 'penny', even though Hawke derives it from the coin game 'heads and tails' (*pen* means 'head'). In Cornish 'penny' is *dynar* (which like the Yugoslavian *dinar* – takes its name from the Roman coin *denarius*).

Cornish Penny Post Set up in 1823 to Lifton and Lewdon (in Devon) but worked from Launceston (see O.C. VIII, 10,1978, p.502).

Cornish Pepper A moist cream cheese sprinkled with peppercorns. See *Cornish Blue*.

Cornish pheasant A magpie. So called due to its abundance in Cornwall (Swainson 1886:76). In Cornwall a magpie was called a *maggoty pie* (Jago 1882:213) which is not to be confused with the *muggety pie* of calf's/sheep's entrails. Another dialect name is *johnner* (Hawke 1989:24) while in Cornish it is *pyasen* (cf.W. *pioden*). The universal rhyme said on seeing magpies, i.e. "One for sorrow, two for joy, three four a girl and four for a boy" was different in Cornwall. It went as follows:

> "One for sorrow; two for mirth
> Three for a wedding; four for a birth.." (Couch 1871:83).

A scolding woman was dubbed a *magpie* and a hat was always doffed when seeing a magpie to turn away anger (Deane and Shaw 1975:131). Even though hats are not so popular today, the magpie is still saluted (Hawke 1989:10). See *Cornish bantam*, *Cornish bird*, *Cornish Chough*, *Cornish eagle* and *Cornish Game*.

Cornish Philosopher Davies Giddy (Gilbert) of St Erth (1767–1839) (for his epithet see Best in the section 'Men and Women', question 6 and Payton 1996:210). He discovered Humphery Davy and was acquainted with *Cornish engineers* and important figures. He was M.P. for Helston and later Bodmin and is remembered for his publication of *curls* (i.e. carols) in 1822 entitled *Some Ancient Christmas Carols*.

Cornish Phoenix The phrase is applied to the (desired revival of the) Cornish mining industry (C.W. 16, 1998, p.31). The phoenix was a bird in the Arabian desert which died every 500 years and then reemerged from its ashes.

Cornish pick Like the *Cornish shovel* (q.v.) this was a distinct tool (Payton 1999:167). Carew mentions "pickaxes of holm, box and hart's horn" used by Jews for mining (1602:19). Piran Pewter have designed a souvenir *Cornish pick* and shovel brooch. The *Cornish dialect* word for pick is *visgey* (Bottrell 1873:52). There was also a double pick called a *touble* (Thomas 1895:130) or a *biddix* with "one end pointed, the other flattened" (Jago 1992:116). Moreover, another tool the *dag* (which normally meant an axe) also had connotations of "a miner's pick" (Ivey 1976:19). Ivey also gives *gad* as a "miner's pick" (ibid. p.28) but it was originally a wedged tool used with a hammer to split rocks. The ambiguity of some tool names might be due to similar tool names in the original Cornish. For instance, *pygal* is a pick, mattock or hoe (cf. dial. *piggal* "beat axe" – Bottrell 1873:52), *pyk* is a pick whereas *pykyn* is a mason's/slater's hammer. *Pick and Gad men* is a nickname for the *spriggans* (a form of elf akin to the *Cornish knockers*) as they held a Christmas Eve mass in the mines (O.C. June 1990:14).

Cornish Pig A breed of pig (Mason 1951:157). In Cornwall *chug chug !* is used to call a pig and children call it a *chuggy pig* (Phillipps 1993:25). A suckling pig is a *veer*. See *Cornish Large Black*.

Cornish pig's head pudding The head is left for a fortnight in brine and is heavily seasoned with mixed spices, bay leaves and nutmeg. Chopped hard boiled eggs are added (for ref. see *Cornish burnt cream*).

Cornish pilchard (*sardina pilchardus*) Since the pilchard has always been such a vital food source the word 'Cornish' is often prefixed (e.g. by Caine and Gorton 2001:36). When eating pilchards "It was unlucky to eat a pilchard from the head towards the tail. Doing this will keep the head of the pilchard away from the coast" so the tail was eaten first so that the pilchards would swim to the shore (C.W. 36, 2003/4, p.11). In dialect pilchards are called *pilchurs* or *pilshies* (Hawke 1989). When they are smoked they are called *fairmaids* (also *fermades* or *fumades*), if they are marinated with bay leaves and spices they are called *marinaded pilchards* (Jago 1882:215), if broiled called *scrowlers* (Thomas 1895:119) and if decayed called *pesak*. In Cornish a pilchard is *hernen* (pl. *hern*) whereas *herngwyn* or 'white pilchards' are 'herring'. See *Cornish duck*.

Cornish Pilgrims of St. James (*Bredereth Sen Jago*). Pilgrims who followed a particular route on their visits to St. James in Santiago de Compostela.

Cornish Pilgrim's Progress Alan Kent's novel *Yowann and the Knot of Time* (Lyonesse, 1996) has been called "a sort of *Cornish Pilgrim's Progress*" (C.W.W. 19, 1996, p.29). *Pilgrim's Progress* was written by John Bunyan (see *Cornish Bunyan*).

Cornish Pine A new year dessert apple. It is large with a dull red flush and according to Spiers, it may have been a seedling of *Cornish Gilliflower* (1996:63). See *Cornish Aromatic*.

Cornish Pineapple Not a pineapple but a synonym of the *Cornish Pine* (q.v.).

Cornish piper (Corn. *pyber*, pl. *pyboryon* or *pybyth*, pl.*pybydhyon*) A player of the *Cornish bagpipes* (q.v.). The most prestigious position for a *Cornish piper* is that of *Pybor Gorseth Kernow* (i.e. Piper of the *Cornish Gorsedd*) which is held at present by Merv Davey. The Pipers are two stones located near the Hurlers on Craddock Moor/the Merry Maidens at St. Buryan (see Davey 1983:5; Woodhouse 1994:60).

Cornish pipes An alternative name for the *Cornish bagpipe*.

Cornish Pipes in D Larger *Cornish pipes* made by Julian Goodacre in the key of D (http://www.goodbagpipes.co.uk/cornish_bagpipe.htm).

Cornish Pipes in G Smaller version of above and also made by Julian Goodacre, playing in G a fourth higher.

Cornish piskey 1 The word 'Cornish' is often prefixed to this peculiarly Cornish variety of pixy (See J.R.I.C. Vol. 1 Part 3, 1864–65, p.51). The piskey was believed to be "not good enough for Heaven, not bad enough for Hell" (*The Cornish Magazine* 1, 1898, p.181). It has some good qualities like the ability to turn tin into silver. Perhaps this was why some people left *piskey holes* in the walls for good luck (Courtney 1890:125) yet they were also deterred by placing *pisky's paws/feet* (large tiles with knobs of lead – to stop piskies dancing on the roof). The *Cornish piskey* is mischievous and likes to *maze* people or lead them astray through quagmires. and to ride horses (in this capacity a piskey is sometimes called a *night rider* [see O.C, X1, 11, 1996, p.572] and a horse thus ridden is said to be *piskey-ridden*). Thus *piskey stirrups* are tangled pony manes (Deane & Shaw 1975:91). Someone can protect themselves from the piskey by turning their coat inside out. The mischievous tendency of the *piskey* to laugh is seen in the Cornish expression "laughing like a *piskey*" (Hawke 1973). Other expressions include *piskey-stool* (mushroom) and *piskey grinding stone* (small round stone part of spindle). For *piskey purse* see *Cornish mermaid*. **2** A *piskey* is also the name for a greenish bug found on blackberries (see Bottrell 1873:157; cf. the Irish *Pooka* who urinates on blackberries after Hallowe'en). **3** The common clothes' moth is also called the *piskey* (Jago 1882:235).

Cornish piskey people Another way of saying *Cornish piskies* (C.W. 38, 2004, p.58).

Cornish piskie Singular form of *Cornish piskies* (used e.g. by Briggs 1976:328).

Cornish piskies The plural of *Cornish piskey*, usually favoured over the form *piskeys* and often prefixed by the word 'Cornish' (e.g. by Rawe 1986:31).

Cornish piskies, Queen of the *Joan the Wad* (Alexander 2002:152 and 218). *Joan the Wad* is another name for *Jack o' Lantern*, i.e the Will o'the Wisp – the "phosphorescent lights seen over marshland" (Deane and Shaw 1975:91).

Cornish pixie 1 Spelling of *Cornish pixy* (q.v.) (used e.g. by Edwards 1974:156; Jenkin 1984:71 and Pearse & Fry 2000:37). **2** In the new Harry Potter 'mythology' the term *Cornish pixies* has been altered to mean "blue pests about 8 inches high that can fly" (see http://www.potter-connection.com/creatures.htm).

Cornish pixy The form used by Hazlitt (1905:146) and Edwards (1976:156) to refer to the *Cornish piskey* (q.v.).

Cornish Pizza It has "a pastry crust, turnips and rutabagas for the filling with clotted cream on top" (see internet page http://archiver.rootsweb.com/th/read/CORNISH/2000-06/0961712851).

Cornish plane The Hungarian word *simítógyalu* or 'smooth plane' – i.e. the cooper's or jointing plane is also translated as *'Cornish plane'* in one Hungarian-English dictionary (Országh László et al *Magyar Angol Nagyszótár*, Kiado, Budapest, 1998, p.1268).

Cornish play As *Cornish wrestling* has been called since 'fair play' (Corn. *gwary tek*) is prized as in *Cornish hurling*. This is opposed to the 'dirty' *'Devon style'* of 'wrestling' which included kicking (the term is used in W.B. 27 Oct. 1826).

Cornish players As *Cornish wrestlers* (q.v.) have also been called (W.B. 22nd July, 1831).

Cornish playing place As Nance called the *Plen an Gwary* (cited by Deane and Shaw 1975:13). This open air theatre was used for the performance of *Cornish miracle plays* (q.v.). This is a literal translation of *plen* (plain, open area of playing place) *an* (the definite article) and *gwary* (game, play; cf. W. *chwarae*, Bret. *c'hoari*).

Cornish plough The conservative Cornish used a distinct "old *Cornish wooden plough*" as opposed to those ploughs operated by the ploughman without a driver to lead horses or oxen. It was also used for ploughing matches (W.B. 28 Feb.,1840 ; term also used by Payton 1996:234). In Cornish 'plough' is *ar(a)dar* (pl. *erder*). The first Monday after Twefth Night was called *Plough Monday* and this was when *Cornish guisers* (q.v.) would go to houses asking for *Plough money* (C.T. 2,6, 1996, p.2). In many parts of Britain a plough was decorated on this day or taken to church.

Cornish plunger pump A type of fixed pump used by *Cornish clayworkers* (Arthur 1955:16). It worked in conjunction with a *Cornish plunger lift* (Arthur ibid. p.15) and *Cornish plunging poles* which "were plunging up and down" (Arthur, ibid. p.80).

Cornish Poet, the John Harris, for whom see *'Cornish' Burns*.

Cornish poet-parson, the As Rev. Robert Stephen Hawker has been called (Martin 1951:97). See *Cornish anthem*.

Cornish Point 1 Area in Bannockburn, New Zealand. **2** Red wine from this region made with *pinot noir* grapes (see internet site http://www.cornishpoint.com).

Cornish poles As the *Cornish maypoles* (q.v.) is called (Deane and Shaw 1975:172).

Cornish Political Party, the As Loveday Jenkin dubs *Mebyon Kernow* (C.W.W. 1995, p.6). See *Cornish Party, the*.

Cornish pony Courtney (1880:25) used the term *Cornish pony* for the native *Cornish horse* (q.v). Perhaps these *Cornish ponies* were the same as the *gossies* or small ponies from the Goss and Tregon Moors that were rounded up and sold at the October fair (see Phillipps 1976:77). However, what the Cornish call a *Jerusalem pony* is a donkey (Hawke 1975:31). See *Cornish goonhilly*.

Cornish portal dolmens Prehistoric structure which consists of two or more upright stones which support a flat stone on top. In Cornish it is called *cromlegh* (from *crom* crooked + *legh* flat rock, slab). The word 'portal' suggests its use as a kind of 'door' or gateway. The word *dolmen* is not to be confused with the *Cornish tol men* (q.v.).

Cornish postmark Postmark in Cornish on 8th May at Helston (see Deane and Shaw 1975:14). It has become a tradition for the Post Office to stamp all mail with a special *Cornish postmark* on this day in commemoration of the Floral dance. See *Cornish Furry Dance*.

Cornish potato As potatoes were still something of a rarity in 1676, since Cornwall grew potatoes they were called '*Cornish potatoes*' (Payton 1996:169). See *Cornish king*.

Cornish potato cake Dish of mashed potatoes baked with suet (Kittow, p.31).

Cornish po'tes Actually spelt '*Cawnish po'tes*' and seems to refer to Cornish pottery (Nance 1956: 60) for which see *Cornish ware*.

Cornish Poultry A synonym of *Cornish Game*.

Cornish pound 1 In the context of cider-making Spiers refers to the *Cornish pound* "or apple-crusher with its huge circular granite trough and granite 'edge' roller" (1996:24). **2** In Cornwall "a custom long prevailed ... of selling 18 ounces to the pound of fresh butter" as opposed to the convention of sixteen ounces elsewhere (W.B. 24 April, 1818). Similarly the *ingrossers* "bought wheat at eighteen gallons the bushel and delivered the same at sixteen gallons the bushel" (Jago 1882:194).

Cornish Powder An explosive like gelignite used in mining (Earl 1978:238). See *Cornish Cut*.

Cornish Prayer Book Rebellion The Rebellion of 1549 led by Humphrey Arundell as a result of Edward VI's imposition of an English Book of Common Prayer on the Cornish people. The Cornishmen besieged Exeter (see *Cornish University*) but were defeated. See *Cornish Commotion*.

Cornish Primrose Dance Composition for woodwind ensemble by Jean Jeandell.

Cornish Prince A rose hybrid (of Talisman rose, hybrid tea).

'Cornish' Private Eye The magazine *Free Cornwall* (published by Allen Forster 1987–1991) has been described as "Cornwall's answer to *Private Eye*" (Deacon et al 2003:84).

Cornish Prosodic Shift Linguistic term referring to the shortening of vowel sounds in the *Cornish Language* (q.v.) that is evident from the *Old Cornish* (q.v. appendix 1) to the *Middle Cornish* (q.v.) periods. Prior to the work of Williams (1995:281) this change was believed to have occurred much later (i.e. between the periods of *Middle Cornish* and *Late Cornish*).

Cornish Problem Phrase which suggests the pressure put on the British government (particularly in the last few decades) for the establishment of a *Cornish Assembly* etc. and is thus analogous with the so-called 'Irish Problem' of the last century. American sociologists once wondered why there "should be so much of a Welsh problem, yet so little of a Cornish one" (M. Hechter and M. Levi 1979, cited by deacon et al 2003:1). However, due to the growing awareness of Corniah national conscience, Deacon rephrases this and states "the issue becomes not why there was so little of a *Cornish problem* but why, as the second half of the twentieth century unfolded, there was so much of one" (ibid., p.1).

Cornish proto-Alignment Trev Crago's term for the era just after W.W.1 when Labour was losing ground in Cornwall and many women were becoming involved in the movement for emancipation (C.S. 2nd, 8, 2000. p.147 and passim).

Cornish pump A steam driven pumping engine used in deep mines to raise underground water. See *Cornish engine*.

Cornish pump, double Some *Cornish engines* had four sets of "double *Cornish pumps*" (C.W. 18, 1998, p.11).

Cornish pump engine Term used by Payton (1999:175) as synonymous with the *Cornish pumping engine* (q.v.).

Cornish pumping engine A type of engine (Crowley 1976:24). A single cylinder engine which replaced Woolf's engine. So called as this engine worked with steam that raised the pump rod. See *Cornish engine*.

Cornish pumping engine house The place where the *Cornish pumping engine* (q.v.) was kept (C.W. 15, 1997/8, p.14). See *Cornish engine house*.

Cornish punch Drink made with rum, cognac, lemon juice and sugar (Waller 1994:45).

Cornish Puzzle Song Category of song (Davey 1983:39 and 44) with some hidden meaning e.g. *My Ow Mos* (see *Cornish Three Men's song*) which refers to *pysk bras naw y-lostow* (a 'huge fish with nine tails'). Rather than an actual fish, this obviously represented something else in the same way that the 'cat o'nine tails' was a whip. In this instance, it is unlikely that the allusion is to an octopus (from Gk. 'eight legs') but is possibly a kind of *creeper* or *centipede* – large anchor-shaped hooks with several spikes that were used by the hated *revenue men* to lift casks of smuggled brandy that had been hidden on the sea bed with an anchor (see Vivian 1969:6).

'Cornish' pyramids, The The *Cornish alps* (q.v.) have also been described as "The pyramids of Cornwall" (see the pamphlet *Cornwall of Mine*, pub. Cornwall of Mine Ltd., Pentridge Cresc., London).

'Cornish' Quaker saint Or rather 'The Quaker Saint of Cornwall'. The epithet of Loveday Hambly C17th Quaker woman who was a devout philanthropist and prison reformer and for George Fox the foremost personality among the Cornish Society of Friends (for epithet see John 1981: 100 and C.T. summer 1997, p.7)

Cornish Queen 1 A *Cornish Rex* (q.v.) female as opposed to a *ram-cat* (i.e. tom-cat) (for use of this term see J. Anne Helgren's internet article *Choosing a Devon Rex*). The word 'queen' is etymologically correct since, although it seems to relate to *rex* (Lat. king), it is fact derived from the O.E. *cwen* meaning woman or wife and a cognate of the Swedish *hona* or female (for which see Cornish rexhona). **2** Queens were also a type of slate used in Cornwall (W.B.10 July, 1840). **3** Queens are scallops or *gweans* (Jago 1882: 246). **4** du Maurier refers to Iseult as "The *Cornish Queen*" (1967:36). Her love Tristan died when he saw the black sails on her ship. When she landed and saw him dead she died as well. The Cornish legend seems a conflation of the Romeo and Juliet theme and the story of Aegeus, father of Theseus who jumped into the (Aegean) Sea on seeing the black sails of his son's ship.

Cornish Question, The Usually in modern usage the phrase refers to the demand for a *Cornish Assembly*. It is used in this context by several writers e.g. by Mark Sandford (C.S. Vol. 11, 2003, p.44). The phrase is also used in the title of John Angarrack's book *Our Future is History: Identity, Law and the Cornish Question*.

Cornish Quickstep A dance and its melody (Davey 1983:6). According to the intenet site http://www.heirloommusic.com/celticcornersnotes.html it is a march (and the music for it).

Cornish rag slate A kind of slate used for roofs (C.W. 40, 2004, p.8). See *Cornish slate*.

Cornish range The unique Cornish stove, also called a *slab* (see Merrick 1998:3 and 4). Tricia Rowe says that apart from cooking, it was also used to display brassware and each week was cleaned by being *black-leaded* (O.C. Vol. XII, No. 12, 2003, pp.12–3). It has also been called the *Cornish kitchen* or *Cornish apparatus*. The kitchen grate near the *Cornish range* was called the *fringle*. The *clavel* or *cravel* was a beam over the *Cornish range* (Ivey 1976:14) and the *shevver* or *shiver* was a flat iron plated in the oven of the range (Ivey ibid. p.59).

Cornish Ratepayers' Association Disparaging term applied to *Mebyon Kernow* not by its opponents but by memebers who feared that its aims could be adulterated by becoming just "a glorified *Cornish Ratepayers' Association* which merely grumbles about present grievances and loses sight of the long-term aims" (from letter by R.G. Jenkin to Robert Dunstone, June 1996 in *MK Collection* – cited by Deacon et al 2003:55).

Cornish Rebellion 1 The *Cornish Rebellion* (1497) was fought against Henry VII's taxes to finance his war in Scotland. The rebellion was led by Michael Joseph of St. Keverne, Thomas Flamank of Bodmin and Lord Audley. The leaders were tortured and executed and 2,000 Cornishmen were defeated at Blackheath by a force of 10,000 men. **2** Beer brewed by Redruth Brewery. See *Cornish Blonde* and *Cornish Knocker*.

Cornish Rebellion, home of the As St. Keverne has been called since it was the home of An Gof and where *Cornish Rebellion* begun (Payton 1996:166). Each year on 27th June *Mebyon Kernow* place a wreath on the monument of An Gof and Thomas Flamank in St Keverne (see *Cornish National Day*).

Cornish Rebellion, the last As Carew referred to the rebellion which started in St. Keverne (1602:111). However, the *Cornish Prayer Book Rebellion* (q.v.) had broken out nearer Carew's own life time.

Cornish Rebellion, the Second 1497 led by Perkin Warbeck (C.W. 12, 1997, p.29). Warbeck landed at Whitesands Bay in September 1497 and in Bodmin was proclaimed Richard IV. Warbeck claimed to be the brother of Edward V. He led the Cornishmen on a siege of Exeter but was defeated.

Cornish Rebellion, the Third The *Cornish Prayer Book Rebellion* (q.v.). Cf. *Cornish Rebellion, the Second*.

Cornish rebels Those brave Cornishmen who took part in either An Gof's *Cornish Rebellion* (q.v.) or in the *Cornish Prayer Book Rebellion* (q.v.). The term is used e.g. by Jenkin (1984:75).

Cornish Red A giant hybrid of rhododendron that can grow up to 50 ft and is in bloom from March to May. See *Cornish Cracker*.

Cornish Red Baron, the Reference to a Fokker triplane "built in Cornwall some 66 years after the original" (C.W. 38, 2004, central page). Actually the Red Baron was not the red triplane but the German pilot ace who flew it.

Cornish Red-billed Chough As the *Cornish chough* (q.v.) is sometimes called (e.g. by Westwood 1992).

Cornish red ensign Unlike the ordinary *Cornish ensign* (q.v.), this is a red flag and in the top left hand corner there is a the *Cornish flag* (i.e. St. Piran's flag of a white cross on a black background).

Cornish Red-legged Chough As the *Cornish Chough* (q.v.) is sometimes called.

Ivey refers to a *"rid-leg chawk"* (1976:55).

Cornish Regiment Name given to **1** The 32nd Cornwall Regiment. They defended Lucknow in the Indian Mutiny of May 1857. **2** The Duke of Cornwall's Light Infantry 46th Foot who killed 400 Americans in a single night in the American War of Independence in 1777. They were called *The Cornwalls*. A Cornish Regiment also fought in W.W.1. (C.W. 28, 2002, pp.24–5).

Cornish Regional Assembly An alternative name for the proposed *Cornish Assembly* (C.W. 38, 2004, p.49).

Cornish Religious Rebellion As Salmon refers to the *Cornish Rebellion* (1903:245).

Cornish Revival (*An Dasserghyans Kernewek*) **1** The name for the revival of the *Cornish Language* and culture. **2** Payton uses the phrase 'Cornish revival' in the context of Methodism in Australia in 1935 (1999: 285).

Cornish Revival, father of the. As Whetter calls Henry Jenner (1977:54) for whom see *Cornish language revival, father of.*

Cornish Revival, leader of the R. Morton Nance (1873–1959) was an author, lexicographer and *Cornish Grand Bard* (q.v.) from 1934 until his death. His bardic name was Mordon (Corn. 'Sea wave') (for his epithet see the cover of his posthumously published work 1963)

Cornish Revivalist Movement, father of the Payton's term (1999:96) for which see *Cornish language revival, father of the.*

Cornish revivalists Those active in the *Cornish Revival* i.e. in reviving the *Cornish Language* and culture (C.S. 2nd Vol. 4,1996, p.172).

Cornish Revolt Alternative term (used e.g. by Jenkin 1984:56) for the *Cornish Rebellion* (q.v.).

Cornish Revolution 1 A synonym of the *Cornish Revolt* **2** By analogy to the Industrial Revolution, Phil Hosken in the 2001 Trelawny lecture refers to the use of steam in Cornwall as "the *Cornish Revolution*" (C.W. 27, 2001, p.27).

Cornish Rex A breed of cat that was bred in 1950s in Cornwall as a result of genetic mutations and is similar to the Devon Rex yet the *Cornish Rex* is said to have a distinct cheesy smell. Unlike the Selkirk Rex which has a normal coat of fur, the Cornish Rex only has the downhair (i.e. undercoat). It does not have the other two cat coats: the guard hairs (outer fur) and the awn hair (middle layer). A tom cat would be called a *ram* cat while a kitten is a *chet* in Cornwall (yet confusingly *kittens* mean kidneys – as does the word *linuth*). 'Rex' is the Latin for 'king' but this is no relation to the *Cornish King* (q.v.).

Cornish Rexhona The Swedish name for the female *Cornish Rex* (see *Cornish queen*). In Swedish the male or *ram* cat is called simply *Cornish Rex*.

Cornish Rhapsody Musical score commissioned in 1944 for 'A Lady Surrenders' starring Margaret Lockwood and Stewart Granger (C.T. May 1999, p.12).

Cornish ribbon Ribbon of *Cornish tartan*, used in catering etc to decorate tables (O.C. XIII, 4, spring 2005, pp.62–63).

'Cornish' Richard Rufus Or rather 'Richard of Cornwall' (Richard de Cornouailles / Richard Cornubiensis). Friar and theologian (fl. early C13th) who lived in Paris.

Cornish ringers "*Cornish ringers* usually employ call-changes and not method ringing, and the bells have no 'stays', which means they can be more easily turned over than in England and therefore are more dangerous" (*Discover Cornwall 1992 Cornwall's Official Holiday Guide*, p.14). *Cornish ringers* would ring bells on the eve of Guy Fawkes Day. Hence in Cornwall the eve of Bonfire Night was called *Ringing Night*.

Cornish Rising As the *Cornish Rebellion* (q.v.) is sometimes called (C.W. 14, 1997, p.13).

Cornish Riviera 1 The southern coastline of Cornwall. In an endeavour to promote tourism, brochures at the turn of the century had tended to exaggerate the comparatively mild Cornish climate. For many this epithet is applicable to all of Cornwall. Thus Cornwall itself was also dubbed "*Britain's Riviera*" (Jenkin 1945:124). The epithet "the English Riviera" was also used (cited by Bradley in C.S. 2nd, 8, 2000: 137). **2** A synonym of the *Cornish Riviera Express*.

Cornish Riviera Express It was once the longest non-stop train service to London Paddington.

Cornish Riviera Run Show of vintage cars passing through Penzance promenade in September, 1995.

Cornish Riviers A Frenchified (rather than French) spelling of the *Cornish Riviera* (see C.S. 2nd, 1995, p.96).

'Cornish' Robin Hood Robin Hood took from the rich to give to the poor. Cornishman Barry Flamank dubbed 'Robin Flamank Hood' "imported some beer and baccy from the continent and sold it to pensioner friends at prices far less than those charged in the shops" (C.W. 20, 1999, p.28). On the day of the *Cornish Furry dance* (q.v.) Robin Hood is mentioned in the verses and songs (Jones 1997 c:6, 20, 30, 31). See *Cornish fair traders*.

Cornish rock 1 (C.W. 3,1994/5, p.28) Cornish stone. **2** Synonym of *Rock Cornish* (appendix 1).

Cornish roadstone Type of Cornish rock used for roads (Jenkin 1984:36). See *Cornish paving*.

Cornish rod In the entry for *lace* Curnow writes "*Cornish rod*. 160 *lace* to a *Cornish acre*, 36sq. rods" (2002:15). In Cornish 'rod' is *gwelen* or *lorgh*. See *Cornish land rod*.

Cornish Romantic, the Tangye gives Edward John Trelawny the epithet "the colourful *Cornish Romantic*" (1978:186). Like the great Romantic poet Byron, he also took part in the Greek Revolution against the Turks.

Cornish rooster (U.S.) *Cornish cockerel* (q.v.).

Cornish rotative beam engine. An engine in the *Cornish cycle* could become rotative by using a *sweep rod* (a heavy connecting rod) "to induce half the crank's rotation by gravity". Such an engine was used to hoist ore (Crowley 1976:23).

'Cornish' rough music Deane and Shaw (1975:54) compare the Cornish custom of the *shallal* with *rough music* (and synonymous terms like *riding the stang* or *skimmington* and *cwlstrin* in Wales). This referred to ways of mocking an unpopular couple on their wedding night, such as a widow who remarried. In Cornwall it was also called *shivaree* (Phillipps 1993:51) a term from the Fr. *charivari* which was a serenade with tin pans (i.e. *lattice pans*).The 'musicians' were called the *shillally band* (Hawke 1975:52). Indeed other European parallels include the Basque *tobera* and Catalan *esquellotada* on the night of a widow(er)'s wedding. In Cornwall this type of revelry was not always conducted for purposes of mockery and, like the tying of tin pots and pans to the *weddiners'* car, other pranks were played like whitewashing windows and blocking chimneys (Hawke 1973:24. In Morvah the couple were taken out of their bed and beaten with a sack of sand while *Cornish Furze* (q.v.) was placed on their mattress (Bird 1988:75). At the *Hal-an-tow* (see *Cornish furry dance*) at Helston a party playing a fife, "crazy drum" and tin pans "begging from door to door, and with them was a boy attired as a woman, decorated in flowers and greens and seated on a donkey" (W.B. 12th May, 1865). Moreover, there was also a custom to *prall* people (i.e. "attach tin pans, kettles. to the tail of an animal or cards, bits of paper to a person's coat" – Thomas 1895:113). This was known as *tail-piping* which also occurred on April Fool's day.

Cornish round In *Cornish dialect* the word *round* (also *roundago*) was a circle of stones within which the druids supposedly danced in imitation of the dragon (see *Cornish dragon*) (Jago 1882: 251). Sometimes used in plural – see *Cornish rounds.*

Cornish round-headed cross Another name (used e.g. by Pearse p.10) for the *Cornish wheel* (q.v.).

Cornish round houses The houses at Veryan (Bird 1989: 49). These houses were commissioned in the early C19th by Rev. Jeremiah Twist. He "built these round houses so the devil couldn't hide in the corners" (Merton 2003:33).

Cornish rounds Hartnoll & Found define the *'Cornish Round's* as the circular earthworks where the *Cornish miracle plays* (q.v.) were performed (1992:108).

'Cornish' rounders A bat and ball game called *Littlemount* which was "a sort of rounders" played on St. Michael's Mount (q.v. *Cornish Mount*) on Easter Monday (Thomas 1895: 102. Jago also records the game *rounders* in Cornwall (1882:252). Day refers to the game of *"Cornish rounders"* that was played on Christmas morning at St. Ives, the idea of which was to hit the ball through four *bickens* (piles of sand) – another game called *catchers* was also played but with only one *bicken* (2000:183).

Cornish round theatre (Corn. *plen an gwary*) The place where the *Cornish miracle plays* were performed.

Cornish Royalist cause, darling of the As Payton dubs Sir Bevill Grenville (1996:159) commander of the *Cornish Royalists* in the Civil War.

Cornish Royalists The term *Cornish Royalists* (used e.g. by Deane and Shaw 1975:100) is normally limited to those Cornishmen who fought for Charles I in the civil war. Charles I's portrait can still be seen in several churches in Cornwall and a short pointed beard is still called a *charley* (Whinray 1997:32), not to be confused with a *charlie* which is a chamber pot (Hawke 1973:33).

Cornish rugby shirt With gold and black stripes. It is popular with many young Cornishmen for just casual wear and is not worn exclusively by the *Cornish XV*. See *Cornish All Blacks*.

'Cornish' Rumpelstiltskin Weatherhill and Devereux describe the story of Duffy and the Devil as "a very Cornish version of 'Rumpelstiltskin'"(1994:106; Day also make this comparison 2000:180). This story tells how Squire Lovell marries the peasant girl Duffy believing her to be the finest needleworker (the work is in fact done by a devil on condition that she will be his if she cannot discover his name within three years). His name is Terrytop (or Tarraway in another Cornish version of the story). See *Cornish Cinderella*.

Cornish Ruodlieb As the Cornish tale of *John of Chyanhor* has been called because of its vicissitudes (C.S. Vol. 4, 1996, pp.45–63 and C.S. 2nd, 10, 2002, p.223, p.236, n. 83). *Ruodlieb* was the title of a romance in Latin verse written c.1030 by an anonymous German poet. It was unfinished and cut up into pieces which were gradually discovered after 1807. Bottrell also made use of the *Ruodlieb*'s "three proverb tale" (i.e. in which the hero is rewarded not with a coin but with wise advice).

Cornishry The term is used (e.g. by Rowse 1942:168 and in C.T. 3, 3 Jan. 1997:33) to refer to Cornish culture and heritage. By analogy to the *Welshry* (Edwards 1998:129) and *Irishry* (Edwards 2004:151) one might infer that it also means an area where Cornish people live.

Cornish saffern cake Alternative dialect spelling of *Cornish saffron cake* (q.v.).

Cornish saffron *Cornish saffron cake* (q.v.). Sometimes the word 'cake' is dropped. For instance, in Warren's ad there is '*Cornish saffron* by post' (C.T. April 1988, p.54).

Cornish saffron bread An alternative name for *Cornish saffron cake* (q.v.).

Cornish saffron cake A cake flavoured with saffron. At Christmas saffron buns were made in the shape of birds called *dilly birds* (see Xmas book.). Saffron is the most expensive spice thus the Cornish expression "as dear as saffern (i.e. saffron)". Because of its yellow colour, this cake was also called *canary duff* (O.C. X. 2., spring 1986, p.90). *Cornish saffron cake* was sent to relatives and friends for good luck "and carefully cut … so each member of the family would share the 'Good luck'" (C.W. 10, 1996, p.21). A large saffron bun is called a *faggon* (Ivey 1976:24). A *cheel-fuggan* was a saffron cake "given to the first person met on returning from a christening"(Hawke 1975:10). This was also called a *kimbly* which was given at weddings too – see Couch 1871:58 and Jago 1882:201). Asala records that the saffron used in Cornish saffron cakes could have magic power enabling one to raise storms, make a love potion or to gain clairvoyant abilities (1998:335).

Cornish saffron cake, plain See *Cornish saffron cake, rich*.

Cornish saffron cake, rich A *Cornish saffron cake* in which the ingredients are soaked, as opposed to a *plain Cornish saffron cake* (Kittow uses the term – pp.14–15).

'Cornish' saffron tea Apart from Cornish saffron cake (q.v.), saffron was boiled in Cornwall for an infusion and this *saffron tea* was a cure for measles (Jenkin 1984:71).

'Cornish' sailcloth jacket See *Cornish wrestling jacket*.

Cornish saint, historian *par excellence* of the As S. Baring Gould, leading expert in *Cornish hagiography* (q.v.) has been dubbed (C.S. 7, 1999, p.91).

Cornish St. Michael's Mount Cunnack intentionally prefixes the word 'Cornish' to the Mount in order to distinguish it from its sister Mont St. Michel in Brittany (1975:7). See *Cornish Mount*.

Cornish saints, the age of David Wright's phrase for the period 200–700 A.D. (C.T. Jan. 1999, p.17).

Cornish saints, father of Rawe uses this epithet to refer to St. Petroc (fl.C6th) of Padstow and Bodmin with monasteries on the North coast (C.W. 30, 2002, p.46). He became a hermit on an island in the Indian Ocean (see John 1981:50). His feast day is on 4th June. There were so many saints in Cornwall that, like Ireland, it has been called "Land of the Saints" (Jenkin 1984:21). See *Cornish ecclesiastical capital*.

Cornish Saints' play Another name for *Cornish miracle play* (q.v.).

'Cornish' Sampson, the Michael Tangye uses the epithet 'the Wendron Sampson' to refer to John Pearce (C.T. 1994, pp.48–49). Pearce (1862–1896 was *Cornish wrestling* champion. He defeated American (of Cornish extraction) world champion Tom Carkeek in 1887. In 1885 when the *Cornish Needle* (q.v.) had fallen John and his brothers re-erected it.

Cornish sandwich Jam on a scone (Walker 1994:41) whereas a *jamie maw* is bread and jam (James 1979:49). Similarly a piece of bread and butter is a *tabm* (Jago 1882:286) and treacle on bread with cream was called *thunder and lightning* (Thomas 1895:129) whereas *bread and dippy* was bread and thin cream (Thomas, ibid. p.71). When making sandwiches it is "unlucky to cut butter or bread both ends" (Hawke 1973:19).

Cornish sardine The pilchard (Noall p.47). See *Cornish duck* and *Cornish pilchard*.

Cornish sausage 1 Sausage soaked in milk and dipped in flour, served with apple purée or gooseberries (Heard 1984:57). **2** Sausage made with a mixture of minced bacon and beef with tomato sauce and chutney (Butcher & Annand 1994:25).

Cornish Saxon A brand of beer brewed by Skinners, Truro. The word 'Saxon' is derived from the Old High German word *sahs* (knife or short sword) and it is from this word that the Cornish take their word *Saws* for an Englishman (cf. W. *Sais*, Bret. *Saoz* and the Gaelic *Sassenach/Sasunnach*). England is *Pow Saws* or 'Land of the Saxon' (cf. Bret. *Bro Saoz*, Van. *Bre/Bro Sauz*) and the English language is *Sawsnek* or '(Anglo-) Saxon' (cf. Bret. *Saozneg*, W. *Saesneg*). See *Cornish Blonde*.

Cornish scalded cream Another name for *Cornish cream*, i.e. clotted cream (see Payton 1999:151). To *scaald* means to scald (Ivey 1980). Once milk was scalded it was then *unreamed* (skimmed) with a *reamer* (a skimmer like a shovel) that would remove the clotted /*clouted* cream from the *scald milk* (see Jago 1882: 249, 255 and 302). Cream form milk that has not been scalded is called *raw ream* (Thomas 1895:116).

Cornish Scot The Penzance train service introduced in 1987 to Edinburgh and

Glasgow (see Railway Dictionary. p.64). See *Cornish Mail, Cornishman* and *Cornish Riviera Express.*

Cornish scrumpy Synonym of *Cornish cider* (q.v.). According to Heard the word 'scrumpy' is "named from '*scrump*', small apple" (1984:123).

Cornish Sea, the Bucca Boo of the A phrase used by Tregarthen (1940:140) as synonymous with *the Neptune of the Cornish Sea* (q.v.).

Cornish Sea, the Neptune of the As Tregarthen called the *Bucca Boo* (1940:129). Around Mevagissey he was accompanied by nine mermen and if anyone saw their boat they would be lucky. Normally in Cornish dialect *bucca boo* refers to a bugbear or scarecrow. Talking of Neptune (the Roman name for the Greek sea god Poseidon who, like the Cornish mermen, had a fish's tail), it was the Cornishman John Couch Adams (1819–92) of Laneast who discovered the planet Neptune (named after this sea god). Yet another connection of Neptune with Cornwall is that the *Neptune* was the name of a phantom ship sunk off the coast of St. Ives (see Underwood 1983:78). See '*Cornish*' *banshee, Cornish brownie, Cornish guardian of the bees, Cornish knocker, Cornish mine goblin, Cornish piskey* and *Cornish tommyknocker.*

Cornish sea dogs, doyen of the Richard Grenville who in 1591 confronted a whole Spanish fleet (Payton 1996:146).

Cornish Sea Fencibles The word 'Cornish' is often prefixed to this naval body (C.S. 1st, 1973:60). Hawke mentions the Say Fencible as "the old coastguard" (1975:50).

Cornish sea monster, the As Day refers to the *Morgawr* (2003:225) for which see *Cornish Nessie.*

Cornish sea names Another name for *Cornish taboo names* (q.v.).

'Cornish' Sea Trout In 1792 Walbaum recorded fish *Salmo trutta* as *Salmo cornubiensis.*

Cornish serpentine A kind of stone found on the Lizard and very popular in Victorian times. It was often carved into lighthouses. In Cornish it is *sarfven* (*sarf* snake + *ven* mutated from of *men* stone). *Sarfek* is 'serpentine' in the sense of snake-like yet *men sarfek* is another name for this stone. It is also a type of dance e.g. The *Snail's Creep* in June around St. Roche in which dancers coil inwards like a snake.

Cornish Service The so-called Cornish service was really the Latin service that was replaced by the English Prayer Book (see Daniell 1988).

Cornish Shades 1 As the mythological otherworld of *Annown* has been called (Spacey 1985:22). It is the equivalent of the Welsh *Annwn*. **2** Donald R. Rawe uses the phrase *Cornish shades* to refer to the distinct colours of *Cornish tartan* (C.W. 6, 1995, p.19).

Cornish shaft Type of mine shaft. With reference to Botallack mine, Brown and Acton observe that "like most *Cornish shafts* it is not vertical and develops a seaward underlie to follow the lode" (1994:108).

Cornish Shark One of the Latin names of the porbeagle (*Lamna nasus*) is also *Squalus conubiensis* (i.e. 'Cornish shark', cf. It. *squalo* shark). Turk records the earlier name *Lamna cornubica* (1971:94). Interestingly the word 'porpoise' is believed to be a *Cornish loan word* (q.v.) and according to an internet site is possibly derived from a portmanteau of 'porpoise' and 'beagle' or the words *porgh* and *bugel* (http://www.flmnh.ufl.edu). Actually the Cornish word *porghel* means piglet and *bugel* is shepherd while *bygel* would mean hobgoblin. The prefix *porghel* (piglet) at least seems to tally with the Cornish word for porpoise which is *morhogh* (i.e. sea pig). Nance also provides the word *porbugel* which he translates "bottle nosed shark" (1978). *The mermaid's comb* was made of shark's teeth (see *Cornish mermaid*).

Cornish shawl Shawl with *Cornish tartan* pattern. The *Cornish hunting shawl*, for instance, has the *Cornish hunting tartan*. The *Cornish national shawl* is with the *Cornish national tartan*. A *turnover* was a shawl "worn cornerways" (Hawke 1975:65).

Cornish Sheep A breed of sheep (or *shaip*) unique to Cornwall and known for its poor quality wool. Yet, as Carew observed, hornless specimens of *Cornish Sheep* had better wool and there were also *Cornish Sheep* with four horns. The breed was preferred for its "speedy fattening, and price of sale and ... sweetness in taste" (1602:39). The Improved Dartmoor Sheep is descended from it. A *yow* is an ewe (Courtney 1890:137) and a *bowjey* is a sheepfold (Bottrell 1873:156). When the Cornish people spoke about this breed over two centuries ago they would have used the word *davas* (pl. *deves*) or 'sheep' (cf. Van *davad*, pl. *deved*, Bret. *dañvad*, pl. *deñved* ; W. *dafad*, pl. *defaid*). At Christmas *Cornish Sheep* were believed to bow towards the East (*Folklore* 3, 1885:186). See *Cornish hair*.

Cornish shepherdess, the An epithet of Thomasine Bonaventura recorded on the internet page (http://www.cornwall.gov.uk/history/ab-hi01a.htm). See *Cornish Cinderella*.

Cornish shibboleths "Such sentences are often used as test of the Cornishness of anyone claiming to belong to our ancient race" (O.C. June 1990:35). An example is "There's a *muryon* on thy *nuddick*" (i.e. there's an ant on your neck). Yet in east *Cornish dialect*, the word for ant would not be *muryan* (or *meryon* which also meant unbaptised children and was a term of endearment – see Courtney 1890:125) but rather *emmet* (yet the word *emmet* also has connotations of the Devon *grockle* when applied to a holidaymaker – see Downes 1986:59). The word 'shibboleth' (Heb. ear of corn) comes form the Old Testament Book of Judges 12 v.6. In this passage the Gileadites asked their enemies the Ephraimites to pronounce the word 'shibboleth'. However, the latter could not pronounce the initial 'sh' but only the sibilant 'ss', i.e. 'sibboleth' whereupon they were killed.

Cornish shield It has fifteen bezants (see *Cornish coat of arms*). The Cornish word for 'shield' is *scos* which also connotes coat of arms and is a cognate of the former Portuguese currency the *escudo* (Port. and Sp. 'shield' – since the coin originally had a shield or crest). There is also the *Cornish Gorsedd* (q.v.) Shield awarded for music.

Cornish shortcake Like several other 'Scottish' aspects of modern Cornish culture, e.g. the *Cornish kilt* and *Cornish tartan*. there is also *Cornish shortcake*.

Cornish shorts The name given to short Cornish films with cultural content (C.S. 11, 2003, pp.112, 118 & 123).

Cornish shovel A unique Cornish tool which has a longer handle than an ordinary shovel and the blade is shaped like a shield. In *Cornish dialect* it is sometimes called a *showl* (Courtney 1890:51), *shouell* (Hawke 1975:53) or *shouell* (Ivey 1976:60) and the past participle is *shoulled* (i.e. shovelled – see Hawke, ibid. 53). Its length is seen in the dialect saying "feet like hafe-crown shovels" (Hawke 1973:4). Moreover, a *sifter* was a small shovel (Clemo p.104) and a *fire-pan* was a "fire shovel" (Thomas 1895:85). A *maglen* was an implement like a shovel with bars for lifting *fumadoes* for washing before barrelling (O.C. XI. 5, 199, p.25). In the Cornish language (as in Welsh and Breton) it was *pal* (cf. Sp. and It. *pala*) – related to the word *bal* meaning mine (see *Cornish bal maiden*). The other Cornish word for 'shovel' *ref* also meant 'oar' (a dual meaning shared by the Tk. word *kürek*. *Ref* is a cognate with W. *rhaw* and Bret. *rañv* – spade; cf. Sp. and It. *remo* – oar). Moreover, *vanning* was washing tin ore on a shovel to test it (Jago 1882:304) and to *spit* meant to cut up the top soil with a shovel (Thomas 1895:124).The *Cornish shovel* is also used for *Cornish hedging*.

Cornish shovel hilt The hilt of an old *Cornish shovel* (q.v.) was often cut down to make a punching stick for washing clothes (Hawke 1989:1). In *Cornish dialect* Nance gives us *showl-hilt* (1956:108). To *stank* means to step on a shovel (Phillipps 1993:52). The notion of stepping is implied in the Cornish word for 'hilt' which is *tros* (literally 'foot'). The similarity of the Cornish *shovel hilt* to certain Cornish crosses e.g. at Parc an Growse has been noted (O.C. XII, 10, 2002, p.30).

Cornish Shrimper A type of gaff-rigged boat that is easy to sail. See *Cornish Crabber*.

Cornish signposts Roadsign written in Cornish (or written over in Cornish by members of *Cornish Solidarity*, q.v.).

Cornish slab A synonym of the *Cornish range* (C.T. April 1998, p.49). In Cornwall the word *slab* itself can sometimes be sufficient. However, strictly speaking the slab was the right part of a *Cornish kitchen range* where the *fringle* (container for the fire) was built. In Cornish *slabba* is the name for the cooking range (Nance 1978:139) whereas in dialect *slab* also means a tombstone (Ivey 1976:61).

Cornish slate Also called blue *Cornish slate*.

Cornish slate, blue dark slate from Cornwall used for roofs or folk art. It is also called *Cornish Blue* (q.v.).

Cornish slate, the Land of As Delabole has been dubbed (C.W. 16, 1998, p11).

Cornish smock The Cornish fisherman's smock (*la vareuse de pecheur*) is really based on a Breton design.

'Cornish' snakestone 1 The *myl pryv* which in dialect is *mill-proo* and which is sometimes anglicised as *millpreve* e.g. by Deane and Shaw (1975:118) who describe the charm as a blue holed stone that is believed to protect from snakebites and translate it as meaning "1,000 snakes", yet it does in fact mean '1,000 worms' (from Corn. *myl* 1,000 + *pryf* worm). While in Welsh the words are identical (*mil* – 1,000 + *pryf* worm ;cf. Bret. *preñv*) in Wales it is called *maen magl* or *glain y nadroedd*. **2** Etymologically this is the *Cornish serpentine* stone (q.v.).

Cornish Snow A variety of camellia (produced by crossing *C. saluenensis* with *C. cuspidate* – related to the Chinese tea plant). It blooms in early to mid spring and has dainty single white flowers with a pink flush. See *Cornish Spring*.

Cornish Social and Economic Research Group (CoSERG) Founded in 1987; the objectives were "to stop the brain drain of our dynamic young people, guarantee the right of future generations to be Cornish and retain local communities by human-scale development that respects the environment" (Deacon et al 2003:84).

Cornish Society 1 The name first suggested for the Old Cornwall Societies in 1920. It was not adopted (O.C. June 1990:3).**2** A society founded by Cornishmen at Oxford University (C.S. 1st, Vol. 8, 1980, p.37).

Cornish Society, The Celtic (*Cowethas Kelto-Kernuak*). Society founded in 1901 to revive the *Cornish language*(q.v), to establish a *Cornish Gorsedd* (q.v.) and to promote sports like *Cornish wrestling* (q.v.) and *Cornish hurling* (q.v.). It was the brainchild of L.C. Duncombe Jewell and Hennry Jenner was vice president. It collapsed in W.W.1.

Cornish Soft A soft cheese with added double cream. See *Cornish Blue* for other cheeses.

Cornish Solidarity (*Unverth Kernewek*) Cornish activist group who campaign for a *Cornish Assembly* (q.v.).

Cornish spade Another name for the *Cornish shovel* (q.v.) (See O.C. VIII,10, 1978, p.467). Courtney suggests that the Cornish miners were called *spadiards* "from their spades" (1890:53).

Cornish speak As *Cornish dialect* speech is sometimes called (O.C. Vol. XI, No. 9, autumn, 1995, p.451).

Cornish speaker In Cornish only one word is necessary for this person (Nance did not record this term but in K.K. it is *kerneweger*, pl. *kernewegoryon*).

Cornish speaker, the last Dolly Pentreath/Dorothy Jeffery (1685–1777), *Cornish fish jouster* (q.v.) from Mousehole is acknowledged as the last Cornish speaker. However, it is not certain that Cornish died with her. As Pool says, "Cornish, like Charles II was 'an unconscionable long time dying' " (1975:5). There are reports of Cornish speakers even after Dolly's death. For instance, in 1777 (the year Dolly died) Barrington met John Nancarrow who could speak Cornish but he had learnt the language (cited by Baring-Gould 1908:32) and in 1794 Bodener purportedly knew of five people in Mousehole who still spoke Cornish. Hence it might be safer to qualify that Dolly was the last *monoglot* Cornish speaker. See also *Cornish Wonder, the*.

Cornish speaking heartland The phrase is used by Payton (1996:125) for the area around St. Keverne. No doubt in the C16th and C17th when English was fast encroaching in east Cornwall, the *Cornish language* in the Western regions then would have been analogous with the *Gaeltachtaí* (pl.)in Ireland or *Y Fro Gymraeg* in Wales today. While it would be an anachronism to apply this term to Modern Cornwall, the word *Kerewegva* (i.e. place of the Cornish language) has been coined by analogy with the Breton *Brezhonegva* by Kendratiev (*Carn* 83, winter 1993/4, p.18.) for an imagined enclave for speakers of the revived *Cornish language*.

Cornish speech As the *Cornish language* (q.v.) is sometimes called (Bottrell:1873).

Cornish spiller See *Cornish boulter*.

Cornish split (Corn. *splytys kernewek*; in L.C. *torrow-bean kernowak*) A Cornish bun made usually split and spread with jam and *Cornish clotted cream*.

Cornish sporran To accompany the *Cornish tartan* (q.v.) outfit there is alo a *Cornish sporran* (mentioned by Payton 1999:395). The *Cornish sporran* is usually of black leather with fifteen brass bezants. It is worn infront of the Cornish *kilt* (q.v.). The word '*sporran*' means 'purse' or 'pouch'(Gaelic *sporan*, Scots *sporran* and cf. Ir. *sparán* – as in *sparán na scillinge*– a leprechaun's purse that is never empty).

Cornish Spring A deep pink variety of camellia *Cornish Spring Camellia williamsii* which has a mass of small single pink flowers. See *Cornish Snow*.

Cornish spring celebration, the As Alison Jones refers to the *Cornish furry dance* (q.v.) (1995:193).

Cornish squab pie 1 Originally a *Cornish pasty* not made with squab (baby pigeon) meat but mutton and apples. The confusion between birds (i.e. squabs) and apples can also be seen in the word *larks* which meant apples (Wright 1986:29). So popular was this pasty that Cornwall has been called "*The Land of Squab pies*" (W.B.11 Sept. 1829). Similarly *lamby* pie did not have lamb in it (Jago 1882:204). **2** Recently the meaning has been changed and a "pigeon pie" (Davey 1983:77n.3) or a "squab pasty" (Merton 2003:29) contain exactly what they suggest.

Cornish stamps 1 Used to crush small pieces of ore into powder. Whereas smaller stamps were powered by waterwheels, the larger stamps received their power from steam engines (See Brown and Acton 1994: 137). The *Cornish stamp* had square feet which did not revolve as opposed to the later Californian stamp. Similarly, a *muller* was a stone used to reduce tin ore to powder (Hawke 1989). See *Cornish crusher*. **2** Just as there have been some Cornish coins such as the *Cornish penny* (q.v.) and even a *Cornish penny post* (q.v.), since the 1960s there has also been a Cornish postage campaign for distinct *Cornish stamps* with a symbol like the *Cornish Chough* in the corner (i.e. where the Welsh, Scottish or Ulster stamps have the dragon, thistle or hand respectively). Yet many Cornish people would like to have completely different stamps similar to the Manx, Jersey or Guernsey stamps.

Cornish stampses According to Courtney the word 'stamps' (i.e. *Cornish stamps*) was always plural. However, she also provides a *Cornish double plural* (q.v.) form (1890:56). This is why Benney refers to "a very ancient Cornish stamps" (1972:85).

Cornish standard A synonym of the *Cornish flag* (q.v.) used by Hunt (2nd, p.475–478). Also called "the Standard of Cornwall" (Hunt, ibid. p.476). In *Cornish wrestling* a *standard* is a wrestler who has thrown two opponents (Jago 1882:277).

Cornish stannaries See *Cornish Stannary Parliament*.

Cornish Stannary Court See *Cornish Stannary Parliament*.

Cornish Stannary Parliament Parliament of the twenty four *Cornish stannators* (q.v.). This was the assembly representing the Cornish tinners. (from Lat. *stannum*, cf. *sten*). It was suspended in 1752.

Cornish stannators Members of the *Cornish Stannary Parliament*.

Cornish steam cycle Alternative name of the *Cornish cycle* (q.v.).

Cornish steam engine See *Cornish engine*. Perhaps the word 'steam' is sometimes added to distinguish it from the *man-engine* which was used to carry Cornish miners up and down the shafts.

Cornish steam pump Name sometimes used (C.W. 9, 1996) for the *Cornish pump* (q.v.).

Cornish step dancing As Neil Davey calls *scoot dancing* performed with *scoots* (metal plates – called in W. Cornwall *Qs* and *toe plates*) placed at the bottom of shoes (C.W. 38, 2004, p.31). The same word *scute* is also used for the iron point of a wooden plough (Courtney 1890:49). Moreover, *scoot* also meant to rush or hurry (Thomas 1895:119 – Thomas spells the iron heel caps as *skutes*, ibid. p.122). Perhaps there is a connection with *scat* meaning beat in music (Phillipps 1993:50). Confusingly in Cornish dialect, *to tap* boots does not mean to do 'tap' (step) dancing but to put *tingles* (small nails) on them for repair (Phillipps ibid. 54–5). Davey says that a step dancer was called a *lappyor* (1983:79), a word which originally meant leaper, acrobat or dresser of refuse ore (Nance 1978). The leaping suggests the dance movements.

Cornish stew As Courtney calls the dish *tetty rattle* (1890:58). The word *tetty* means potato. Other old dialect word for stew were *chod* and *scabby-gullion*.

'Cornish' stick According to E. Sidney Hartland in Cornwall three yards square was a *stick*. Moreover, four *sticks* equaled a *lease* and 8 score lease was an acre (see *Cornish acre*) (*Folklore* 9, 1898, p.189).

Cornish stile A distinct type of stile "consisting of four or five horizontal slabs of stone, possibly with a pit underneath … sometimes known as a *Cornish stile*. It can claim to be a prototype of the modern cattle grids" (O.C. XII, 5, 1999, p.41).

Cornish Sting, Operation Launched by the Tesco supermarket chain "to find producers willing to grow nettles that are used to give *Cornish Yarg* cheese its distinctive citrus taste" (C.W. 34, 2003, p.9). On May morning Cornish girls would use nettles to thrash anyone still in bed (Bird 1988:53). If someone is stung by a nettle then a *dock leaf* is applied (Hawke 1973:31).

Cornish stone 1 As kaolin is called. **2** A colourful stone stained dark red by iron deposits for building (C.W. 15, 1997/8, p.9). Not to be confused with the 'Cornwall Stone' which was a meeting place for ther gentry near Godolphin

Manor (Courtney 1990:93–4). **3** A synonym for *Cornish diamond* (q.v.) (O.E.D.).

Cornish Stone, the A monument in Australia erected by the C.A.N.S.W. (Cornish Association of New South Wales) to honour the past, present and future generations of Cornish people The inscription reads:

> "We name this stone *'The Cornish Stone'* and dedicate it
> to those Cornish Australians that have gone before us …
> We dedicate this *Cornish Stone* to the Cornish of today …
> We dedicate this *Cornish Stone* to the future …"

(cited in C.W. 1994,12, p.9). Moreover, Leggat uses the phrase *"Cornish stone"* to refer to *moorstone* (1987:8,30).

Cornish stone-built hedge Jenkin's term (1945:141) for a *Cornish hedge* (q.v.).

Cornish stone-faced hedge A term used (O.C. VI, 7, 1964) for the *Cornish hedge* (q.v.).

Cornish stone hedge See *Cornish hedge.*

Cornish stonehedging Another term for *Cornish hedging* (O.C. VI, 12, 1967, p.543 and Nicholls1986:9).

'Cornish stories' *'Cousin Jack stories'* or *'Cousin Jack narratives'* are given to the literary genre of Corrnish dialect about Cornishmen (Alan M. Kent uses the terms in C.S. 2nd, 12, 2004, p.106). See *Cornish novel.*

Cornish storm god Bucca (Jones 1997:14). See *Cornish Bucca.*

Cornish style *Cornish wrestling* (q.v.) as opposed to the similar Breton style and the Cumberland style, not to mention the free style or the old Devon style with kicking.The term is used by Jenkin (1984:71).

Cornish sub-committee (*Is kesedhek Kernow*) the body which represents the *Cornish language* at the European Bureau for Lesser Used Languages.

Cornish Sucker 1 (*L.lepadogaster*) Also called the *shore clingfish* or according to Borlase, the *suck-fish.* Turk believes that although this fish is common throughout the British west coast as far as the Hebrides, it is called 'Cornish' merely as it was first discovered by Borlase (1971:86). It is a reddish fish which is found in shallow water, slightly similar to Conch's sucker yet in this latter species the dorsal and anal fins are not joined to the tail fin (see Nance 1963:155). It has two eye-like marks on the back of its head and usues its pelvic fins to cling to rocks. **2** In Cornish dialect a *sucker* is another word for a piglet – like *slip* or *veer* (Hawke 1989:31).

Cornish Summer School (*Scol Haf Kernewek*) School for learning Cornish in the summer (C.S. 1st, Vol. 6, 1978, p.49).

Cornish Sunday Closing Bill There was a campaign to close pubs on Sunday in 1883 to follow the Welsh Sunday Closing Act of 1881 (see C.S. 2nd, 1997, p.138).

Cornish Super Giant, White Another name for the *Rock Cornish* Game (see appendix 1). It is used by the Hoffman Hatchery, Pennsylvania (on the internet site http://www.geocities.com/Heartland/Lake/5128/chickenbreeders.html).

Cornish Supper 1 A supper with a *Cornish pasty* (Wright 1986:16). **2** A dinner usually with talks and slide shows as often held by the Old Cornwall Societies (O.C. XII, 1, 1997, p. 47).

Cornish surfboard In the 1920s at Perranporth (and long before the sport was popular in the rest of Britain) "planks of wood were nailed together by the local coffin maker were the very first *Cornish surfboards*" (C.T. October 1998, p.8). The local names for surfing with these boards were *surf-riding* or *body-shooting* (O.C. XIII, 4, spring 2005, pp.13–14).

Cornish system, the Another name for *Cornish wrestling* (W.B. 22nd July, 1831).

Cornish taboo name The term is used by R. Morton Nance (J.R.I.C. Vol. 21, No. 72, 1925, p. 476). It applies to a form of language, especially used by fishermen in which words that applied to land objects or animals were given special names in order to avoid bad luck. For instance, a fox was *lostek* (Corn. 'big-tailed') and a hare *scovernak* (perhaps not as Nance suggests meaning 'long-eared' but a cognate of W. *ysgyfarnog*) (see Nance, ibid. pp.475–6). Yet the word *rabbit* refers to a streaked gurnard (Nance 1963:133) whereas *shore rabbits* are limpets (Turk 1971:19 ; cf. Dev. *longtailed rabbit is* a pheasant – Marten 1992:29). Often the word 'Cornish' is prefixed in order to distinguish it from taboo languages used also by Manx, Shetland and Orcadian fishermen which likewise substitute the names of land objects for taboo names but these names (called *haaf names* in the Shetlands) are very different.

Cornish tarot (Corn. *tarot Kernow*) A Cornish form of tarot cards with bilingual names (in *Kemmyn Kernewek* as well as English) and scenes depicting aspects of Cornish culture designed by Jonathan Kereve-Clarke. For more on cards see *Cornish whist*.

Cornish tartan Long before the recent *Cornish tartan* emerged, tartan was called in Cornish dialect *plod* or *plad* (i.e. plaid) (Jago 1882:237). For *Cornish kilt* (q.v.) designs see *Cornish hunting tartan* and *Cornish national tartan*. The use of a tartan is contrary to the idea of members of *Mebyon Kernow* in the 1950s: that the *Cornish kilt* should be of a plain dark colour (Deacon et al 2003:46).

Cornish tartan consciousness A new term that indicates the philosophy of some Cornish people who choose to wear a specific form of tartan dress, e.g. a *Cornish kilt* as an expression of their *Cornishness* (C.W. 37, 2004, p.30).

Cornish Tax Rebellion Term used for the *Cornish Rebellion* (q.v.) by Colin Allen (C.W. 1994, 11, p.33).

Cornish tea 1 Tea without sugar. Traditionally the Cornish do not put sugar in their tea. According to Merrick this custom is derived from Wesley's boycott of sugar as a protest against the slave trade (1995:9). However, if sugar is added the bubbles in tea that come from the sugar are called *shugger kiss* (Hawke 1975:53). The Cornish drink a *drop of warm* (Hawke 1989:19) or a *dish of tay* (i.e. cup of tea) (yet in Cornwall a *dish* was also a gallon of black tin paid to the mine lord). A *waiter* is a tea tray (Thomas 1895:133), a *milk cup* is the cream jug (Ivey 1976:44) and *browshams, groushams, grishens, grudgings* and *growts* (i.e. 'grounds') were some of the many Cornish names for the dregs of tea leaves with which fortunes were told. *Soddled* tea is tea made some time ago (Hawke ibid. 55) whereas with weak tea one says "water bewitcht tea begricht" (Hawke 1973:8) and to *vamp* a cup of tea is to fill it up (Phillipps 1993:58). There are several Cornish superstitions connected with tea drinking: tea leaves floating on tea are a sign of visitors and if one is served half a cup of tea they will be widowed whereas "if more than one lady pours from the teapot there may be family increases" (Hawke 1973: 14–5,18 and 20). Moreover, "stirring tea with aknife will cause trouble, especially if the blade is used" (C.W. 40, 2004, p.11). S 2 The *Cornish cream tea* (q.v.). Jenkin observes that generally the Cornishman does not take sugar with tea except when eating *Cornish pasties* (1984:71).

Cornish tea cakes Cakes made with flour, dripping, currants, milk, candied peel and mixed spice (Pascoe 1995).

Cornish Teeny Tiny As Hunt (1881:2nd, 452) refers to the story of the old woman who found gold teeth in the sands of Perranzabuloe. When a voice came at night asking for the teeth, she threw them away. In Halliweel's original story of Tenny Tiny an old woman takes bones from the churchyard to make soup but someone comes to demand their return. On a related note, Rosamund Venning recorded the unusual custom of the "burial of the teeth with the body" at Mawgan, Cornwall – the teeth being preserved in a box until the day of Resurrection (*Folklore* 5, 1984, p.343). Moreover, in contrast with English children who expect the tooth fairy to bring a coin (formerly a sixpence) for a milk tooth left under the pillow, Cornish "children's first teeth are burnt to prevent dog's teeth or *snaggles* – irregular teeth coming in their stead" (Courtney 1890:156–157).

Cornish Tertia, New As Stoyle refers to Sir Richard Grenville's armed regiment in 1644–6 (C.S. Vol. 4, p.26).

Cornish testament As Tangye describes the ballad by Rev. Hawker (1978:33). See *Cornish anthem*.

Cornish than Cornwall itself, more Phrase applied by W.G. Spence in 1889 to the Cornish immigrants of Moonta and Wallaroo, Australia (cited by Payton 1999:281). See next entry.

Cornish than the Cornish, more Allen Buckley uses this expression to refer to miners not born in Cornwall (C.T. 2, 1, August 1995, p.8). In an editorial Philip M.Hosken also uses this phrase (C.W. 20, p.20). The phrase seems coined by analogy to *more Irish than the Irish* (see Edwards 2004:170). See previous entry.

Cornish theatre in the round Term used by Lynette Olson (C.S. 2nd 5, 1998, p.54) for the *Cornish Rounds* (q.v.).

Cornish three hand reel Dance for a few people (not necessarily only three) to a lively tune and with *scoots* (see *Cornish step dancing*). The English Folk Dance and Drama Society have decided to include the "*Cornish 3-hand reel*" in their Key Stage 2 curriculum for children (see *E.F.D.S.S. Newsletter*, summer, 1995, p.2).

Cornish three-lives system An old form of village tenure (Rowse 1942:24).

Cornish Three Men's Song Type of fishermen's song with a three-part harmony and sung in Cornish (Jenkin 1945:131–2; Deane & Shaw 1975:79). One example is *Ha My Ow Mos* (see Davey 1983:35).

Cornish tie Black and gold like the *Cornish rugby shirt* (q.v.).

Cornish time An article from the *West Briton* (15th July, 1859) has been given the title "London Time or *Cornish Time*" (Barton ed. 1972:59). In Hayle the clock of Mr. Sandys indicated *Cornish time* and had another red hand which also showed the official G.M.T. which was twenty minutes earlier. Though this practice might sound rather eccentric it is very logical since Cornwall is to the extreme west and the sun rises later. For the same reason in U.S.A. San Francisco is three hours ahead of New York. The phrase became adapted by Cornishmen overseas. For instance, "*Cornish time*" also came to mean merely that which is two hours ahead of South African time (C.W. 8, 1996, p. 17).

Cornish Tin, Heart of As Lanner has been dubbed because of its rich tin mining heritage. See Sharon P. Schwartz and Roger Parker *Tin Mines and Miners of Lanner – the Heart of Cornish Tin* (pub. Halsgrove, Tiverton).

Cornish tin mine engine house Title of one of the Heritage models of the Trevithick Trust (C.W. 19, 1998/9, p.28). Another name for a *Cornish engine house* (q.v.).

Cornish tin miner See Cornish tinner.

Cornish tin mining evangelist, the Billy Bray (1794–1868) the tin miner (for this sobriquet see the internet site www.merlot-consultancy.co.uk). Like St. Piran – as in the phrase "as drunk as a *Piraner*" (see *Cornish patron saint*), Billy was a great Christian preacher who had some association with drink since he was a drunkard before he became converted (see *Cornish miner, the converted*) while he was reading Bunyan's work (see *Cornish Bunyan*).

Cornish tinner Cornish tin miner. The Cornish word for 'tinner' *stenor* (pl. *–yon*) also means 'wagtail'. By coincidence, another mining word also refers to a bird – since *palores* a 'female digger' also means the Cornish *chough* (q.v.).

Cornish Tinners, Patron saint of As St. Piran has been called (Williams 1987:23) for whom see *Cornish Patron saint*.

Cornish Tinners' holidays Apart from St. *Piran's Day* (5th March) which seems to have merged with the 'first Friday in *Lide*' (i.e. March) there was also *Picrous Day* held on the second Thusday before Christmas (when tin was supposedly discovered) and 'White Thursday' (*Chewhidden Thursday*) on the Thursday before Christmas when 'white tin' was first made in Cornwall. A *troil* was the word for a "tinner's feast" (Hawke – Hotchpotch) as was the word *duggle* (Jago 1882:319).

Cornish tin stamp Term sometimes used (e.g. by Brown and Acton 1994:12) for the *Cornish stamp* (q.v.).

Cornish tin streamer Another name for the *Cornish tinner* (q.v.) and sometimes with the word 'Cornish' prefixed (C.W. 15, 1997/8, p.18). *Streamers* were the miners who looked for *tin stream* or "tin ore found in the form of pebbles in valleys" and *stream works* the places where this tin was washed (Orchard 1990:36).

'Cornish' Titanic The *SS. Schiller* which sank off the Isles of Scilly in 1875 with the loss of 384 passengers (Cornish fishermen managed to save 43 on board). The *SS.Schiller* sank a few decades before the Titanic (which sank in 1912) yet it has been called "*Cornwall's Titanic*" (C.W. 29, 2002, p.4). Similarly a recent book by Keith Austin about the *SS.Schiller* is entitled *The Victorian Titanic* (pub. Halsgrove).

'Cornish' Toadflax There is a rare variety of toadflax the Latin name of which is *Linaria cornubiensis Druce* (C.S. 9, 1981:21).

Cornish toast *Pysk, sten ha cober* (i.e. fish, tin and copper). Ellis writes that "by 1920 a new toast had replaced it: 'china clay and tourists' " (1990:22). See also *Cornish fisherman's toast*.

Cornish together, to A phrase recorded by some (e.g. Courtney 1880:14 and Wright 1898–1905, Vol. 1, p.734) as synonymous with *Cornish a drink* (q.v.).

Cornish to heel An expression to describe a Cornishman or Cornish lady who is thoroughly Cornish 'to the bone' or Cornish 'form head to toe' (O.C. X, 11, 1990, p.561). The phrase is the equivalent of the Welsh *Cymro i'r carn* (i.e. 'Welshman to the heel').

Cornish token A form of coin usually paid to miners. and issued by a particular company. Tokens were often spent in *tommy shops* (like the *truck shops* in S. Wales) "at which men were virtually compelled to deal" (Jenkin 1945:244). In Cornish folklore *tokens* are also warnings of death like tapping (Jenkin ibid. 284). See *Cornish halfpenny*.

Cornish tol men Courtney referred to the "*Cornish tol-men, men-an-tol*" (1890:103) which is a holed stone. People would sometimes go through the hole three or nine time *widdershins* (anticlockwise)to be cured of a disease (Westwood 1992:38) (cf. *Cornish Pebble*). The Cornish term *tol men* is not to be confused with the *dolmen* which is a W. *cromlech*, Corn. *cromlegh*; Bret. *krommlec'h* ; Ir. *cromleac*). The word *toll* means hole (cf. W. *twll*; Bret. *toull*) and a compound with the word *men* or stone (Van. *mén*; W. and Bret. *maen*) would mutate (i.e. it would not be *tol-men* but *tolven*).

Cornish Tom As Dean and Shaw call giant-killer Tom of Bowjeyheer, as opposed to his East Anglian counterpart Tom Hickathrift (1975:99). See *Cornish giant legends*.

Cornish Tommy Knockers Term for the *Cornish knockers* (q.v.) used several times by Ronald M. James (*Western Folklore* 51, 1992, No.2, pp.155, .162 & 172). Perhaps there is a slight discrepancy in the *Cornish American* usage since *tommy-knockers* are described not as Jews or previous mine workers but "ghosts of men killed there" (Cassidy 1985:805).

Cornish ton 21 cwt as opposed to a legal ton of 20 cwt (Orchard (1990:38). Also known as the *Cornish mining ton*. Similarly a *burn* was 21 fish (Jago 1882:125).

Cornish tongue See *Cornish language* (q.v.). Apart from the word *yeth* (language), the other Cornish word for 'language' *tavas* means literally 'tongue' (c.f. W. *tafod* – tongue in the anatomical sense – yet *ar dafod*, i.e. 'on tongue' means 'spoken'). In many languages the word for 'tongue' is used to mean 'language' (e.g. Gk. *glossa*, Albanian *gjuhë*, Tk. *lisan* and Bulgarian *ezik*.). Even our word 'language' derives from the Lat. word for tongue (*lingua*).

Cornish topaz Nickname for the yellow transparent gemstone found on Marazion beach (Ferris p.17). Cf. *Scotch topaz* – a type of cairngorm stone. See *Cornish diamond*.

Cornish Topography, No man's land of "Parcels of land … left unused". and believed to be haunted by the *Cornish Bucca* (q.v.) (Payton 1996:28).

Cornish Tors The phrase *Cornish toors* is used often (e.g. by Tregarthen 1940: 187). A *tor* is a rock, prominence. In Cornwall *tor* also means "light turfy soil" (Thomas 1895:130).

Cornish towans As the Cornish sands have been called (O.C. Vol. VI, No. 10, spring 1996, p.468). The word *towan* (or forms thereof e.g. *towin* and *tewen*) also meant a green hillock (perhaps as there was grass on the dunes– see Jago 1882:197) and it is related to the word *tewas* or 'sand' (cf. W. *tywod*). In Cornwall sand was used to cover the doorstep at Christmas time (Courtney 1890:15) and in Morvah the newly-weds were beaten with a sack of sand (see '*Cornish*' *rough music*). See *Cornish horse* for the transportation of sand and *Cornish hurling* for the match on the sands.

Cornish tower The tower of a traditional *Cornish church* (q.v.). In *Cornish taboo language* (q.v.) the word *tower* was said instead of mentioning a particular church, especially Paul Church, Mount's Bay and St. Buryan's, (Nance 1963:164). Other terms used to avoid mentioning a church tower were *steeple* (even though a Cornish church has a tower – Nance ibid. 153) and *cleeta* (ibid. 59–60 ; from Corn. *cleghtour* i.e. 'bell-tower').

Cornishtown A Cornish neighbourhood in a foreign city where the *Cornish diaspora* has moved, e.g. "At Hill End, famous for its gold, the Cornish made up about one fifth of the population, living in a sector known as *Cornishtown*" (C.W. 10, 1996, p.31).

Cornish Town See *Cornishtown*.

Cornish town, quaint old An epithet of Helston, the venue of the *Cornish Flora Dance*. In Cornish dialect 'quaint' is *ancient* (Phillipps 1993:19).

Cornish towns As opposed to *Cornishtown* (q.v.) the *Cornish Towns* were the three towns of Moonta, Kadina and Wallaroo in an area called the 'Copper Triangle' in the Yorke Peninsula, Australia (C.W.W. 1991, 4, p.4).

Cornish traverse board An instrument shaped like a bellows (see *Cornish organ*) with a compass marked on one side and used to record the speed and direction travelled (Harris 1983:75).

Cornish treacle mines Mines believed to yield treacle (mentioned by Heard 1984:121). Parents told children such stories when treacle became more available and began to replace honey. In dialect it is *dryakel* (Merton 2003:61) and there is even a 'treacle pasty' (Merton ibid. 31).

'Cornish' Tree Nicholls calls the *Cornish Elm* (q.v.) 'Cornwall's native tree' (1986:7).

Cornish Trelawny Type of cheese (see internet site of Shell Bay Seafood Restaurant). See *Cornish Blue* for other cheeses.

Cornish tribute and tutwork system Term used by Payton (1999:245) to refer to the system by which miners worked for *tribute* (i.e. took a percentage of the ore they raised), in dialect form *tribit* (Deane & Shaw 1975:65). Moreover, *tutwork* meant piecework. The miners thus contracted were called *tributers* and *tutmen* respectively.

Cornish tributers The *tributers* were those miners who took the *tribute* (see previous entry).Often it is prefixed by the word 'Cornish' (e.g. in C.S. 2nd, Vol. 3, 1995, p.8 and C.S. 2nd, 9, 2001, p.124, n.32).

Cornish tribute system Term used by Scwartz (C.S. 2nd, 2001, p.114) for which see *Cornish tribute and tutwork system.*

Cornish trifle As Nancy Jonckheere says, this is "not to be confused with an English trifle". Apart from the basic sponge, it is made with *Cornish cream*, fresh fruit and hazelnuts (for ref. see *Cornish Christmas Cake*).

Cornish triskele The Celtic symbol found in ancient Cornish stonework which is similar to the Manx emblem but not so angular and is rather like a three-legged version of the Basque *lauburu* or rounded swastika (Basque *lau* four + *buru* head). The word 'triskele' (Gk. *triskelion*) means literally 'three legs' (Gk. *tri* three [cf. Corn. *try*] + *skelos* – leg.)

Cornish troyl A party with *Cornish step dancing* (q.v.) and *Cornish droll* (q.v.) telling. Jago described *troil* as a "tinner's feast"and a synonym of *duggle* (1882:299 – from Corn. *degol* – holiday). Possibly *troyl* is derived from Corn. *troyll* i.e. circuit, spiral or spin (perhaps from a circular dance movement). The word *troil/troyl* may also have a connection with the dialect word *troll* meaning to walk awkwardly (Phillipps 1993:55) (as though the feet hurt from too much dancing?) and thus corresponds with another meaning of *duggle* (or *doggle*) i.e. "to totter in walking" (Jago ibid.158 and 153).

'Cornish' turnip In Cornwall a turnip (*turmot* or *turmut*) is a swede (Merrick 2003:13).

Cornish turquoise As opposed to the greenish blue semi-precious turquoise, "*Cornish turquoise is* very pale blue… and not of true gem quality" (see Ferris p.21).

Cornish tye With reference to mining, Scwartz mentions a *Cornish tye* which was "a long trough to separate roughs from slimes by washing" (C.S. 2nd, 9, 2001, p.119). The word is derived from O.E. *teag* meaning chest or case. In Cornwall *tye* also means a feather bed (Thomas 1895:131).

Cornish tynner Old spelling of *Cornish tinner*.

Cornish type beam engine A synonym of the *Cornish beam engine* (q.v.).

Cornish Uitlanders The Cornish of South Africa (Payton 1999:360). Like the term *Cornish Afrikanders* (q.v.) it is pejorative in meaning since the Cornishmen's neutrality in the Boer War (1899–1902) was viewed by some as being pro-Boer. The Afrikaans/Dutch word *uitlander* was applied to the English settlers in Transvaal and is a cognate of the English word '*outlander*' which in Cornish dialect means a foreigner (Jago 1882:228). Cf. *Cornish foreigners*.

Cornish Underground Resistance Movement Epithet given to *Mebyon Kernow* by Arthur Caddick (C.S. 2nd, 7, 1999, p.133). See *Cornish Party*.

Cornish underheave A term for a move unique to *Cornish wrestling*. *Cornish wrestlers* themselves may just call it the *underheave* and, like the *pull-under*, it is a move used to counter the *fore crook* (throw over side of legs). There is also the *back heave* and the *fore heave* (as a counter to an attack).

Cornish underroast A dish of chunks of beef and kidney with onions. which is baked with potatoes in the oven. It is included in most good Cornish cookery books (e.g. Walker 1994:24 and Merrick 1995:6).

Cornish under roast Alternative spelling of *Cornish underroast* (which can also be spelt hyphenated – i.e. *Cornish under-roast* – see Merick 1995:6). The separate word form is used by some writers eg. Kittow (p.23).

Cornish undershot wheels In the water mill "*Cornish undershot wheels* were ... usually endowed with elm floats or paddles" (Benney 1972:29). These paddles were used in place of buckets common elsewhere. The undershot wheel was used where "a fierce fall of water was not available" and used in conjunction with a millpond or head weir to store water.

Cornish Unionists Those Cornish people who are not *Cornish Nationalists*

Cornish unit house Rawe refers to "the not unattractive *Cornish unit house*, half-tiled in most cases(slates being considered too expensive) and utilizing blocks made from china clay sand, went up on housing estates all over the Duchy" (1986:203).

Cornish University (Corn. *Unyversyta Kernow*) Just as there is a call in Cornwall for a *Cornish Assembly*, many would like to see a *Cornish University*. Apart from encouraging young Cornish people to stay nearer home, the establishment of a *Cornish University* provides a great support for Cornish culture. In K.K. instead of *unyversyta* the word *pennskol* is used (*penn* head + *skol* school; W. *prifysgol* – *prif* chief + *ysgol* school; Bret. *skol veur* 'big school'). Recently the Combined Universities in Cornwall (CUC) has been established with the hub at Tremough, Penryn. This is a partnership of universities and colleges serving Cornwall including Camborne School of Mines, University College, Falmouth and the Department of Cornish Studies of Exeter University. At present CUC offers over 400 university level courses.

Cornish Uprising As the *Cornish Rebellion* (q.v.) is sometimes called (C.W. 13, 1997, p.25 and C.T. summer 1997, p.7).

Cornish valve the double – beat valves of a *Cornish engine* (q.v.) (*The Encyclopedia Americana*, Vol.27, p.654).

Cornish van Jenkin refers to the '*Cornish van*' at one time used for both passengers and mail (1945:239). He writes "in its appearance the van resembled a long, four-wheeled spring cart, covered with canvas stretched over a framework and having curtains both at the back and at the front" (ibid. 237).

Cornish vandals, anti- *Mebyon Kernow* chairman Richard Jenkin denounced the activist group *An Gof* (see *Cornish Braveheart*) as "*anti-Cornish vandals*, not nationalists" (Deacon et al 2003:78).

Cornish vargord As opposed to the *fore-gourd*, a *Cornish vargord* is a spar with two forks set against the foremast of a boat (Nance 1963:170).

Cornish Vegetable soup with Hog's pudding Hog's pudding with soup of swedes, parsnips, carrots celery, red lentils and cream (Butcher & Annand 1994:7).

'Cornish' Velásquez, the Sir Joshua Reynolds hailed John Opie (for whom see the *Cornish Wonder*) as "like Caravaggio and Velásquez in one". Diego Velásquez (1599–1660) was the greatest Spanish artist and famous for his portraits.

Cornish vernacular The *Cornish dialect* (q.v.). Richard Gendall uses this term to refer to Cornish speech (O.C. X, 11, 1990, p.535) and Lyonesse Press also uses the same term to refer to its editions of dialect verse.

Cornish vexillology (*baneronieth Kernow*) "A project to gather information on Cornish flags, banners, ensigns, burgees." (C.W. 22, 2000, p.27). In Latin *vexillum* was a Roman standard. See *Cornish arms, Cornish ensign* and *Cornish flag*.

Cornish village Roose in Furness, Cumbria which housed labour demanded by the local mine in 1873 (see Bryn Trescatheric *Roose – A Cornish Village in Furness* (Barrow, 1983).

Cornish wafer A type of biscuit. It is even made by the Jacob's company.

Cornish wagon or barrel roof See *Cornish barrel roof*.

Cornish wain A unique type of Cornish cart. In 1840 Baker Peter Smith in *Trip to the Far West* described it thus: "The *Cornish wain*, on which they carry their crops, is a stage or floor or two wheels, having no side, front, or tail-boards. There is a semi-circular piece of wood-work placed over, and within the upper part of the wheel, which rises higher than the wain; and the load of corn or hay is secured on the wain by two ropes drawn from front to rear, which are strained tightly over the load, by means of a wind lass, attached to the tail of the wain" (cited in O.C. XII, 2001, p.60). A small donkey-driven cart with two wheels was called a *shay* (Ivey 1980:59). See *Cornish butt*, *Cornish cart*, *Cornish haywain*, *Cornish jackwain* and *Cornish wagon*.

Cornish Ware *Cornish china* ware but the term is often used mainly as a synonym of *Cornish Blue* (C.W. 16,1998, p.13).

Cornish wassailers Unlike the Devon and Somerset wassailers (who wassailed apple trees), the *Cornish wassailers* also visited homes (See Gendall and Gendall 1991:8). The wassailers often knocked the door with this rhyme:

> "Now Christmas is comen and New Year begin
> Pray open your door and let us come in."

Before visiting they would take a *clomben* cup of cider or *lambswool* (hot milk, eggs, sugar and nutmeg; cf. *Cornish eggyot*) to the apple trees. Some was drunk and the rest was thrown over the trees (Hunt 1881, 2nd, 387). In east Cornwall the *Warsail Boys* begged for money "in exchange for hot spiced ale" (Day 2000:189). The word *wassail* is derived form O.N. *ves heill* (be in health). Apart from wassailing, apple-growers would ensure a good crop by not picking all the fruit. Some were left for the *piskies* (C.W. 40, 2004, p.11). Possibly the ritual of wassailing was originally performed for the good yield of all fruit trees. The apple merely represented fruit in general (in O.E. *æppel* meant any kind of fruit not just an apple).

Cornish water god, the With reference to St. Nectan, Dan Bloomfield writes "there never was a St. Nectan: the name is a Christianised form of the *Cornish water god* – Nechtan" (C.W. 40, 2004, p.46).

'Cornish' water horse Cornish folklore may not have an exact equivalent of the Welsh *ceffyl dŵr* or the Irish *each/capall uisce*, Manx *cabbyl-ushtey* and Scottish *each uisage* or *kelpie* who sometimes drown their riders. Nevertheless, Deane and Shaw refer to a "phantom white horse" whose rider "was swept away and drown" (1975:110). However, unlike its Celtic counterparts, instead of drowning its rider, it was seen "patiently waiting on the beach for its master". *Cornish horses* (q.v.) are sometimes victims of the rider – i.e. are *piskey-ridden* (see *Cornish piskey*). Thus one farmer was afraid of his horse drowning him in a *piskey bog* (Tregarthen 1940:62).

Cornish water mill Benney describes the "typical *Cornish water mill*" as being adjoined by a miller's dwelling. The wheel was positioned on the side wall (1972:69). See *Cornish mill*.

Cornish water wheel The word 'Cornish' is sometimes prefixed to indicate the specific water wheel that was used in mining (e.g. on the internet page of *The Gold Pan City* about Quesnel in British Columbia). The wheel was fitted with buckets or paddles and driven by weight or water force.

Cornishway Spelt as one word. In 1979 the Mebyon Kernow candidate Len Truran had the slogan:

> "Lib-Lab –Tory have had their day
> Vote *Mebyon Kernow* the *Cornishway*" (cited in C.S. 2nd, 9, 2001, p.199).

Cornish Way, Royal Rawe writes that "Launceston was the beginning of the *Royal Cornish Way* – for kings, earls and dukes of Cornwall entered via Polson" (1986:41).

Cornish weather Light continuous rain with mild temperatures. Rawe writes "they had their share of *'Cornish weather'* – being told that the fine drizzle could last a fortnight" (1986:104). See *Cornish mist*. The Cornish expression *hurling-weather* means "drying weather" (Thomas 1895:95). In *Cornish dialect* weather is *wedder* (Ivey 1976:74).

Cornish weather dog The broad rainbow on the horizon which is a sign of rain (Stevens prefixes the word *'Cornish'*, p.20). In the Cornish language this phenomenon was called *lagas awel* (Nance 1963:104) from *lagas* (eye or patch of blue sky) and *awel* (air or wind) (c.f. the Welsh cognates *llygad* – eye and *awel* – breeze; Bret. *lagad + avel*). See *Cornish mist*, *Cornish time* and *Cornish weather*.

Cornish wedding 1 A wedding in which the groom wears a *Cornish kilt*. **2** Wedding in which the service is conducted in Cornish with the couple both saying '*Mynnaf*' (I will). Such a wedding took place at St. Piran's Church, Perran-ar-worthal yet the service was bilingual since English had to be used as well (*W.B.* 1 Oct, 1964).

Cornish well As the *peeth* is described (C.W. 34, 2003, p29). "It was a well about four feet in circumference … there was stone all the way round to stop the earth coming in … across the well was a fixture, a piece of wood about a foot in circumference with an iron chain … the depth of the *peeth*. We used to tie the bucket handle to the chain and we would lower it down" (ibid. p.28). Many *peeths* in Cornwall were associated with saints and known for cures, e.g the leeches in Boscawell Well. Courtney refers to wells such as a *boussening well* and a "*ducking well* for the cure of a mad person" (1890:61). Rags or *clooties* could be hung on trees near wells as votive offerings (see Leggat 1987:15) and pins were also dropped into wells.

Cornish well house Small house at a well built of rectangular *Cornish stone* blocks with a high roof and pointed arch (Leggat 1987:30).

Cornish wheel The round headed Celtic stone cross (Pearse uses the term twice, p.10). This kind of cross is said to combine the symbols of the cross and the sun.

Cornish wheelbarrow "The wheelbarrows are six feet long and about fifteen inches wide, being well adapted to carrying heavy metals and ores in the mines, by reason of the long handle acting as a lever, while the narrowness is adapted to the confined passages and *adits* in which they work" (O.C. Vol. XII, No. 9, 2001, p.60; Payton also refers to the *Cornish wheelbarrow* – 1999:167). In dialect the wheelbarrow is a *wheel-barra/berrer* (Ivey 1976: 75) while a *gurry* was a "large hand-barrow for carrying fish" (W.B. 23 Nov.1821). Sometimes an *anker and dandy* (barrel) would be fixed onto the wheelbarrow (see Hawke 1989), especially by *Cornish fairtraders* (q.v.). Sometimes a 'foreigner' from a neighbouring village who courted a local girl was forced to ride in a dirty wheelbarrow by the girl's fellow-villagers (Deane & Shaw 1975:53–4). A wheelbarrow also took a *stan* (barrel for water) (Hawke 1975:58).

Cornish wheel cross See *Cornish wheel.*

Cornish whiddle A tale (or whim) that would perhaps be told by a *Cornish droll* (q.v.). The phrase is used in Mrs. Frank Morris' *Cornish Whiddles for Teenin' Time* (1898). Perhaps the word has some connection with *lidden* (an often told tale) (Jago 1882:208). *Whiddle* is not to be confused with *widdle* (to wriggle or squirm – Thomas 1895:134). The word is from the Cornish *whethel* meaning tale or story (cf. W. *chwedl*).

Cornish whim A machine which raises ores. It can be worked by steam, water or by horse. The *Cornish whim* worked slowly and therefore there were fewer accidents.

Cornish whist The game of *euchre* as it is played mainly in Cornwall (see Payton 1999:303). Euchre is so called as *Yewker* is a corruption of the 'Joker' card which in Cornwall is called *Benny* (C.W.W. 21, 1997, p.42). From this game there is even the dialect word *euchered* i.e. 'cornered' (James 1979:48). *Whist with swabs* was another Cornish variation of whist played (like *Board'em* and *Ranter-go-round* or *Miss Joan*) at Christmas (Day 2000:181).

Cornish White 1 An old breed of poultry (Caine and Gorton 2001: 8 and 34). **2** A white violet hybrid. **3** A breed of pig. See *Cornish White, Lop-eared.* **4** A variety of *Cornish Heather* (for ref. see *Cornish Gold*). See *Cornish Cream* for other heather varieties.

Cornish White, Lop-eared A breed of pig (Mason 1951). See *Cornish Large Black*.

Cornish white clay As *Cornish clay* (q.v.) is sometimes called. Indeed in Cornish the word for clay is *pry gwyn* (literally 'white clay').

'Cornish' white gold Or rather *"Cornwall's white gold"* as *Cornish clay* (q.v.) has been called (C.W. 9, pp.8–9). See *Cornish gold*.

Cornish White Laced Red See *white laced red Cornish* in appendix 1.

'Cornish' Whuppity Stoorie Weatherhill and Devereux describe the story of Duffy and the Devil (See *Cornish Rumpelstiltskin*) as the "Cornish version" of the Scottish Whuppity Stoorie (1994:106).

Cornish-wide That which pertains to all of Cornwall (term is used by Whetter 1977:69).

'Cornish' wild hunt Deane and Shaw (1975:110) compare the wild dogs of Cornish legends with the Norse hounds. Such dogs include the *Cheney hounds*, *Dando's dogs*, *wish hounds*, *yell/yeth hounds* (like the Dev. *zet ounds*) and the *Bargest* (see Hunt 1881). Their Welsh equivalents are the *cŵn Annwn* or 'dogs of Shades' (cf. *Cornish Shades*). See *Cornish ghost-dog*.

Cornish wild pony As the *Cornish Goonhilly* pony has been called (C.S. 1st, 1973:11).

'Cornish' William Tell White informs us that one "Mr Trefusis gave the boy a guinea for allowing him to shoot a mark directkly above the boy's head in the style of William Tell but with a pistol" (1994:14–15). William Tell was the Swiss hero (fl. early C14th) who was ordered by the Duke of Austria's steward Gessler to hit an apple on his son's head with an arrow.

Cornish Wine Apple A variety cultivated by Dorothy Pelling and Ted and Sheila Jeffries at a vineyard and cider farm near St. Keverne. They aimed to take grafts to make a pink apple wine (C.W. 7, 1995/6, p.36). See *Cornish Aromatic* for other apple varieties.

Cornish wit As Ian Glanville refers to the distinct "Cornish (*Cousin Jack*) style of humour" involving the "misplacement of words" which is the hallmark of a *Cornish joke* (q.v.) (*St. Just's Point*, Bendigo, Victoria, n.d. cited by Kent in C.S. 2nd, 2004, p.141).

Cornish witch The traditional *Cornish witch* was said to ride on stalks of ragwort not a broom (just like the Turkish witch who rides on a *küp* or large earthenware vessel not unlike the Cornish *bussa*). In Cornish a witch is called *colyoges* a diviner or soothsayer (from *col* divination or omen), *pystryores* (from *pystry* sorcery, magic) and more commonly the word is *gwragh*. This word *gwragh* can connote a hag or the fish wrasse (see *Cornish loan words* – significantly the Bret. *gwrac'h* for 'witch' also refers to a type of fish). Interestingly the Welsh cognate *gwrach* or hag, witch is also the word used for the last sheaf of harvest (i.e. the neck in Cornwall) and the Irish word *cailleach* has identical nuances. It is thus possible that the Cornish harvest *neck* was named after the word *gwar* (Corn. 'neck') when it could easily (as in Wales and Ireland) have been named 'hag' after the *gwragh*. Clemo gives us the dialect word *witnick* meaning "witch or mad person" (p.106). Witches can also turn into hares. See *Cornish coven*.

Cornish Witch Finder, the Sobriquet of the folklorist William Henry Paynter (1901–76) whose research in the 1920s and 1930s saved many already dying traditions and practices of *Cornish cunning folk*. The epithet is recorded by Jason Semmens (*Folklore* 116, April2005, p.79). See *Cornish Charmer*.

Cornishwoman (Corn. *kernewes*, pl. *–ow*) Spelt as one word.

Cornishwoman, the Big (Fr. *La Grande Cornouallaise*) As the Bretons called famous Cornish folk singer Brenda Wooton (see C.W. 1994, 12, p.16). Perhaps the 'Great Cornish Lady' would be a more appropriate epithet, especially since in Cornish dialect *large* can mean 'conceited' (Phillipps 1993:39). See *Cornish Folk Music, the Queen of*.

Cornishwomen Spelt as one word. See *Cornishwoman*.

Cornish Wonder, the John Opie (1761–1807). According to Brewer (1870) this epithet was given by 'Peter Pindar' (John Wolcot). Selleck calls him the "Wondrous Cornishman" (1992). Artist famous for his portraits. He painted Dolly Pentreath (see *Cornish speaker, last*) while still a teenager. He was noted for his rich use of colours and shade. When someone asked him what he used to mix those colours, he replied " I mix them with my brains, sir". In *Cornish dialect* the word *wonders* means "fingers shaking with cold" (Curnow 2002:23). See *'Cornish' Caravaggio* and *'Cornish' Velásquez*.

Cornish wool See *Cornish hair*.

Cornish wrassler Alternative spelling of *Cornish wrestler*.

Cornish wrasslin' Alternative dialect form of *Cornish wrestling* (q.v.) The similar Devon dialect forms are *rasselin* (Downes 1986:26) or *wrassling* and *wraxling* (Downes ibid. 82).

Cornish wrastler In C18th the poet Chatterton used this dialect spelling for *Cornish wrestler* (q.v.) (cited by Deane and Shaw 1975:167).

Cornish wrastling A *Cornish dialect* from of *Cornish wrestling* (q.v.). Phillipps gives the spelling *wrassling* (1993:60). W.T. Hooper also uses the word wrasting (J.R.I.C., Vol. 2, 1953–56, p.88).

Cornish wrestler (Corn.*omdowlor, gwrynyer*)An athlete of *Cornish wrestling* (q.v.). The Cornish principle of 'fair play' (as seen in the *Cornish hurling motto*) also applies to the *Cornish wrestler* who is noted for his sportsmanship (any wrestler who bargained to lose a contest was shunned as a *fagot*). The *Cornish wrestler* has to learn a variety of complicated moves and be very strong and fit. Sometimes a *Cornish wrestler* has been placed to wrestle against wrestlers of similar styles e.g. Breton and Cumberland.

Cornish wrestler's standard The colours are gold and royal blue (C.W. 37, 2004, p. 29).

Cornish wrestling Style of wrestling popular in Cornwall. Unlike the dirty Devon style of 'wrestling' in which kicking was allowed, the art of *Cornish wrestling* is defined by strict rules. Each wrestling match is refereed by a *stickler*. See *Cornish hug* and *Cornish underheave*.

Cornish wrestling, Cornish carols, Cornish pasties and saffron cake, home of Long Gully, Australia where Cornish miners emigrated (Payton 1999:234). It was also called 'Bendigo's Little Cornwall'.

Cornish wrestling jacket A white sailcloth jacket with loose sleeves worn by *Cornish wrestlers* (the term is used in C.T. 9,1995, p.39). *Marks* (good points in school but bad points in *Cornish wrestling*) are given against a wrestler who slips out of his jacket to avoid being thrown. If a wrestler performs the *crowbar hitch* (by passing his arm inside an opponent's jacket for leverage) it is a foul. Another foul is when the opponent pulls the jacket too tight and does what is known as the *cross collar*. Moreover, the *flying mare* is performed by gripping the jacket on the top cords and swinging. In fact the jacket is very important for this sport – hence the term "jacket wrestling" (C.W. 24, 2001, p.16).

Cornish wrestling meet A tournament of *Cornish wrestling* (Payton uses the term 1999:218). In Cornish a wrestling match is *fyt omdowl*. The word *meet* is also used for a fox hunters' gathering e.g. at St. Just on the Monday nearest to 31st October.

Cornish XV The Cornish rugby team (C.T. 8,1995, p.15). See *Cornish rugby shirt*. The Cornish rugby supporters have been dubbed *Trelawny's Army* (C.S. 2nd, 12, 2004, p.5). Cf. the *Green Army* (supporters of the Irish football team) and the *Tartan Army* (supporters of the Scottish football team).

Cornish-Yankee accent A hybrid accent which in the *Cornish Cousin Jack* communities of America was "the natural twang among the miners" (Payton 1999:377). See *Cornish brogue*.

Cornish yard In dialect the *gunnies* (a word meaning literally a yard – i.e. three feet) was used without refence to feet. Hence four and a half feet would be '*a gunnies an a half*' (Jago 1882:321). In Cornish 'yard' is *lath* (cf.W. *llath*) or *gwelen* (literally 'rod' or 'pole') and *kevelyn* was half a yard or cubit.

Cornish Yarg A cow's milk cheese produced at Lynher Dairies, Netherhorn. The name derives from the surname 'Gray' spelt backwards since it was Allan and Jenny Gray who gave the recipe to Netherton Farm. See *Cornish Sting, Operation*. For other cheese varieties see *Cornish Blue*.

Cornish yeast buns Buns made with milk and currants (see internet site *Cornish Recipes*).

Cornish Yellow Like *Cornish Green*, this is a variation of the original *Cornish Blue* crockery. This type of *Cornishware* has characteristic stripes of 'yellow' or *yalla* in dialect (actually more like a creamy beige than yellow) and white.

Cornish yeomanry A force of Cornish freeholders or yeomen (the term is used in C.S. 1, 1973 pp.63–4). The word yeoman is Middle English (*yoman*, *yeman* probably means 'young man').

'Cornish' Yes Like Welsh, Cornish does not have a word for either 'yes' or 'no'. Instead affirmative replies correspond with the tense. For instance, 'Are you Cornish?' 'I am', 'Can he drive?' 'He can'. So apart from *aye* another way evolved. Jago wrote: "A Cornishman has a way of answering 'yes' which cannot be written or spelt. It is thus done. The teeth a little apart and the mouth rounded, a sudden and sibilant inspiration is made. The sound produced is meant for 'yes' and is equivalent to a nod" (1882:314). Hawke records this unique sound as *Shh* – a "sound made by drawing the breath in sharply"(1975:53).

Cornish yule log "The *Cornish yule log* was called a '*mock*' or '*block*' and was usually ignited with a piece of the previous year's log, sometimes with the figure of a man engraved upon it" (Deane & Shaw 1975:187). It was also called a *mot* (O.C. Vol. XI, No. 9, autumn 1995, p.466). The name *block* is also seen in the Irish *bloc na Nollag* (i.e. Christmas log) and another Cornish dialect word for it was *stock* (Courtney 1890:7). In the Cornish language the term is *etew Nadelek*. While the Yule log is found in most European countries, the unusual Cornish custom of drawing a human form on the *mock* can also be seen in the *Cailleach Noillaich* ('Christmas Old Hag') in the Scottish Highlands (Day 2000:175). The Catalan custom is to make a *tió de Nadal* (also called *tronca*) which is a hollowed

Christmas log on which a smilng face and red *barretina* (little sock hat) is placed. It gives children a present if they strike it. In Cornish dialect confusingly the word *yule* is the east Cornish form of *evil* (a manure fork – Phillipps 1993:29) and *mock* is also apple cheese in cider making (Jago 1882:220). See *Cornish Bush* and *Cornish Christmas tree.*

Cornish zaffern cake Alternative form of *Cornish saffron cake* (q.v.) often heard since "the Cornish letter 's' is commonly pronounced as 'z'" (Dean &Shaw 1975:162) like the case of the choir clerk Hawke mentions who would "zing any zong" (1989:13). *Zaffern* or *saffern* is *Cornish dialect* for saffron (cf. Dev. saffron – Marten 1992:46).

APPENDIX 1
Phrases which end with the word 'Cornish'

A bit Cornish (When applied to a young lady) in slang it means very attractive (for etymology see *Cornish pasty*). By contrast, the apparent compliment *a pretty beauty* refers to "a woman of no reputation" (Phillipps 1993:21).

Acre Cornish Just as one talks of a penny Scots, so the word 'Cornish' can sometimes follow rather than precede a noun. For instance, E. Smirke wrote of an *"acre Cornish"* (J.R.I.C., 1962, p.39). See *Cornish acre*.

Ancient Cornish A pattern (or as the Scotsmen would say 'sett') of *Cornish tartan* in the Aristocratic Cornish Tartans series. Other tartans in this series include *Modern Cornish*, *Modern Hunting Cornish* and *Natural Cornish*.

Anglo-Cornish As some, e.g. Jones (2001:3) and Kent (C.S. 11, 2003, P.130) call the *Cornish Dialect*.

Arbor Acres Cornish Apart from the main varieties of *Cornish Game* (in this appendix) the internet site for the National Poultry Improvement Plan records other subvarieties: *Arbor Acres C.*(i.e. *Cornish*), *Cebe Black C.*, *Cebe Gold C.*, *Cebe Red C.*, *Dominant C.*, *Ideal C.*, *Penobscot Red C.* and *Harman Red C.*

Broken Cornish Incorrect Cornish (language) as opposed to *Cornish dialect*. Ivey uses this term to describe the Cornish expression *nag'os a beej* (i.e. not for the world) (1976:46). The phrase contains the Cornish negative participle *nag* and the *beej* (from the Corn. *bys* world ; cf. W. *byd* and Bret. *bed*). Possibly the 'a' is a contracted form of the article *an*.

Buff Cornish A variety of *Cornish hen*.

Celtic Cornish As Jago referred throughout his glossary to the *Cornish Language* (q.v.) as opposed to the *Cornish Dialect* (e.g. 1882:105, 108, 109, 110).

Celto-Cornish Term used (e.g. by Alan M. Kent in C.S. 2nd 10, 2002, p.226) to refer to the Celtic (i.e. non-English) cultural heritage of Cornwall.

Christian Cornish The pure *Cornish language* (q.v.) With reference to a *Cornish miracle play* (q.v.) of 1611, Jenkin observes "the tradition of putting foreign words – English, Latin and French – into the mouths of unbelievers, torturers or devils, such creatures by an unwritten law being seemingly forbidden to speak good *Christian Cornish*" (1945:130). An analogous use of the word 'Christian' can be seen in O.E. word *cristen* (i.e. Christan) which was applied to "the English as opp[osed to the Danes" (Hall 1894:75). This corresponds exactly with the Spanish phrase *hablar en cristiano* (to speak in the Christain language) – i.e. in Spanish and metaph. straightforwardly).

Common Cornish *(Kernewek Kemmyn)* The spelling form of Cornish devised by Ken George. Initially George's system was welcomed as an ostensible improvement on Nance's spelling system (see *Unified Cornish*). However, *Common Cornish* has received some criticism. Not only has its creation been accused of causing unnecessary division among the small number of Cornish speakers but it has also been attacked on linguistic grounds (see *Unified Cornish Revised*). However, George has robustly defended the system.

Computer Cornish As supporters of *Unified Cornish* have dubbed *Common Cornish* (see C.S. 2nd, 1, 1993, p. 113).

Crockpot Cornish Recipe with *Cornish Game* (q.v.) boiled for six hours with rice underneath and pecan nuts (see internet page http://freefoodrecipes.com/).

Dark Cornish A strain of *Cornish Game* hen.

Double Cornish Term used by Alan M. Kent (C.S. 2nd, 12, 2004, p.142, n.111) and refers to the Cornish people's dual linguistic heritage of their *Cornish language* and their *Cornish dialect*.

Early Cornish An early variety of what was most probably a potato, recorded by James Stevens in late C19th (1977:56 and 75).

Fast Cornish Like *Cornish Slow*, it is a *Cornish Cross* (q.v.) which is a good broiler. It is bred by the Privett Hatchery of New Mexico (for ref. see *Cornish Super Giant*).

Galvinised Cornish In a review of Gage Mckinney's book *When Miners Sang – The Grass Valley Carol Choir*, Ann Trevenen Jenkin observes "McKinney has some interesting comments to make on *Cornishness*. In Grass Valley, those who embrace the Cornish spirit even if they are not Cornish, are known as '*galvinised Cornish*'" (C.W. 28, 2002, p.57). Perhaps this term derives from Payton's words (not used as a phrase) that the arrival of the Chinese in S. Africa "galvinised Cornish opinion" (1999:361).

German 'Cornish' or rather *German Cornwall* A breed of pig (Mason 1951). See *Cornish Large Black* and *Cornish White*, *Lop-eared*.

Insular Cornish Term used by Eugene V. Graves as opposed to Breton (O.C. VI, 7, 1964, p.328).

Last dregs from the cup of Cornish, the As Newton-Webb (cited by Jones

2001:7) refers to the community of Cornish speakers (tin miners, their families and their descendants) who went to the Bay of Biscay area in France in 1771 (i.e. Cornish was apparently still thriving there only six years before the last reputed speaker Dolly Pentreath died in 1777).

Late Cornish (*An Cornoack lebben*) the form of Cornish revived in the first instance by Richard Gendall which represents a realistic evolution of the latest form of the language. Some of the vocabulary still exists, albeit in altered forms in the *Cornish Dialect*. By contrast Nance and others chose to revive the earlier and purer form of the language.

Lop-eared Cornish See *Cornish white, lop-eared*.

Medieval Cornish So *Unified Cornish* is sometimes called.

Middle Cornish The form of Cornish (1200–1575).

Modern Cornish (*Curnoack Nowedga*) **1** Term used by Gendall as a synonym of *Late Cornish*. **2** A pattern of *Cornish tartan* (see *Ancient Cornish* in this appendix).

Modern hunting Cornish A pattern of *Cornish tartan* also called *Cornish hunting tartan* (q.v.). See also *Ancient Cornish* (appendix 1).

Natural Cornish A pattern of *Cornish tartan* (see Ancient Cornish).

Neo-Cornish Glanville Price's term for the modern forms of the *Cornish language* (Williams 1995:8 ; C.S.2nd, 6, 1998, p.191).

New Cornish See *Cornish Tertia, New*

Old Cornish 1 The form of the Cornish Language from 800–1200 as seen in the glosses of the Bodmin gospel and in a Cornish Latin word list (*Vocabularium Cornicum*) **2** The regiment (C.S. 4, p.26).

Phonemic Cornish As *Common Cornish* (q.v.) is also called since "the orthography was so devised as to represent any one phoneme (i.e. basic letter sound) by a unique symbol or a set of symbols" (Williams 1995:99).

Pidgin Cornish 1 Correctly speaking this term should apply to imperfect speech of the *Cornish lanuage* as opposed to *Cornish dialect*. **2** In a cartoon Farmer Tregorrah believes that the Bretons speak "*Pidgin Cornish*" (cited by Whetter 1977:133).

Primitive Cornish The earliest form of Cornish (600–800) of which no written records exist. This form of Cornish was still very similar to early Welsh and almost identical to early Breton.

Revived Cornish As the newly recreated forms of the *Cornish Language* have been called as opposed to the actual forms of the past (e.g. George uses the phrase – cited by Williams 1995:109).

Rock Cornish A poultry hybrid of Plymouth Rock and *Cornish Game* which is plump and has good meat.

Slow Cornish See *Fast Cornish*.

To Cornish See *Cornish a drink* and *Cornish together*.

Tokenistic Cornish Kenneth Mackinnon's term for the systematic use of a smattering of Cornish everywhere as a concession to both tourists and locals (C.S. 2nd, 10, 2002, p.280). It is the equivalent of the *cúpla focal* or few token words of Irish in a speech that is in English.

Traditional Cornish Term used by Gendall as synonymous with *Late Cornish*.

Tudor Cornish As Merfyn Philips (an advocate of *Modern/Late Cornish*) refers to *Unified Cornish* (*The Celtic Pen*, Vol. 3, Issue 1, winter 1995/6, p.8). As Williams observes, by the Tudor period the Cornish language shows evidence of what he calls "the Armorican return" since Breton settlers had added words to Cornish (1995:69).

Unified Cornish (*Kernewek Unyes*) The original revived form of Cornish devised by Morton Nance (hence sometimes also called *Mordonnek* – there is, however, also the adjective *Nancean* see O.C. 2nd, 3, 1995, p.211). As opposed to *Late Cornish*, *Unified Cornish* is based on Cornish words found in earlier texts.

Unified Cornish Revised Modified form of Unified Cornish devised by Williams which is closely derived from Nance and emerged as a reaction against *Common Cornish*.

White Cornish A variety of *Cornish Game*. In America most supermarket chicken broilers are "a cross between *White Cornish* and White Plymouth Rock" (C.W. 23, 2000, p.21).

White Laced Red Cornish A strain of *Cornish Game*.

APPENDIX 2
Phrases with the word
'Cornishman/Cornishman's'

Cornishman's Bible, the An epithet of the *West Briton* newspaper (coined by Ince 2001:5). The full name of the newspaper was *The West Briton and Cornwall Advertiser*. See *Cornish Bible*.

Cornishman's Church, the church of Llangerniw in Denbighshire, Wales has been called "*The Cornishman's Church*" (J.R.I.C. Vol. 6, 1878–81, p.98). Indeed, etymologically the name indicates this since the prefix *llan* (similar to the Corn. *lan*) indicates a place where there is a church (as opposed to an actual church which is *eglwys* or in Corn. *eglos*) and *gerniw* seems a mutated form of *Cernyw* (the Welsh for Cornwall).

Cornishman's disease With reference to 'chronic diabetes'. Alan M. Kent writes "this condition is often called '*Cornishman's disease*' due tio its prevalence among the Cornish" (C.S. 2nd, 12, 2004, p.140, n.42). See *Cornish malaise*.

Cornishman's dream As the *Cornish pasty* is dubbed (C.T. July 1998, p.16)

Cornishman's gift An expression (used e.g. by Hawke 1975:14) which is identical in meaning with *Cornish compliment*. This is not to be confused with the Cousin Jack gift which was the prize for the Cornish miners' running race in C19th Adelaide (Jauncey 2004:94). In Cornish dialect gifts are white patches on the nails. The rhyme goes:

> "A *gift* on the thumb is sure to come
> A *gift* on the finger is sure to linger" (Couch 1871:84).

Another connection between gifts and nails is that "the Cornish believed that if you cut your nails before breakfast on a monday you would have a present next Monday" (Day 2003:182).

Cornishman's handshake Payton informs us that Cornish miners overseas "would recognize each other by the *Cornishman's handshake*, the palm outwards" (1999:356). It is analogous to the *dap* or *soul handshake* used by Afro-Americans (in the Vietnam War this was forbidden on the grounds that it reflected an exclusive bond among certain soldiers – see Clark 1990:478). The Freemasons have also been known to use a special handshake as a form of identification and the hippies used the *brothers' handshake* with the hand held upwards and thumbs locked (McCleary 2002:70). By contrast, a *French handshake* in slang refers to a "suggestive" handshake (Green 1998:447). Moreover, *Cornish wrestlers* give a standard handshake (i.e. not a *Cornishman's handshake*) before a contest, each hitch and each bout. This is done not only out of courtesy but to prevent an unfair grip or foul.

Cornishman's metal As gold has been called since Cornish mining expertise was indispensable in many areas where gold was mined (Payton 1999:300). Yet Payton says that this phrase is also applicable to tin and copper. The largest gold nugget in the world, the Welcome Stranger was found by the two Cornishmen Oates and Deason in Australia in 1869.

Cornishman's tail See *Cornishmen's tails* in main dictionary.

APPENDIX   3
Phrases with the word 'West'

Bath of the West, the As Ian Clark observes, "By the end of the eighteenth century, Truro had become an elegant georgian town, a *'Bath of the West'* " (C.S. 2nd, 12, 2004, p.186). See *Cornish capital* and *Cornish London*.

"Falstaff of the West, the See *Cornish Giant*.

Go the West 'ome "An emphatic way of saying 'Go home' (Thomas 1895:90). Perhaps the analogy is that the person should go right into the sea.

Land of the West Welsh Epithet for Cornwall (Ellis 1985:135).

Paradise of the Western World Scilly (C.T. April 1998).

Rob Roy of the West, the Epithet of Jack Ruttenbury (b. Devon, 1778) (Martin 1951:132 and 164–5).

Song of the Western Men See *Cornish national Anthem*.

South West Term which, like *Devonwall* (for which see *Cornish Dumnonia*) reflects a policy of treating Cornwall only as part of a larger region (See Deacon et al 2003:85 and 109). The phrase can be seen in west country bodies throughout Cornwall such as South West Water and South West Electricity board.

West Barbary, the Land of Cornwall (Jenkin 1945:143). This slightly pejorative epithet perhaps derives from allusions to wreckers. The name *Barbary* really means land of the Berbers (of N. Africa) and is not to be confused with 'barbarian' (from Gk. *barbaros* – someone who speaks a foreign language, i.e. not Greek).

West Briton 1 A Cornishman – hence the name of the popular newspaper. **2** The same phrase in Hiberno-English has the pejorative connotations of an Irishman who is pro-British.

Western Gorse See *Cornish fuzz*.

Western Land Another epithet for Cornwall. It is seen in *Cornish Bells* (q.v.).

Westernmost town in England See *Cornishmost town in Cornwall*.

West-ome Way home (Ivey 1980:74). See *Get the West 'ome*.

West Welsh The Cornish (for which see *Cornish foreigners*).

BIBLIOGRAPHY

Alexander, Marc (2002) *A Companion to the Folklore, Myths and Customs of Britain* (Sutton, Bath).

Arthur, M. M. Marshel (1955) *The Autobiography of a China Clay Worker* (Federation of Old Cornwall Societies).

Asala, Joanne (1998) *Celtic Folklore Cooking* (Llewellyn Publications).

Ayto, John (2002) *Oxford Dictionary of Rhyming Slang* (rep. 2003, O.U.P.).

Baker, Margaret (1996) *Discovering the Folklore of Plants* (Shire Publications).

Baring-Gould, S. (1908) *Cornish Characters and Strange Events* (John Lane:The Bodley Head, London, rep. as *Strange Cornish Characters* (Oakmagic, Penzance, 1997).

Barber, Richard and Anne Riches (1971) *A Dictionary of Fabulous Beasts* (Boydell Press, Woodbridge, rep. 2000).

Baron, Stanley (1934) *Westward Ho! From Cambria to Cornwall* (Jarrolds, London).

Barton, D.B. (1989) *Cornwall Engine Houses* (Tor Mark,Penryn).

Barton, R.M. (ed.) (1970) *Life in the Early Nineteenth Century* (extracts from *The West Briton 1810–35*), (D.Bradford Barton, Truro).

Barton,R,M, (ed.) (1971) *Life in Cornwall in the Mid-nineteenth Century* (extracts from the W.B.1835–1854) (D.Bradford Barton, Truro).

Barton, Rita M. (ed.) (1972) *Life in Cornwall in the Late Nineteenth Century* (extracts from the *West Briton* 1855–1875) (D.Bradford Barton, Truro).

Benney, D.E. (1972) *An Introduction to Cornish Water Mills* (D. Bradford Barton, Truro).

Best, R.S. (no date) *Cornish Quiz* (Dyllansow Truran, Redruth).

Bird, Sheila (1988) *The Books of Cornish Villages* (The Dovecote Press, Wimborne).

Bird, Sheila (1989) *Cornish Curiosities* (The Dovecote Press, Wimborne).

Bissell, Frances (1996) *West Country Kitchen* (Macmillan, London).

Bottrell, W.B. (1873) *Traditions & Hearthside Stories of West Cornwall* (Beare and Son, facsimile rep. Llanerch, Lampeter, 1989).

Bowen, Geraint and Sonia Bowen (1991) *Hanes Gorsedd y Beirdd* (Barddas, Dinbych, Clwyd, Wales).

Bowley, E.L (1945) *The Fortuanate Islands: The Story of the Isles of Scilly* (W.P. Kennedy, St. Mary's).

Brewer, Ebenezer Cobham (1870) *Dictionary of Phrase and Fable.*

Briggs, Katherine (1976) *A Dictionary of Fairies* (Allen Lane, rep. Penguin 1979).

Brown, Kenneth and Bob Acton (1994) *Exploring Cornish Mines Vol. 1* (Landfall Publications, Truro, 2nd edition 1996).

Buckley, J.A. (1989) *Cornish Mining – Underground* (Tor Mark, Penryn).

Butcher, Ann and Kenneth Fraser Annand (1994) *Recipes and Ramblings*

(Tredinnick Press, St. Day).

Caine, Margaret and Alan Gorton (2001) *The Cornwall Quiz Book* (A Comfy Jack Book, Cotswold Quality, Blackwell, Warwickshire).

Carew, Richard (1602) *The Survey of Cornwall* (John Inggard, London, rep. Tamar Books, Redruth, 2000).

Cassidy, Frederic G. (ed.) (1985) *Dictionary of Regional American English (Vol.1)* (Belknap Press, Harvard University Press, Cambridge, Massachusetts).

Cornish Pumping Engines and Rotative Beam Engines: An Illustrative Survey (Cornish Engines Preservation Society, 1953, rep. The Trevithick Society, 1991).

Clemo, Jack (no date) *The Bouncing Hills* (Dyllansow Truran, Redruth).

Clark, Gregory R. (1990) *Words of the Vietnam War* (McFarland, Jefferson, Carolina).

Couch, Jonathan (1871) *The History of Polperro* (facsimile rep. 1965 by Dyllansow Truran, Redruth).

Courtney, M.A. (1880) *Glossary of Words in use in Cornwall* (Trubner, London, rep. Oakmagic, 2000).

Courtney, M.A. (1890) *Folklore and Legends of Cornwall* (facsimile rep. of *Cornish Feasts and Folklore*, by Cornwall Books, Wheaton, Exeter, 1989).

Crowley, T.E. (1976) *Beam Engines* (Shire Publications, rep. 1996).

Cunnack, Edward M. (1975) *The Helston Furry Dance* (Flora Day Assoc. & Stewards of the Helston Furry Dance).

Curnow, Gladys (2002) *'Ere 'Tez: The Dialect of St. Just and Pendeen* (Gladys Curnow, St. Just).

Daniell, S. V. (1988) *The Story of Cornwall's Churches* (Tor Mark, Penryn).

Darke, T.O. (1971) *The Cornish Chough* (D. Bradford Barton, Truro).

Davey, Gwenda Beed & Grahan Seal (2003) *A Guide to Australian Folklore* (Kangaroo Press, Syndney).

Davey, Merv (1983) *Hengan* (Dyllansow Truran, Redruth).

Davidson, Alan (1999) *The Oxford Companion to Food* (Oxford University Press).

Day, Brian (2003) *The Celtic Calendar* (C.W. Daniel, Saffron Walden).

Day, Brian (2000) *Chronicle of Celtic Folk Customs* (Hamlyn, London).

Deacon, Bernard, Dick Cole and Garry Tregida (2003) *Mebyon Kernow & Cornish Nationalim* (Welsh Academic Press, Cardiff).

Deane, Tony & Tony Shaw (1975) *The Folklore of Cornwall* (Batsford, London).

Downes, John (1986) *A Dictionary of Devon Dialect* (Tabb House, Padstow).

du Maurier, Daphne (1967) *Vanishing Cornwall* (Victor Gollancz, rep. Penguin, Harmondsworth, 1974).

Earl, Bryan (1978) *Cornish Explosives* (Trevithick Society).

Edwards, Gillian (1974) *Hobgoblin and Sweet Puck: Fairy Names* (Geoffrey Bles, Lomdon).

Edwards, T.B. (1998) *Welsh Nots, Welsh Notes and Welsh Nuts: A Dictionary of Phrases with the word 'Welsh'* (Gwasg Carreg Gwalch, Llanrwst, Wales).

Edwards, Thornton B. (2004) *Irish! A Dictionary of Phrases, Terms & Epithets beginning with the word 'Irish'* (Mercier Press, Cork, Ireland).

Ellis, P. Beresford (1985) *The Celtic Revolution* (Y Lolfa, Talybont, Wales).
Ellis, P. Berresford (1990) *The Story of the Cornish Language* (Tor Mark, Penryn).
Ernault, Emile (1919) *Dictionnaire Breton-Français du Dialecte de Vannais* (Ti Lafoyle Frères, Gwened, rep. Brud Nevez, Brest, 1991).
Ferris, L.C. (no date) *Pebbles on Cornwall's Beaches* (Tor Mark, Penryn).
Fudge, Crysten (1982) *The Life of Cornish* (Dyllansow Truran, Redruth/Kesva an Tavas Kernewek)
Gendall, J.E. & R.R.M. Gendall (1991) *Nadelik Kernowak/ A Cornish Christmas* (Teere ha Tavaz, Liskeard).
Gendall, Jan (1995) *Scat-ups, Shags and Shagdowns: A Glossary of Cornish Community Nicknames* (Teer ha Tavas, Liskeard).
George, Ken (1993) *Gerlyver Kernewek Kemmyn: Kernewek-Sowsnek/An Gerlyver Meur* (The Cornish Language Board, Callington).
Green, Jonathon (1998) *Cassell's Dictionary of Slang* (Cassell, London, paperback edn. 2000).
Hall, J.R. Clark (1894) *A Concise Anglo-Saxon Dictionary* (C.U.P., 4th edn. University of Toronto Press).
Halliwell, J.O (1847) *Dictionary of Archaic and Provincial Words* (Routledge, N.Y., 7th edn., 1924).
Harris, K. (1983) *Hevva !* (Dyllansow Truran, Redruth).
Hartnoll, Phyllis & Peter Found (1992) *The Concise Oxford Companion to the Theatre* (O.U.P., Oxford).
Hawke, Kathleen (1973) *Cornish Sayings, Superstitions and Remedies* (Dyllansow Truran, Redruth, 4th edn.1987).
Hawke, Kathleen (1975) *A Glossary of Cornish Dialect Words* (unpublished manuscript).
Hawke, Kathleen (1989) *A Cornish Hotchpotch* (Dyllansow, Truran, Redruth).
Hazlitt, W.C. (1905) *Dictionary of Faiths and Folklore: Beliefs, Superstitions and Popular Customs* (Reeves and Turner, London, rep. Bracken Books, 1995).
Heard, Vida (1984) *Cornish Cookery* (Dyllansow Truran, Redruth).
Hemon, Roparz (1985) *Nouveau Dictionnaire Breton-Français* (Al Liamm, Brest, 7th edn.).
Hendickson, Robert (1983) *Animal Crackers: A Bestial Lexicon* (Penguin, Harmondsworth).
Hincks, Rhisiart (1991) *Geriadur Kembraeg-Brezhoneg/Geiriadur Cymraeg-Llydaweg* (Mouladurioù Hor Yezh, Lesneven).
Hodge, James (1995) *Richard Trevithick* (Shire Publications Ltd., Princes Risborough).
Holmes, Julyan (1983) *1000 Cornish Place Names Explained* (Dyllansow Truran, Redruth).
Hunt, Robert (1881) *The Drolls, Traditions, and Superstitions of Old Cornwall*: 1st Series.
Ince, Catharine (2001) *Life in Cornwall 1939–42: Extracts from the West Briton*

Newspaper (Truran, Truro).

Ivey, W.F. (1976) *A Dictionary of Cornish Dialect Words* (Helston Printers, 5th enlarged edn., 1980).

Jago, Fred W.P. (1882) *The Ancient Language and Dialect of Cornwall* (Netherton &Worth, Truro).

James, Beryl (1979) *Cornish Faist* (Dyllansow Truran, Redruth).

Jauncey, Dorothy (2004) *Bardi Grubs and Frog Cakes: South Australian Words* (Oxford University Press).

Jenkin, A.K. Hamilton (1945) *Cornwall and its People: Cornish Seafarers, Cornwall and the Cornish, Cornish Homes and Customs* (J.M. Dent & Sons, London).

Jenkin, John (1984) *A First History of Cornwall* (Dyllansow Truran, Redruth).

John, Catherine Rachel (1981) *The Saints of Cornwall* (Dyllansow Truran, Redruth).

Jones, Alison (1995) *Larousse Dictionary of World Folklore* (Larousse, Edinburgh).

Jones, Craig Owen (2001) *The Writings of Marcus S. Treverns: Was Laval-Sur-Mer The Last Bastion of the Corntish Language?* (Catchpenny Publications, Mold, Wales).

Jones, Kelvin I. (ed.) (1996) *Cornish Fairy Folk* (Oakmagic, Penzance).

Jones, Kelvin I. (ed.) (1997) *Strange Cornish Customs* (Oakmagic, Penzance).

Jones, Kelvin I. (ed.) (1997b) *Penzance Customs and Superstitions* (Oakmagic, Penzance).

Jones, Kelvin I. (ed.) (1997c) *The Furry Dance: An Ancient Tradition* (Oakmagic, Penzance).

Kirk, David (1994) *Snowdonia: A Historical Anthology.*

Kittow, June (no date) *Favourite Cornish Recipes* (J. Salmon, Sevenoaks).

Leggat, P.O. and D.V. Leggat (1987) *The Healing Wells:Cornish Cults and Customs* (Dyllansow Truran, Redruth).

MacLeay, J. (1977) *Cornish Witchcraft* (James Pike Ltd., St. Ives).

McCleary, John Bassett (2002) *The Hippie Dictionary* (Ten Speed Press, Berkeley, California).

Marten, Clement (1992) *The Devonshire Dialect* (Peninsula Press, Newton Abbot).

Martin, Carolyn (1993) *Our Daily Bread: Secrets from the Bakers of Cornwall* (Tabb House, Padstow).

Martin, E.W. (1951) *A Wanderer in the West Country* (Phoenix House, London).

Mason, I.L. (1951) *A World Dictionary of Livestock Breeds, Types and Varieties* (4th edn., CAB International, Wallingford 1996).

Mayne, J.A.D. & J.A. Williams (1985) *Coins & Tokens of Cornwall* (Constantine, Exeter).

Merrick, Hettie (1995) *The Pasty Book* (Tor Mark, Penryn).

Merrick, Hettie (1998) *Fed Fitty: Recipes from a Cornish Kitchen* (Tor Mark, Redruth).

Merton, Les (2003) *The Official Encyclopaedia of the Cornish Pasty* (Palores Publications, Redruth).

Monteleone, Vincent J. (1949) Criminal Slang: *The Vernacular of the Underworld Lingo* (Christopher Publications, Boston; rep.(2003) The Lawbook Exchange, New Jersey).

Nance, R. Morton (1956) *The Cledry Plays: Drolls and Old Cornwall for Village Actors and Home Reading* (Federation of Old Cornwall Societies, Marazion and Penzance).

Nance, R. Morton (1963) *A Glossary of Cornish Sea-Words* (The Federation of Old Cornwall Societies).

Nance, R. Morton (1978) *An English-Cornish and Cornish-English Dictionary* (The Cornish Language Board, Penzance).

Nicholls, Dorothy Delancey (1986) *Gleanings from a Cornish Notebook* (Dyllansow, Truran).

Noall, Cyril (no date) *Cornish Seines and Seiners* (Bradford Barton, Truro).

ÓMuirithe, Diarmaid (1997) *A Word in your Ear* (Four Courts, Dublin).

Orchard, W.G. (ed.) (1990) *A Glossary of Mining Terms* (Dyllansow Truran, Redruth).

Partridge, Eric (1937) *The Penguin Dictionary of Historical Slang* (Penguin Books, Middlesex, rep. 1988).

Pascoe, A.M. (1995) *Cornish Recipes* (Tor Mark, Penryn).

Payton, Philip (ed.) (1993) *Cornwall Since the War* (Institute of Cornish Studies/Dyllansow Truran).

Payton, Philip (1996) *Cornwall* (Alexander Associates, Fowey).

Payton, Philp (1999) *The Cornish Overseas* (Alexander Associates, Fowey).

Pearse, Keith & Helen Fry (eds.) (2000) *The Lost Jews of Cornwall:From the Middle Ages to the Nineteenth Century* (Redcliffe, Bristol).

Pearse, Richard (no date) *The Land Beside the Celtic Sea* (Dyllansow, Truran).

Penn, Peter (ed.) (1906) *Bizarre Cornish Beliefs* (rep. from the *Cornish Telegraph*, pub. Elliot Stock, London, rep. Oakmagic, Weston Super Mare, 2002).

Phillipps, K.C. (1976) *West Country Words and Ways* (David & Charles, Newton Abbot).

Phillipps, K.C. (1993) *A Glossary of the Cornish Dialect* (Tabb House, Padstow).

Pool, P.A.S. (1975) *The Death of Cornish* (rep. The Cornish Language Board, 1982).

Puxley, Ray (2003) *Britslang: An Uncensored A–Z of the People's Language including Rhyming Slang* (Robson Books, London).

Quigley, Christine (1994) *Death Dictionary* (McFarland, Jefferson, N. Carolina).

Rawe, Donald R. (1984) *Cornish Hauntings and Happenings* (Robert Hale, London).

Rawe, Donald (1986) *A Prospect of Cornwall* (Robert S. Hale, London).

Rendell, Joan (1983) *North Cornwall in the Old Days* (Bossiney Books, St.Teath, Bodmin).

Richards, Jack (no date) *Memories of a Cornish Countryman* (Packet Publishing,

Ponsharden).
Robinson, Mairi (1985) *The Concise Scots Dictionary*.
Rose, Carol (1998) *Spirits, Fairies, Gnomes and Goblins: An Encyclopedia of the Little People* (ABC–CLIO, Santa Barbara./Oxford).
Rothwell, Catherine (1989) *Old Cornwall Recipes* (Hendon).
Rowse, A.L. (1942) *A Cornish Childhood* (Jonathan Cape, London, 5th imp., 1945).
Rowse, A.L. (1986) *The Little Land of Cornwall* (Alan Sutton, rep. Dyllansow Truran, Redruth).
St. Clair, Sheila (1971) *Folklore of the Ulster People* (Mercier, Cork).
Salmon, Arthur L. (1903) *Cornwall* (Methuen, London, 8th revised edn., 1938).
Selleck, Douglas (1992) *Another Cornish Bedside Book* (Dyllansow Truran, Redruth).
Share, Bernard (1997) *Slanguage: A Dictionary of Irish Slang* (Gill & Macmillan, Dublin).
Smith, D.J.M. (1988) *A Dictionary of Horse-drawn Vehicles* (J.A. Allen, London).
Smylie, Mike (1998) *The Herring Fishers of Wales* (Gwasg Carreg Cwalch, Llanrwst, Wales).
Spacey, A.W. (1985) *The Bird, the Beast and Fishes Tail* (Truran).
Spiers, Virginia (1996) *Burcombes, Queenies and Colloggetts* (West Brendon).
Stevens, G.A. (no date) *Do You Know Cornwall?* (Tor Mark, Penryn).
Stevens, James (1977) (ed. P.A.S. Pool) *A Cornish Farmer's Diary* (Selections from the diary of James Stevens of Sancreed 1847–1918) (P.A.S.Pool, Pennzance).
Swainson, Charles (1886) *The Folklore and Provincial Names of British Birds* (facsimile rep. Llanerch, Lampeter).
Tangye, Nigel (1978) *Voyage into Cornwall's Past* (William Kimber, London).
Thomas, Joseph (1895) *Randigal Rhymes and a Glossary of Cornish Words* (F. Rodda, Penzance).
Thurlow, Charles (1990) *China Clay* (Tor Mark, Penryn).
Treenoodle, Uncle Jan (1846) *Specimens of Cornish Provincial Dialect* (John Russell, London).
Tregarthen, Enys (1940) *Pixie Folklore and Legends: A Book of Cornish Piskey Tales* (collected by Elizabeth Yates, Gramercy Books, rep. Random House, New Jersey, 1996).
Tremain, Robert (1992) *Oyez! Oyez! Oyez! Bells and Yells: The Town Crier's Story* (Tremain, Launceston).
Trevail, B. (1990) *Introducing Cornwall* (Tor Mark, Penryn).
Tuck, Brian (1988) *Thus we live: Poems from Cornwall* (Pedn-an-drea Books).
Turk, Stella M. (1971) *Seashore Life in Cornwall* (D.Bradford Barton, Truro).
Underwood, Peter (1983) *Ghosts of Cornwall* (Bossiney Books, St. Teath, Bodmin).

Venable, Roger (1993) *The Hooting Carn and other Cornish Tales* (Men Scryfa Press, Penzance).

Vivian, John (1969) *Tales of the Cornish Smugglers* (Tor Mark, Penryn, rep. 1992).

Wakelin, Martyn (1994) *Discovering English Dialects* (Shire Publications, Ltd.).

Waller, Betty (1994) *Granny's Kitchen: Cornish Cooking from Back along* (Whistletop, Calstock).

Weatherhill, Craig and Paul Devereux (1994) *Myths and Legends of Cornwall* (Sigma Press, Wilmslow).

Westwood, Jennifer (1992) *Gothick Cornwall* (Shire Publications, Ltd., Princes Risborough).

Whetter, James (1977) *Cornish Essays 1971–76* (CNP Publications, St. Austell).

Whinray, James (1997) *Down 'long weth We* (Tor Mark, Penryn).

White, Paul (1994) *Classic Cornish Anecdotes* (Tor Mark, Penryn).

Williams, Douglas (1987) *Festivals of Cornwall* (Bossiney Books, St. Teath, Bodmin).

Williams, Michael (1982) *Superstitions and Folklore* (Bossiney Books, St. Teath, Bodmin).

Williams, N.J. (1995) *Cornish Today* (KDL, Sutton Coldfield).

Woodhouse, Harry (1994) *Cornish Bagpipes: Fact or Fiction* (Dyllansow Truran, Redruth).

Wright, Joseph (ed.) (1898–1905) *The English Dialect Dictionary* (rep. O.U.P., London, 1970).

Wright, Mary (1986) *Cornish Treats* (Alison Hodge).